CREATIVE INTELLIGENCE

ESSAYS IN THE PRAGMATIC ATTITUDE

BY

JOHN DEWEY
ADDISON W. MOORE
HAROLD CHAPMAN BROWN
GEORGE H. MEAD
BOYD H. BODE
HENRY WALDGRAVE STUART
JAMES HAYDEN TUFTS
HORACE M. KALLEN

PREFATORY NOTE

The Essays which follow represent an attempt at intellectual coöperation. No effort has been made, however, to attain unanimity of belief nor to proffer a platform of "planks" on which there is agreement. The consensus represented lies primarily in outlook, in conviction of what is most likely to be fruitful in method of approach. As the title page suggests, the volume presents a unity in attitude rather than a uniformity in results. Consequently each writer is definitively responsible only for his own essay. The reader will note that the Essays endeavor to embody the common attitude in application to specific fields of inquiry which have been historically associated with philosophy rather than as a thing by itself. Beginning with philosophy itself, subsequent contributions discuss its application to logic, to mathematics, to physical science, to psychology, to ethics, to economics, and then again to philosophy itself in conjunction with esthetics and religion. The reader will probably find that the significant points of agreement have to do with the ideas of the genuineness of the future, of intelligence as the organ for determining the quality of that future so far as it can come within human control, and of a courageously inventive individual as the bearer of a creatively employed mind. While all the essays are new in the form in which they are now published, various contributors make their acknowledgments to the editors of the *Philosophical Review*, the *Psychological Review*, and the *Journal of Philosophy, Psychology and Scientific Methods* for use of material which first made its appearance in the pages of these journals.

CONTENTS

CREATIVE INTELLIGENCE

THE NEED FOR A RECOVERY OF PHILOSOPHY

JOHN DEWEY

Intellectual advance occurs in two ways. At times increase of knowledge is organized about old conceptions, while these are expanded, elaborated and refined, but not seriously revised, much less abandoned. At other times, the increase of knowledge demands qualitative rather than quantitative change; alteration, not addition. Men's minds grow cold to their former intellectual concerns; ideas that were burning fade; interests that were urgent seem remote. Men face in another direction; their older perplexities are unreal; considerations passed over as negligible loom up. Former problems may not have been solved, but they no longer press for solutions.

Philosophy is no exception to the rule. But it is unusually conservative—not, necessarily, in proffering solutions, but in clinging to problems. It has been so allied with theology and theological morals as representatives of men's chief interests, that radical alteration has been shocking. Men's activities took a decidedly new turn, for example, in the seventeenth century, and it seems as if philosophy, under the lead of thinkers like Bacon and Descartes, was to execute an about-face. But, in spite of the ferment, it turned out that many of the older problems were but translated from Latin into the vernacular or into the new terminology furnished by science.

The association of philosophy with academic teaching has reinforced this intrinsic conservatism. Scholastic philosophy persisted in universities after men's thoughts outside of the walls of colleges had moved in other directions. In the last hundred years intellectual advances of science and politics have in like fashion been crystallized into material of instruction and now resist further change. I would not say that the spirit of teaching is hostile to that of liberal inquiry, but a philosophy which exists largely as something to be taught rather than wholly as something to be reflected upon is conducive to discussion of views held by others rather than to immediate response. Philosophy when taught inevitably magnifies the history of past thought, and leads professional philosophers to approach their subject-matter through its formulation in received systems. It tends, also, to emphasize points upon which men have divided into schools, for these lend themselves to retrospective definition and elaboration. Consequently, philosophical discussion is likely to be a dressing out of antithetical traditions, where criticism of one view is thought to afford proof of the truth of its opposite (as if formulation of views guaranteed logical exclusives). Direct preoccupation with contemporary difficulties is left to literature and politics.

If changing conduct and expanding knowledge ever required a willingness to surrender not merely old solutions but old problems it is now. I do not mean that we can turn abruptly away from all traditional issues. This is impossible; it would be the undoing of the one who attempted it. Irrespective of the professionalizing of philosophy, the ideas philosophers discuss are still those in which Western civilization has been bred. They are in the backs of the heads of educated people. But what serious-minded men not engaged in the professional business of philosophy most want to know is what modifications and abandonments of intellectual inheritance are required by the newer industrial, political, and scientific movements. They want to know what these newer movements mean when translated into general ideas. Unless professional philosophy can mobilize itself sufficiently to assist in this clarification and redirection of men's thoughts, it is likely to get more and more sidetracked from the main currents of contemporary life.

This essay may, then, be looked upon as an attempt to forward the emancipation of philosophy from too intimate and exclusive attachment to traditional problems. It is not in intent a criticism of various solutions that have been offered, but raises a question *as to the genuineness, under the present conditions of science and social life, of the problems.*

The limited object of my discussion will, doubtless, give an exaggerated impression of my conviction as to the artificiality of much recent philosophizing. Not that I have wilfully exaggerated in what I have said, but that the limitations of my purpose have led me not to say many things pertinent to a broader purpose. A discussion less restricted would strive to enforce the genuineness, in their own context, of questions now discussed mainly because they have been discussed rather than because contemporary conditions of life suggest them. It would also be a grateful task to dwell upon the precious contributions made by philosophic systems which as a whole are impossible. In the course of the development of unreal premises and the discussion of artificial problems, points of view have emerged which are indispensable possessions of culture. The horizon has been widened; ideas of great fecundity struck out; imagination quickened; a sense of the meaning of things created. It may even be asked whether these accompaniments of classic systems have not often been treated as a kind of guarantee of the systems themselves. But while it is a sign of an illiberal mind to throw away the fertile and ample ideas of a Spinoza, a Kant, or a Hegel, because their setting is not logically adequate, is surely a sign of an undisciplined one to treat their contributions to culture as confirmations of premises with which they have no necessary connection.

I

A criticism of current philosophizing from the standpoint of the traditional quality of its problems must begin somewhere, and the choice of a beginning is arbitrary. It has appeared to me that the notion of experience implied in the questions most actively discussed gives a natural point of departure. For, if I mistake not, it is just the inherited view of experience common to the empirical school and its opponents which keeps alive many discussions even of matters that on their face are quite remote from it, while it is also this view which is most untenable in the light of existing science and social practice. Accordingly I set out with a brief statement of some of the chief contrasts between the orthodox description of experience and that congenial to present conditions.

(i) In the orthodox view, experience is regarded primarily as a knowledge-affair. But to eyes not looking through ancient spectacles, it assuredly appears as an affair of the intercourse of a living being with its physical and social environment. (ii) According to tradition experience is (at least primarily) a psychical thing, infected throughout by "subjectivity." What experience suggests about itself is a genuinely objective world which enters into the actions and sufferings of men and undergoes modifications through their responses. (iii) So far as anything beyond a bare present is recognized by the established doctrine, the past exclusively counts. Registration of what has taken place, reference to precedent, is believed to be the essence of experience. Empiricism is conceived of as tied up to what has been, or is, "given." But experience in its vital form is experimental, an effort to change the given; it is characterized by projection, by reaching forward into the unknown; connexion with a future is its salient trait. (iv) The empirical tradition is committed to particularism. Connexions and continuities are supposed to be foreign to experience, to be by-products of dubious validity. An experience that is an undergoing of an environment and a striving for its control in new directions is pregnant with connexions. (v) In the traditional notion experience and thought are antithetical terms. Inference, so far as it is other than a revival of what has been given in the past, goes beyond experience; hence it is either invalid, or else a measure of desperation by which, using experience as a springboard, we jump out to a world of stable things and other selves. But experience, taken free of the restrictions imposed by the older concept, is full of inference. There is, apparently, no conscious experience without inference; reflection is native and constant.

These contrasts, with a consideration of the effect of substituting the account of experience relevant to modern life for the inherited account, afford the subject-matter of the following discussion.

Suppose we take seriously the contribution made to our idea of experience by biology,—not that recent biological science discovered the facts, but that it has so emphasized them that there is no longer an excuse for ignoring them or treating them as negligible. Any account of experience must now fit into the consideration that experiencing means living; and that living goes on in and because of an environing medium, not in a vacuum. Where there is experience, there is a living being. Where there is life, there is a double connexion maintained with the environment. In part, environmental energies constitute organic functions; they enter into them. Life is not possible without such direct support by the environment. But while all organic changes depend upon the natural energies of the environment for their origination and occurrence, the natural energies sometimes carry the organic functions prosperously forward, and sometimes act counter to their continuance. Growth and decay, health and disease, are alike continuous with activities of the natural surroundings. The difference lies in the bearing of what happens upon future life-activity. From the standpoint of this future reference environmental incidents fall into groups: those favorable to life-activities, and those hostile.

The successful activities of the organism, those within which environmental assistance is incorporated, react upon the environment to bring about modifications favorable to their own future. The human being has upon his hands the problem of responding to what is going on around him so that these changes will take one turn rather than another, namely, that required by its own further functioning. While backed in part by the environment, its life is anything but a peaceful exhalation of environment. It is obliged to struggle—that is to say, to employ the direct support given by the environment in order indirectly to effect changes that would not otherwise occur. In this sense, life goes on by means of controlling the environment. Its activities must change the changes going on around it; they must neutralize hostile occurrences; they must transform neutral events into coöperative factors or into an efflorescence of new features.

Dialectic developments of the notion of self-preservation, of the *conatus essendi*, often ignore all the important facts of the actual process. They argue as if self-control, self-development, went on directly as a sort of unrolling push from within. But life endures only in virtue of the support of the environment. And since the environment is only incompletely enlisted in our behalf, self-preservation—or self-realization or whatever—is always indirect—always an affair of the way in which our present activities affect the direction taken by independent changes in the surroundings. Hindrances must be turned into means.

We are also given to playing loose with the conception of adjustment, as if that meant something fixed—a kind of accommodation once for all (ideally at least) of the organism *to* an environment. But as life requires the fitness of the environment to the organic functions, adjustment to the environment means not passive acceptance of the latter, but acting so that the environing changes take a certain turn. The "higher" the type of life, the more adjustment takes the form of an adjusting of the factors of the environment to one another in the interest of life; the less the significance of living, the more it becomes an adjustment to a given environment till at the lower end of the scale the differences between living and the non-living disappear.

These statements are of an external kind. They are about the conditions of experience, rather than about experiencing itself. But assuredly experience as it concretely takes place bears out the statements. Experience is primarily a process of undergoing: a process of standing something; of suffering and passion, of affection, in the literal sense of these words. The organism has to endure, to undergo, the consequences of its own actions. Experience is no slipping along in a path fixed by inner consciousness. Private consciousness is an incidental outcome of experience of a vital objective sort; it is not its source. Undergoing, however, is never mere passivity. The most patient patient is more than a receptor. He is also an agent—a reactor, one trying experiments, one concerned with undergoing in a way which may influence what is still to happen. Sheer endurance, side-stepping evasions, are, after all, ways of treating the environment with a view to what such treatment will accomplish. Even if we shut ourselves up in the most clam-like fashion, we are doing something; our passivity is an active attitude, not an extinction of response. Just as there is no assertive action, no aggressive attack upon things as they are, which is all action, so there is no undergoing which is not on our part also a going on and a going through.

Experience, in other words, is a matter of *simultaneous* doings and sufferings. Our undergoings are experiments in varying the course of events; our active tryings are trials and tests of ourselves. This duplicity of experience shows itself in our happiness and misery, our successes and failures. Triumphs are dangerous when dwelt upon or lived off from; successes use themselves up. Any achieved equilibrium of adjustment with the environment is precarious because we cannot evenly keep pace with changes in the environment. These are so opposed in direction that we must choose. We must take the risk of casting in our lot with one movement or the other. Nothing can eliminate all risk, all adventure; the one thing doomed to failure is to try to keep even with the whole environment at once—that is to say, to maintain the happy moment when all things go our way.

The obstacles which confront us are stimuli to variation, to novel response, and hence are occasions of progress. If a favor done us by the environment conceals a threat, so its disfavor is a potential means of hitherto unexperienced modes of success. To treat misery as anything but misery, as for example a blessing in disguise or a necessary factor in good, is disingenuous apologetics. But to say that the progress of the race has been stimulated by ills undergone, and that men have been moved by what they suffer to search out new and better courses of action is to speak veraciously.

The preoccupation of experience with things which are coming (are now coming, not just to come) is obvious to any one whose interest in experience is empirical. Since we live forward; since we live in a world where changes are going on whose issue means our weal or woe; since every act of ours modifies these changes and hence is fraught with promise, or charged with hostile energies—what should experience be but a future implicated in a present! Adjustment is no timeless state; it is a continuing process. To say that a change takes time may be to say something about the event which is external and uninstructive. But adjustment of organism to environment takes time in the pregnant sense; every step in the process is conditioned. by reference to further changes which it effects. What is going on in the environment is the concern of the organism; not what is already "there" in accomplished and finished form. In so far as the issue of what is going on may be affected by intervention of the organism, the moving event is a challenge which stretches the agent-patient to meet what is coming. Experiencing exhibits things in their unterminated aspect moving toward determinate conclusions. The finished and done with is of import as affecting the future, not on its own account: in short, because it is not, really, done with.

Anticipation is therefore more primary than recollection; projection than summoning of the past; the prospective than the retrospective. Given a world like that in which we live, a world in which environing changes are partly favorable and partly callously indifferent, and experience is bound to be prospective in import; for any control attainable by the living creature depends upon what is done to alter the state of things. Success and failure are the primary "categories" of life; achieving of good and averting of ill are its supreme interests; hope and anxiety (which are not self-enclosed states of feeling, but active attitudes of welcome and wariness) are dominant qualities of experience. Imaginative forecast of the future is this forerunning quality of behavior rendered available for guidance in the present. Day-dreaming and castle-building and esthetic realization of what is not practically achieved are offshoots of this practical trait, or else practical intelligence is a chastened fantasy. It makes little difference.

Imaginative recovery of the bygone is indispensable to successful invasion of the future, but its status is that of an instrument. To ignore its import is the sign of an undisciplined agent; but to isolate the past, dwelling upon it for its own sake and giving it the eulogistic name of knowledge, is to substitute the reminiscence of old-age for effective intelligence. The movement of the agent-patient to meet the future is partial and passionate; yet detached and impartial study of the past is the only alternative to luck in assuring success to passion.

II

This description of experience would be but a rhapsodic celebration of the commonplace were it not in marked contrast to orthodox philosophical accounts. The contrast indicates that traditional accounts have not been empirical, but have been deductions, from unnamed premises, of what experience *must* be. Historic empiricism has been empirical in a technical and controversial sense. It has said, Lord, Lord, Experience, Experience; but in practice it has served ideas *forced into* experience, not *gathered from* it.

The confusion and artificiality thereby introduced into philosophical thought is nowhere more evident than in the empirical treatment of relations or dynamic continuities. The experience of a living being struggling to hold its own and make its way in an environment, physical and social, partly facilitating and partly obstructing its actions, is of necessity a matter of ties and connexions, of bearings and uses. The very point of experience, so to say, is that it doesn't occur in a vacuum; its agent-patient instead of being insulated and disconnected is bound up with the movement of things by most intimate and pervasive bonds. Only because the organism is in and of the world, and its activities correlated with those of other things in multiple ways, is it susceptible to undergoing things and capable of trying to reduce objects to means of securing its good fortune. That these connexions are of diverse kinds is irresistibly proved by the fluctuations which occur in its career. Help and hindrance, stimulation and inhibition, success and failure mean specifically different modes of correlation. Although the actions of things in the world are taking place in one continuous stretch of existence, there are all kinds of specific affinities, repulsions, and relative indifferencies.

Dynamic connexions are qualitatively diverse, just as are the centers of action. *In this sense*, pluralism, not monism, is an established empirical fact. The attempt to establish monism from consideration of the very nature of a relation is a mere piece of dialectics. Equally dialectical is the effort to establish by a consideration of the nature of relations an ontological Pluralism of Ultimates: *simple and independent beings.* To attempt to get results from a consideration of the "external" nature of relations is of a piece with the attempt to deduce results from their "internal" character. Some things are relatively insulated from the influence of other things; some things are easily invaded by others; some things are fiercely attracted to conjoin their activities with those of others. Experience exhibits every kind of connexion1 from the most intimate to mere external juxtaposition.

Empirically, then, active bonds or continuities of all kinds, together with static discontinuities, characterize existence. To deny this qualitative heterogeneity is to reduce the struggles and difficulties of life, its comedies and tragedies to illusion: to the non-being of the Greeks or to its modern counterpart, the "subjective." Experience is an affair of facilitations and checks, of being sustained and disrupted, being let alone, being helped and troubled, of good fortune and defeat in all the countless qualitative modes which these words pallidly suggest. The existence of genuine connexions of all manner of heterogeneity cannot be doubted. Such words as conjoining, disjoining, resisting, modifying, saltatory, and ambulatory (to use James' picturesque term) only hint at their actual heterogeneity.

Among the revisions and surrenders of historic problems demanded by this feature of empirical situations, those centering in the rationalistic-empirical controversy may be selected for attention. The implications of this controversy are twofold: First, that connexions are as homogeneous in fact as in name; and, secondly, if genuine, are all due to thought, or, if empirical, are arbitrary by-products of past particulars. The stubborn particularism of orthodox empiricism is its outstanding trait; consequently the opposed rationalism found no justification of bearings, continuities, and ties save to refer them in gross to the work of a hyper-empirical Reason.

Of course, not all empiricism prior to Hume and Kant was sensationalistic, pulverizing "experience" into isolated sensory qualities or simple ideas. It did not all follow Locke's lead in regarding the entire content of generalization as the "workmanship of the understanding." On the Continent, prior to Kant, philosophers were content to draw a line between empirical generalizations regarding matters of fact and necessary universals applying to truths of reason. But logical atomism was implicit even in this theory. Statements referring to empirical fact were mere quantitative summaries of particular instances. In the sensationalism which sprang from Hume (and which was left unquestioned by Kant as far as any strictly empirical element was concerned) the implicit particularism was made explicit. But the doctrine that sensations and ideas are so many separate existences was not derived from observation nor from experiment. It was a logical deduction from a prior unexamined concept of the nature of experience. From the same concept it followed that the appearance of stable objects and of general principles of connexion was but an appearance.2

Kantianism, then, naturally invoked universal bonds to restore objectivity. But, in so doing, it accepted the particularism of experience and proceeded to supplement it from non-empirical sources. A sensory manifold being all which is really empirical in experience, a reason which transcends experience must provide synthesis. The net outcome might have suggested a correct account of experience. For we have only to forget the apparatus by which the net outcome is arrived at, to have before us the experience of the plain man—a diversity of ceaseless changes connected in all kinds of ways, static and dynamic. This conclusion would deal a deathblow to both empiricism and rationalism. For, making clear the non-empirical character of the alleged manifold of unconnected particulars, it would render unnecessary the appeal to functions of the understanding in order to connect them. With the downfall of the traditional notion of experience, the appeal to reason to supplement its defects becomes superfluous.

The tradition was, however, too strongly entrenched; especially as it furnished the subject-matter of an alleged science of states of mind which were directly known in their very presence. The historic outcome was a new crop of artificial puzzles about relations; it fastened upon philosophy for a long time the quarrel about the *a priori* and the *a posteriori* as its chief issue. The controversy is to-day quiescent. Yet it is not at all uncommon to find thinkers modern in tone and intent who regard any philosophy of experience as necessarily committed to denial of the existence of genuinely general propositions, and who take empiricism to be inherently averse to the recognition of the importance of an organizing and constructive intelligence.

The quiescence alluded to is in part due, I think, to sheer weariness. But it is also due to a change of standpoint introduced by biological conceptions; and particularly the discovery of biological continuity from the lower organisms to man. For a short period, Spencerians might connect the doctrine of evolution with the old problem, and use the long temporal accumulation of "experiences" to generate something which, for human experience, is *a priori*. But the tendency of the biological way of thinking is neither to confirm or negate the Spencerian doctrine, but to shift the issue. In the orthodox position *a posteriori* and *a priori* were affairs of knowledge. But it soon becomes obvious that while there is assuredly something *a priori*—that is to say, native, unlearned, original—in human experience, that something is *not* knowledge, but is activities made possible by means of established connexions of neurones. This empirical fact does not solve the orthodox problem; it dissolves it. It shows that the problem was misconceived, and solution sought by both parties in the wrong direction.

Organic instincts and organic retention, or habit-forming, are undeniable factors in actual experience. They are factors which effect organization and secure continuity. They are among the specific facts which a description of experience cognizant of the correlation of organic action with the action of other natural objects will include. But while fortunately the contribution of biological science to a truly empirical description of experiencing has outlawed the discussion of the *a priori* and *a posteriori*, the transforming effect of the same contributions upon other issues has gone unnoticed, save as pragmatism has made an effort to bring them to recognition.

III

The point seriously at issue in the notion of experience common to both sides in the older controversy thus turns out to be the place of thought or intelligence in experience. Does reason have a distinctive office? Is there a characteristic order of relations contributed by it?

Experience, to return to our positive conception, is primarily what is undergone in connexion with activities whose import lies in their objective consequences—their bearing upon future experiences. Organic functions deal with things as things in course, in operation, in a state of affairs not yet given or completed. What is done with, what is just "there," is of concern only in the potentialities which it may indicate. As ended, as wholly given, it is of no account. But as a sign of what may come, it becomes an indispensable factor in behavior dealing with changes, the outcome of which is not yet determined.

The only power the organism possesses to control its own future depends upon the way its present responses modify changes which are taking place in its medium. A living being may be comparatively impotent, or comparatively free. It is all a matter of the way in which its present reactions to things influence the future reactions of things upon it. Without regard to its wish or intent every act it performs makes some difference in the environment. The change may be trivial as respects its own career and fortune. But it may also be of incalculable importance; it may import harm, destruction, or it may procure well-being.

Is it possible for a living being to increase its control of welfare and success? Can it manage, in any degree, to assure its future? Or does the amount of security depend wholly upon the accidents of the situation? Can it learn? Can it gain ability to assure its future in the present? These questions center attention upon the significance of reflective intelligence in the process of experience. The extent of an agent's capacity for inference, its power to use a given fact as a sign of something not yet given, measures the extent of its ability systematically to enlarge its control of the future.

A being which can use given and finished facts as signs of things to come; which can take given things as evidences of absent things, can, in that degree, forecast the future; it can form reasonable expectations. It is capable of achieving ideas; it is possessed of intelligence. For use of the given or finished to anticipate the consequence of processes going on is precisely what is meant by "ideas," by "intelligence."

As we have already noted, the environment is rarely all of a kind in its bearing upon organic welfare; its most whole-hearted support of life-activities is precarious and temporary. Some environmental changes are auspicious; others are menacing. The secret of success—that is, of the greatest attainable success—is for the organic response to cast in its lot with present auspicious changes to strengthen them and thus to avert the consequences flowing from occurrences of ill-omen. Any reaction is a venture; it involves risk. We always build better or worse than we can foretell. But the organism's fateful intervention in the course of events is blind, its choice is random, except as it can employ what happens to it as a basis of inferring what is likely to happen later. In the degree in which it can read future results in present ongoings, its responsive choice, its partiality to this condition or that, become intelligent. Its bias grows reasonable. It can deliberately, intentionally, participate in the direction of the course of affairs. Its foresight of different futures which result according as this or that present factor predominates in the shaping of affairs permits it to partake intelligently instead of blindly and fatally in the consequences its reactions give rise to. Participate it must, and to its own weal or woe. Inference, the use of what happens, to anticipate what will—or at least may—happen, makes the difference between directed and undirected participation. And this capacity for inferring is precisely the same as that use of natural occurrences for the discovery and determination of consequences—the formation of new dynamic connexions—which constitutes knowledge.

The fact that thought is an intrinsic feature of experience is fatal to the traditional empiricism which makes it an artificial by-product. But for that same reason it is fatal to the historic rationalisms whose justification was the secondary and retrospective position assigned to thought by empirical philosophy. According to the particularism of the latter, thought was inevitably only a bunching together of hard-and-fast separate items; thinking was but the gathering together and tying of items already completely given, or else an equally artificial untying—a mechanical adding and subtracting of the given. It was but a cumulative registration, a consolidated merger; generality was a matter of bulk, not of quality. Thinking was therefore treated as lacking constructive power; even its organizing capacity was but simulated, being in truth but arbitrary pigeon-holing. Genuine projection of the novel, deliberate variation and invention, are idle fictions in such a version of experience. If there ever was creation, it all took place at a remote period. Since then the world has only recited lessons.

The value of inventive construction is too precious to be disposed of in this cavalier way. Its unceremonious denial afforded an opportunity to assert that in addition to experience the subject has a ready-made faculty of thought or reason which transcends experience. Rationalism thus accepted the account of experience given by traditional empiricism, and introduced reason as extra-empirical. There are still thinkers who regard any empiricism as necessarily committed to a belief in a cut-and-dried reliance upon disconnected precedents, and who hold that all systematic organization of past experiences for new and constructive purposes is alien to strict empiricism.

Rationalism never explained, however, how a reason extraneous to experience could enter into helpful relation with concrete experiences. By definition, reason and experience were antithetical, so that the concern of reason was not the fruitful expansion and guidance of the course of experience, but a realm of considerations too sublime to touch, or be touched by, experience. Discreet rationalists confined themselves to theology and allied branches of abtruse science, and to mathematics. Rationalism would have been a doctrine reserved for academic specialists and abstract formalists had it not assumed the task of providing an apologetics for traditional morals and theology, thereby getting into touch with actual human beliefs and concerns. It is notorious that historic empiricism was strong in criticism and in demolition of outworn beliefs, but weak for purposes of constructive social direction. But we frequently overlook the fact that whenever rationalism cut free from conservative apologetics, it was also simply an instrumentality for pointing out inconsistencies and absurdities in existing beliefs—a sphere in which it was immensely useful, as the Enlightenment shows. Leibniz and Voltaire were contemporary rationalists in more senses than one.[3]

The recognition that reflection is a genuine factor within experience and an indispensable factor in that control of the world which secures a prosperous and significant expansion of experience undermines historic rationalism as assuredly as it abolishes the foundations of historic empiricism. The bearing of a correct idea of the place and office of reflection upon modern idealisms is less obvious, but no less certain.

One of the curiosities of orthodox empiricism is that its outstanding speculative problem is the existence of an "external world." For in accordance with the notion that experience is attached to a private subject as its exclusive possession, a world like the one in which we appear to live must be "external" to experience instead of being its subject-matter. I call it a curiosity, for if anything seems adequately grounded empirically it is the existence of a world which resists the characteristic functions of the subject of experience; which goes its way, in some respects, independently of these functions, and which frustrates our hopes and intentions. Ignorance which is fatal; disappointment; the need of adjusting means and ends to the course of nature, would seem to be facts sufficiently characterizing empirical situations as to render the existence of an external world indubitable.

That the description of experience was arrived at by forcing actual empirical facts into conformity with dialectic developments from a concept of a knower out side of the real world of nature is testified to by the historic alliance of empiricism and idealism.4 According to the most logically consistent editions of orthodox empiricism, all that can be experienced is the fleeting, the momentary, mental state. That alone is absolutely and indubitably present; therefore, it alone is cognitively certain. It alone is *knowledge*. The existence of the past (and of the future), of a decently stable world and of other selves—indeed, of one's own self—falls outside this datum of experience. These can be arrived at only by inference which is "ejective"—a name given to an alleged type of inference that jumps from experience, as from a springboard, to something beyond experience.

I should not anticipate difficulty in showing that this doctrine is, dialectically, a mass of inconsistencies. Avowedly it is a doctrine of desperation, and as such it is cited here to show the desperate straits to which ignoring empirical facts has reduced a doctrine of experience. More positively instructive are the objective idealisms which have been the offspring of the marriage between the "reason" of historic rationalism and the alleged immediate psychical stuff of historic empiricism. These idealisms have recognized the genuineness of connexions and the impotency of "feeling." They have then identified connexions with logical or rational connexions, and thus treated "the real World" as a synthesis of sentient consciousness by means of a rational self-consciousness introducing objectivity: stability and universality of reference.

Here again, for present purposes, criticism is unnecessary. It suffices to point out that the value of this theory is bound up with the genuineness of the problem of which it purports to be a solution. If the basic concept is a fiction, there is no call for the solution. The more important point is to perceive how far the "thought" which figures in objective idealism comes from meeting the empirical demands made upon actual thought. Idealism is much less formal than historic rationalism. It treats thought, or reason, as constitutive of experience by means of uniting and constructive functions, not as just concerned with a realm of eternal truths apart from experience. On such a view thought certainly loses its abstractness and remoteness. But, unfortunately, in thus gaining the whole world it loses its own self. A world already, in its intrinsic structure, dominated by thought is not a world in which, save by contradiction of premises, thinking has anything to do.

That the doctrine logically results in making change unreal and error unaccountable are consequences of importance in the technique of professional philosophy; in the denial of empirical fact which they imply they seem to many a *reductio ad absurdum* of the premises from which they proceed. But, after all, such consequences are of only professional import. What is serious, even sinister, is the implied sophistication regarding the place and office of reflection in the scheme of things. A doctrine which exalts thought in name while ignoring its efficacy in fact (that is, its use in bettering life) is a doctrine which cannot be entertained and taught without serious peril. Those who are not concerned with professional philosophy but who are solicitous for intelligence as a factor in the amelioration of actual conditions can but look askance at any doctrine which holds that the entire scheme of things is already, if we but acquire the knack of looking at it aright, fixedly and completely rational. It is a striking manifestation of the extent in which philosophies have been compensatory in quality.5 But the matter cannot be passed over as if it were simply a question of not grudging a certain amount of consolation to one amid the irretrievable evils of life. For as to these evils no one knows how many are retrievable; and a philosophy which proclaims the ability of a dialectic theory of knowledge to reveal the world as already and eternally a self-luminous rational whole, contaminates the scope and use of thought at its very spring. To substitute the otiose insight gained by manipulation of a formula for the slow coöperative work of a humanity guided by reflective intelligence is more than a technical blunder of speculative philosophers.

A practical crisis may throw the relationship of ideas to life into an exaggerated Brocken-like spectral relief, where exaggeration renders perceptible features not ordinarily noted. The use of force to secure narrow because exclusive aims is no novelty in human affairs. The deploying of all the intelligence at command in order to increase the effectiveness of the force used is not so common, yet presents nothing intrinsically remarkable. The identification of force—military, economic, and administrative—with moral necessity and moral culture is, however, a phenomenon not likely to exhibit itself on a wide scale except where intelligence has already been suborned by an idealism which identifies "the actual with the rational," and thus finds the measure of reason in the brute event determined by superior force. If we are to have a philosophy which will intervene between attachment to rule of thumb muddling and devotion to a systematized subordination of intelligence to preëxistent ends, it can be found only in a philosophy which finds the ultimate measure of intelligence in consideration of a desirable future and in search for the means of bringing it progressively into existence. When professed idealism turns out to be a narrow pragmatism—narrow because taking for granted the finality of ends determined by historic conditions—the time has arrived for a pragmatism which shall be empirically idealistic, proclaiming the essential connexion of intelligence with the unachieved future—with possibilities involving a transfiguration.

IV

Why has the description of experience been so remote from the facts of empirical situations? To answer this question throws light upon the submergence of recent philosophizing in epistemology—that is, in discussions of the nature, possibility, and limits of knowledge in general, and in the attempt to reach conclusions regarding the ultimate nature of reality from the answers given to such questions.

The reply to the query regarding the currency of a non-empirical doctrine of experience (even among professed empiricists) is that the traditional account is derived from a conception once universally entertained regarding the subject or bearer or center of experience. The description of experience has been forced into conformity with this prior conception; it has been primarily a deduction from it, actual empirical facts being poured into the moulds of the deductions. The characteristic feature of this prior notion is the assumption that experience centers in, or gathers about, or proceeds from a center or subject which is outside the course of natural existence, and set over against it:—it being of no importance, for present purposes, whether this antithetical subject is termed soul, or spirit, or mind, or ego, or consciousness, or just knower or knowing subject.

There are plausible grounds for thinking that the currency of the idea in question lies in the form which men's religious preoccupations took for many centuries. These were deliberately and systematically other-worldly. They centered about a Fall which was not an event in nature, but an aboriginal catastrophe that corrupted Nature; about a redemption made possible by supernatural means; about a life in another world—essentially, not merely spatially, Other. The supreme drama of destiny took place in a soul or spirit which, under the circumstances, could not be conceived other than as non-natural—extra-natural, if not, strictly speaking, supernatural. When Descartes and others broke away from medieval interests, they retained as commonplaces its intellectual apparatus: Such as, knowledge is exercised by a power that is extra-natural and set over against the world to be known. Even if they had wished to make a complete break, they had nothing to put as knower in the place of the soul. It may be doubted whether there was any available empirical substitute until science worked out the fact that physical changes are functional correlations of energies, and that man is continuous with other forms of life, and until social life had developed an intellectually free and responsible individual as its agent.

But my main point is not dependent upon any particular theory as to the historic origin of the notion about the bearer of experience. The point is there on its own account. The essential thing is that the bearer was conceived as outside of the world; so that experience consisted in the bearer's being affected through a type of operations not found anywhere in the world, while knowledge consists in surveying the world, looking at it, getting the view of a spectator.

The theological problem of attaining knowledge of God as ultimate reality was transformed in effect into the philosophical problem of the possibility of attaining knowledge of reality. For how is one to get beyond the limits of the subject and subjective occurrences? Familiarity breeds credulity oftener than contempt. How can a problem be artificial when men have been busy discussing it almost for three hundred years? But if the assumption that experience is something set over against the world is contrary to fact, then the problem of how self or mind or subjective experience or consciousness can reach knowledge of an external world is assuredly a meaningless problem. Whatever questions there may be about knowledge, they will not be the kind of problems which have formed epistemology.

The problem of knowledge as conceived in the industry of epistemology is the problem of knowledge *in general*—of the possibility, extent, and validity of knowledge in general. What does this "in general" mean? In ordinary life there are problems a-plenty of knowledge in particular; every conclusion we try to reach, theoretical or practical, affords such a problem. But there is no problem of knowledge in general. I do not mean, of course, that general statements cannot be made about knowledge, or that the problem of attaining these general statements is not a genuine one. On the contrary, specific instances of success and failure in inquiry exist, and are of such a character that one can discover the conditions conducing to success and failure. Statement of these conditions constitutes logic, and is capable of being an important aid in proper guidance of further attempts at knowing. But this logical problem of knowledge is at the opposite pole from the epistemological. Specific problems are about right conclusions to be reached—which means, in effect, right ways of going about the business of inquiry. They imply a difference between knowledge and error consequent upon right and wrong methods of inquiry and testing; not a difference between experience and the world. The problem of knowledge *überhaupt* exists because it is assumed that there is a knower in general, who is outside of the world to be known, and who is defined in terms antithetical to the traits of the world. With analogous assumptions, we could invent and discuss a problem of digestion in general. All that would be required would be to conceive the stomach and food-material as inhabiting different worlds. Such an assumption would leave on our hands the question of the possibility, extent, nature, and genuineness of any transaction between stomach and food.

But because the stomach and food inhabit a continuous stretch of existence, because digestion is but a correlation of diverse activities in one world, the problems of digestion are specific and plural: What are the particular correlations which constitute it? How does it proceed in different situations? What is favorable and what unfavorable to its best performance?—and so on. Can one deny that if we were to take our clue from the present empirical situation, including the scientific notion of evolution (biological continuity) and the existing arts of control of nature, subject and object would be treated as occupying the same natural world as unhesitatingly as we assume the natural conjunction of an animal and its food? Would it not follow that knowledge is one way in which natural energies coöperate? Would there be any problem save discovery of the peculiar structure of this coöperation, the conditions under which it occurs to best effect, and the consequences which issue from its occurrence?

It is a commonplace that the chief divisions of modern philosophy, idealism in its different kinds, realisms of various brands, so-called common-sense dualism, agnosticism, relativism, phenomenalism, have grown up around the epistemological problem of the general relation of subject and object. Problems not openly epistemological, such as whether the relation of changes in consciousness to physical changes is one of interaction, parallelism, or automatism have the same origin. What becomes of philosophy, consisting largely as it does of different answers to these questions, in case the assumptions which generate the questions have no empirical standing? Is it not time that philosophers turned from the attempt to determine the comparative merits of various replies to the questions to a consideration of the claims of the questions?

When dominating religious ideas were built up about the idea that the self is a stranger and pilgrim in this world; when morals, falling in line, found true good only in inner states of a self inaccessible to anything but its own private introspection; when political theory assumed the finality of disconnected and mutually exclusive personalities, the notion that the bearer of experience is antithetical to the world instead of being in and of it was congenial. It at least had the warrant of other beliefs and aspirations. But the doctrine of biological continuity or organic evolution has destroyed the scientific basis of the conception. Morally, men are now concerned with the amelioration of the conditions of the common lot in this world. Social sciences recognize that associated life is not a matter of physical juxtaposition, but of genuine intercourse—of community of experience in a non-metaphorical sense of community. Why should we longer try to patch up and refine and stretch the old solutions till they seem to cover the change of thought and practice? Why not recognize that the trouble is with the problem?

A belief in organic evolution which does not extend unreservedly to the way in which the subject of experience is thought of, and which does not strive to bring the entire theory of experience and knowing into line with biological and social facts, is hardly more than Pickwickian. There are many, for example, who hold that dreams, hallucinations, and errors cannot be accounted for at all except on the theory that a self (or "consciousness") exercises a modifying influence upon the "real object." The logical assumption is that consciousness is outside of the real object; that it is something different in kind, and therefore has the power of changing "reality" into appearance, of introducing "relativities" into things as they are in themselves—in short, of infecting real things with subjectivity. Such writers seem unaware of the fact that this assumption makes consciousness supernatural in the literal sense of the word; and that, to say the least, the conception can be accepted by one who accepts the doctrine of biological continuity only after every other way of dealing with the facts has been exhausted.

Realists, of course (at least some of the Neo-realists), deny any such miraculous intervention of consciousness. But they6 admit the reality of the problem; denying only this particular solution, they try to find some other way out, which will still preserve intact the notion of knowledge as a relationship of a general sort between subject and object.

Now dreams and hallucinations, errors, pleasures, and pains, possibly "secondary" qualities, do not occur save where there are organic centers of experience. They cluster about a subject. But to treat them as things which inhere exclusively in the subject; or as posing the problem of a distortion of *the* real object by a knower set over against the world, or as presenting facts to be explained primarily as cases of contemplative knowledge, is to testify that one has still to learn the lesson of evolution in its application to the affairs in hand.

If biological development be accepted, the subject of experience is at least an animal, continuous with other organic forms in a process of more complex organization. An animal in turn is at least continuous with chemico-physical processes which, in living things, are so organized as really to constitute the activities of life with all their defining traits. And experience is not identical with brain action; it is the entire organic agent-patient in all its interaction with the environment, natural and social. The brain is primarily an organ of a certain kind of behavior, not of knowing the world. And to repeat what has already been said, experiencing is just certain modes of interaction, of correlation, of natural objects among which the organism happens, so to say, to be one. It follows with equal force that experience means primarily not knowledge, but ways of doing and suffering. Knowing must be described by discovering what particular mode—qualitatively unique—of doing and suffering it is. As it is, we find experience assimilated to a non-empirical concept of knowledge, derived from an antecedent notion of a spectator outside of the world.*7

In short, the epistemological fashion of conceiving dreams, errors, "relativities," etc., depends upon the isolation of mind from intimate participation with other changes in the same continuous nexus. Thus it is like contending that when a bottle bursts, the bottle is, in some self-contained miraculous way, exclusively responsible. Since it is the nature of a bottle to be whole so as to retain fluids, bursting is an abnormal event— comparable to an hallucination. Hence it cannot belong to the "real" bottle; the "subjectivity" of glass is the cause. It is obvious that since the breaking of glass is a case of specific correlation of natural energies, its accidental and abnormal character has to do with *consequences*, not with causation. Accident is interference with the consequences for which the bottle is intended. The bursting considered apart from its bearing on these consequences is on a plane with any other occurrence in the wide world. But from the standpoint of a desired future, bursting is an anomaly, an interruption of the course of events.

The analogy with the occurrence of dreams, hallucinations, etc., seems to me exact. Dreams are not something outside of the regular course of events; they are in and of it. They are not cognitive distortions of real things; they are *more* real things. There is nothing abnormal in their existence, any more than there is in the bursting of a bottle.<u>8</u> But they may be abnormal, from the standpoint of their influence, of their operation as stimuli in calling out responses to modify the future. Dreams have often been taken as prognostics of what is to happen; they have modified conduct. A hallucination may lead a man to consult a doctor; such a consequence is right and proper. But the consultation indicates that the subject regarded it as an indication of consequences which he feared: as a symptom of a disturbed life. Or the hallucination may lead him to anticipate consequences which in fact flow only from the possession of great wealth. Then the hallucination is a disturbance of the normal course of events; the occurrence is wrongly *used* with reference to eventualities.

To regard reference to use and to desired and intended consequences as involving a "subjective" factor is to miss the point, for this has regard to the future. The uses to which a bottle are put are not mental; they do not consist of physical states; they are further correlations of natural existences. Consequences in use are genuine natural events; but they do not occur without the intervention of behavior involving anticipation of a future. The case is not otherwise with an hallucination. The differences it makes are in any case differences in the course of the one continuous world. The important point is whether they are good or bad differences. To use the hallucination as a sign of organic lesions that menace health means the beneficial result of seeing a physician; to respond to it as a sign of consequences such as actually follow only from being persecuted is to fall into error— to be abnormal. The persecutors are "unreal"; that is, there are no things which act as persecutors act; but the hallucination exists. Given its conditions it is as natural as any other event, and poses only the same kind of problem as is put by the occurrence of, say, a thunderstorm. The "unreality" of persecution is not, however, a subjective matter; it means that conditions do not exist for producing the *future* consequences which are now anticipated and reacted to. Ability to anticipate future consequences and to respond to them as stimuli to present behavior may well *define* what is meant by a mind or by "consciousness."[9] But this is only a way of saying just what kind of a real or natural existence the subject is; it is not to fall back on a preconception about an unnatural subject in order to characterize the occurrence of error.

Although the discussion may be already labored, let us take another example—the occurrence of disease. By definition it is pathological, abnormal. At one time in human history this abnormality was taken to be something dwelling in the intrinsic nature of the event—in its existence irrespective of future consequences. Disease was literally extra-natural and to be referred to demons, or to magic. No one to-day questions its naturalness—its place in the order of natural events. Yet it is abnormal—for it operates to effect results different from those which follow from health. The difference is a genuine empirical difference, not a mere mental distinction. From the standpoint of bearing on a subsequent course of events disease is unnatural, in spite of the naturalness of its occurrence and origin.

The habit of ignoring reference to the future is responsible for the assumption that to admit human participation in any form is to admit the "subjective" in a sense which alters the objective into the phenomenal. There have been those who, like Spinoza, regarded health and disease, good and ill, as equally real and equally unreal. However, only a few consistent materialists have included truth along with error as merely phenomenal and subjective. But if one does not regard movement toward possible consequences as genuine, wholesale denial of existential validity to all these distinctions is the only logical course. To select truth as objective and error as "subjective" is, on this basis, an unjustifiably partial procedure. Take everything as fixedly given, and both truth and error are arbitrary insertions into fact. Admit the genuineness of changes going on, and capacity for its direction through organic action based on foresight, and both truth and falsity are alike existential. It is human to regard the course of events which is in line with our own efforts as the *regular* course of events, and interruptions as abnormal, but this partiality of human desire is itself a part of what actually takes place.

It is now proposed to take a particular case of the alleged epistemological predicament for discussion, since the entire ground cannot be covered. I think, however, the instance chosen is typical, so that the conclusion reached may be generalized.

The instance is that of so-called relativity in perception. There are almost endless instances; the stick bent in water; the whistle changing pitch with change of distance from the ear; objects doubled when the eye is pushed; the destroyed star still visible, etc., etc. For our consideration we may take the case of a spherical object that presents itself to one observer as a flat circle, to another as a somewhat distorted elliptical surface. This situation gives empirical proof, so it is argued, of the difference between a real object and mere appearance. Since there is but one object, the existence of two *subjects* is the sole differentiating factor. Hence the two appearances of the one real object is proof of the intervening distorting action of the subject. And many of the Neo-realists who deny the difference in question, admit the case to be one of knowledge and accordingly to constitute an epistemological problem. They have in consequence developed wonderfully elaborate schemes of sundry kinds to maintain "epistemological monism" intact.

Let us try to keep close to empirical facts. In the first place the two unlike appearances of the one sphere are physically necessary because of the laws of reaction of light. If the one sphere did *not* assume these two appearances under given conditions, we should be confronted with a hopelessly irreconcilable discrepancy in the behavior of natural energy. That the result is natural is evidenced by the fact that two cameras—or other arrangements of apparatus for reflecting light—yield precisely the same results. Photographs are as genuinely physical existences as the original sphere; and they exhibit the two geometrical forms.

The statement of these facts makes no impression upon the confirmed epistemologist; he merely retorts that as long as it is admitted that the organism is the cause of a sphere being seen, from different points, as a circular and as an elliptical surface, the essence of his contention—the modification of the real object by the subject—is admitted. To the question why the same logic does not apply to photographic records he makes, as far as I know, no reply at all.

The source of the difficulty is not hard to see. The objection assumes that the alleged modifications of *the* real object are cases of *knowing* and hence attributable to the influence of a *knower.* Statements which set forth the doctrine will always be found to refer to the organic factor, to the eye, as an observer or a percipient. Even when reference is made to a lens or a mirror, language is sometimes used which suggests that the writer's naïveté is sufficiently gross to treat these physical factors as if they were engaged in perceiving the sphere. But as it is evident that the lens operates as a physical factor in correlation with other physical factors—notably light—so it ought to be evident that the intervention of the optical apparatus of the eye is a purely non-cognitive matter. The relation in question is not one between a sphere and a would-be knower of it, unfortunately condemned by the nature of the knowing apparatus to alter the thing he would know; it is an affair of the dynamic interaction of two physical agents in producing a third thing, an effect;—an affair of precisely the same kind as in any physical conjoint action, say the operation of hydrogen and oxygen in producing water. To regard the eye as primarily a knower, an observer, of things, is as crass as to assign that function to a camera. But unless the eye (or optical apparatus, or brain, or organism) be so regarded, there is absolutely no problem of observation or of knowledge in the case of the occurrence of elliptical and circular surfaces. Knowledge does not enter into the affair at all till *after* these forms of refracted light have been produced. About them there is nothing unreal. Light is really, physically, existentially, refracted into these forms. If the same spherical form upon refracting light to physical objects in two quite different positions produced the same geometric forms, there would, indeed, be something to marvel at—as there would be if wax produced the same results in contact simultaneously with a cold body and with a warm one. Why talk about *the real* object in relation to *a knower* when what is given is one real thing in dynamic connection with another real thing?

The way of dealing with the case will probably meet with a retort; at least, it has done so before. It has been said that the account given above and the account of traditional subjectivism differ only verbally. The essential thing in both, so it is said, is the admission that an activity of a self or subject or organism makes a difference in the real object. Whether the subject makes this difference in the very process of knowing or makes it prior to the act of knowing is a minor matter; what is important is that the known thing has, by the time it is known, been "subjectified."

The objection gives a convenient occasion for summarizing the main points of the argument. On the one hand, the retort of the objector depends upon talking about *the* real object. Employ the term "*a* real object," and the change produced by the activity characteristic of the optical apparatus is of just the same kind as that of the camera lens or that of any other physical agency. Every event in the world marks a difference made to one existence in active conjunction with some other existence. And, as for the alleged subjectivity, if subjective is used merely as an adjective to designate the specific activity of a particular existence, comparable, say, to the term feral, applied to tiger, or metallic, applied to iron, then of course reference to subjective is legitimate. But it is also tautological. It is like saying that flesh eaters are carnivorous. But the term "subjective" is so consecrated to other uses, usually implying invidious contrast with objectivity (while subjective in the sense just suggested means specific mode *of* objectivity), that it is difficult to maintain this innocent sense. Its use in any disparaging way in the situation before us—any sense implicating contrast with a real object—assumes that the organism *ought* not to make any difference when it operates in conjunction with other things. Thus we run to earth that assumption that the subject is heterogeneous from every other natural existence; it is to be the one otiose, inoperative thing in a moving world—our old assumption of the self as outside of things.10

What and where is knowledge in the case we have been considering? Not, as we have already seen, in the production of forms of light having a circular and elliptical surface. These forms are natural happenings. They may enter into knowledge or they may not, according to circumstances. Countless such refractive changes take place without being noted.11 When they become subject-matter for knowledge, the inquiry they set on foot may take on an indefinite variety of forms. One may be interested in ascertaining more about the structural peculiarities of the forms themselves; one may be interested in the mechanism of their production; one may find problems in projective geometry, or in drawing and painting—all depending upon the specific matter-of-fact context. The forms may be *objectives* of knowledge—of reflective examination—or they may be means of knowing something else. It may happen—under some circumstances it does happen—that the objective of inquiry is the nature of the geometric form which, when refracting light, gives rise to these other forms. In this case the sphere is the thing known, and in this case, the forms of light are signs or evidence of the conclusion to be drawn. There is no more reason for supposing that they *are* (mis)knowledges of the sphere—that the sphere is necessarily and from the start what one is trying to know—than for supposing that the position of the mercury in the thermometer tube is a cognitive distortion of atmospheric pressure. In each case (that of the mercury and that of, say, a circular surface) the primary datum is a physical happening. In each case it may be used, upon occasion, as a sign or evidence of the nature of the causes which brought it about. Given the position in question, the circular form would be an intrinsically *unreliable* evidence of the nature and position of the spherical body only in case it, as the direct datum of perception, were *not* what it is—a circular form.

I confess that all this seems so obvious that the reader is entitled to inquire into the motive for reciting such plain facts.

Were it not for the persistence of the epistemological problem it would be an affront to the reader's intelligence to dwell upon them. But as long as such facts as we have been discussing furnish the subject-matter with which philosophizing is peculiarly concerned, these commonplaces must be urged and reiterated. They bear out two contentions which are important at the juncture, although they will lose special significance as soon as these are habitually recognized: Negatively, a prior and non-empirical notion of the self is the source of the prevailing belief that experience as such is primarily cognitional—a knowledge affair; positively, *knowledge is always a matter of the use that is made of experienced natural events*, a use in which given things are treated as indications of what will be experienced under different conditions.

Let us make one effort more to clear up these points. Suppose it is a question of knowledge of water. The thing to be known does not present itself primarily as a matter of knowledge-and-ignorance at all. It occurs as a stimulus to action and as the source of certain undergoings. It is something to react to:—to drink, to wash with, to put out fire with, and also something that reacts unexpectedly to our reactions, that makes us undergo disease, suffocation, drowning. In this twofold way, water or anything else enters into experience. Such presence in experience has of itself nothing to do with knowledge or consciousness; nothing that is in the sense of depending upon them, though it has everything to do with knowledge and consciousness in the sense that the latter depends upon prior experience of this non-cognitive sort. Man's experience is what it is because his response to things (even successful response) and the reactions of things to his life, are so radically different from knowledge. The difficulties and tragedies of life, the stimuli to acquiring knowledge, lie in the radical disparity of presence-in-experience and presence-in-knowing. Yet the immense importance of knowledge experience, the fact that turning presence-in-experience over into presence-in-a-knowledge-experience is the sole mode of control of nature, has systematically hypnotized European philosophy since the time of

Socrates into thinking that all experiencing is a mode of knowing, if not good knowledge, then a low-grade or confused or implicit knowledge.

When water is an adequate stimulus to action or when its reactions oppress and overwhelm us, it remains outside the scope of knowledge. When, however, the bare presence of the thing (say, as optical stimulus) ceases to operate directly as stimulus to response and begins to operate in connection with a forecast of the consequences it will effect when responded to, it begins to acquire meaning—to be known, to be an object. It is noted as something which is wet, fluid, satisfies thirst, allays uneasiness, etc. The conception that we begin with a known visual quality which is thereafter enlarged by adding on qualities apprehended by the other senses does not rest upon experience; it rests upon making experience conform to the notion that every experience *must* be a cognitive noting. As long as the visual stimulus operates as a stimulus on its own account, there is no apprehension, no noting, of color or light at all. To much the greater portion of sensory stimuli we react in precisely this wholly non-cognitive way. In the attitude of suspended response in which consequences are anticipated, the direct stimulus becomes a sign or index of something else—and thus matter of noting or apprehension or acquaintance, or whatever term may be employed. This difference (together, of course, with the consequences which go with it) is the difference which the natural event of knowing makes to the natural event of direct organic stimulation. It is no change of a reality into an unreality, of an object into something subjective; it is no secret, illicit, or epistemological transformation; it is a genuine acquisition of new and distinctive features through entering into relations with things with which it was not formerly connected—namely, possible and future things.

But, replies some one so obsessed with the epistemological point of view that he assumes that the prior account is a rival epistemology in disguise, all this involves no change in Reality, no difference made to Reality. Water was all the time all the things it is ever found out to be. Its real nature has not been altered by knowing it; any such alteration means a mis-knowing.

In reply let it be said,—once more and finally,—there is no assertion or implication about *the* real object or *the* real world or *the* reality. Such an assumption goes with that epistemological universe of discourse which has to be abandoned in an empirical universe of discourse. The change is of *a* real object. An incident of the world operating as a physiologically direct stimulus is assuredly a reality. Responded to, it produces specific consequences in virtue of the response. Water is not drunk unless somebody drinks it; it does not quench thirst unless a thirsty person drinks it—and so on. Consequences occur whether one is aware of them or not; they are integral facts in experience. But let one of these consequences be anticipated and let it, as anticipated, become an indispensable element in the stimulus, and then there is a known object. It is not that knowing *produces* a change, but that it *is* a change of the specific kind described. A serial process, the successive portions of which are as such incapable of simultaneous occurrence, is telescoped and condensed into an object, a unified inter-reference of contemporaneous properties, most of which express potentialities rather than completed data.

Because of this change, an *object* possesses truth or error (which the physical occurrence as such never has); it is classifiable as fact or fantasy; it is of a sort or kind, expresses an essence or nature, possesses implications, etc., etc. That is to say, it is marked by specifiable *logical* traits not found in physical occurrences as such. Because objective idealisms have seized upon these traits as constituting the very essence of Reality is no reason for proclaiming that they are ready-made features of physical happenings, and hence for maintaining that knowing is nothing but an appearance of things on a stage for which "consciousness" supplies the footlights. For only the epistemological predicament leads to "presentations" being regarded as cognitions of things which were previously unpresented. In any empirical situation of everyday life or of science, knowledge signifies something stated or inferred of another thing. Visible water is not a more less erroneous presentation of H_2O, but H_2O is a knowledge about the thing we see, drink, wash with, sail on, and use for power.

A further point and the present phase of discussion terminates. Treating knowledge as a presentative relation between the knower and object makes it necessary to regard the mechanism of *presentation* as constituting the act of knowing. Since things may be presented in sense-perception, in recollection, in imagination and in conception, and since the mechanism in every one of these four styles of presentation is sensory-cerebral the problem of knowing becomes a mind-body problem.[12] The psychological, or physiological, mechanism of presentation involved in seeing a chair, remembering what I ate yesterday for luncheon, imagining the moon the size of a cart wheel, conceiving a mathematical continuum is identified with the operation of knowing. The evil consequences are twofold. The problem of the relation of mind and body has become a part of the problem of the possibility of knowledge in general, to the further complication of a matter already hopelessly constrained. Meantime the actual process of knowing, namely, operations of controlled observation, inference, reasoning, and testing, the only process with *intellectual* import, is dismissed as irrelevant to the theory of knowing. The methods of knowing practised in daily life and science are excluded from consideration in the philosophical theory of knowing. Hence the constructions of the latter become more and more elaborately artificial because there is no definite check upon them. It would be easy to quote from epistemological writers statements to the effect that these processes (which supply the only empirically verifiable facts of knowing) are *merely* inductive in character, or even that they are of purely psychological significance. It would be difficult to find a more complete inversion of the facts than in the latter statement, since presentation constitutes in fact the psychological affair. A confusion of logic with physiological physiology has bred hybrid epistemology, with the amazing result that the technique of effective inquiry is rendered irrelevant to the theory of knowing, and those physical events involved in the occurrence of data for knowing are treated as if they constituted the act of knowing.

V

What are the bearings of our discussion upon the conception of the present scope and office of philosophy? What do our conclusions indicate and demand with reference to philosophy itself? For the philosophy which reaches such conclusions regarding knowledge and mind must apply them, sincerely and whole-heartedly, to its idea of its own nature. For philosophy claims to be one form or mode of knowing. If, then, the conclusion is reached that knowing is a way of employing empirical occurrences with respect to increasing power to direct the consequences which flow from things, the application of the conclusion must be made to philosophy itself. It, too, becomes not a contemplative survey of existence nor an analysis of what is past and done with, but an outlook upon future possibilities with reference to attaining the better and averting the worse. Philosophy must take, with good grace, its own medicine.

It is easier to state the negative results of the changed idea of philosophy than the positive ones. The point that occurs to mind most readily is that philosophy will have to surrender all pretension to be peculiarly concerned with ultimate reality, or with reality as a complete (i.e., completed) whole: with *the* real object. The surrender is not easy of achievement. The philosophic tradition that comes to us from classic Greek thought and that was reinforced by Christian philosophy in the Middle Ages discriminates philosophical knowing from other modes of knowing by means of an alleged peculiarly intimate concern with supreme, ultimate, true reality. To deny this trait to philosophy seems to many to be the suicide of philosophy; to be a systematic adoption of skepticism or agnostic positivism.

The pervasiveness of the tradition is shown in the fact that so vitally a contemporary thinker as Bergson, who finds a philosophic revolution involved in abandonment of the traditional identification of the truly real with the fixed (an identification inherited from Greek thought), does not find it in his heart to abandon the counterpart identification of philosophy with search for the truly Real; and hence finds it necessary to substitute an ultimate and absolute flux for an ultimate and absolute permanence. Thus his great empirical services in calling attention to the fundamental importance of considerations of time for problems of life and mind get compromised with a mystic, non-empirical "Intuition"; and we find him preoccupied with solving, by means of his new idea of ultimate reality, the traditional problems of realities-in-themselves and phenomena, matter and mind, free-will and determinism, God and the world. Is not that another evidence of the influence of the classic idea about philosophy?

Even the new realists are not content to take their realism as a plea for approaching subject-matter directly instead of through the intervention of epistemological apparatus; they find it necessary first to determine the status of *the* real object. Thus they too become entangled in the problem of the possibility of error, dreams, hallucinations, etc., in short, the problem of evil. For I take it that an uncorrupted realism would accept such things as real events, and find in them no other problems than those attending the consideration of any real occurrence—namely, problems of structure, origin, and operation.

It is often said that pragmatism, unless it is content to be a contribution to mere methodology, must develop a theory of Reality. But the chief characteristic trait of the pragmatic notion of reality is precisely that no theory of Reality in general, *überhaupt*, is possible or needed. It occupies the position of an emancipated empiricism or a thoroughgoing naïve realism. It finds that "reality" is a *denotative* term, a word used to designate indifferently everything that happens. Lies, dreams, insanities, deceptions, myths, theories are all of them just the events which they specifically are. Pragmatism is content to take its stand with science; for science finds all such events to be subject-matter of description and inquiry—just like stars and fossils, mosquitoes and malaria, circulation and vision. It also takes its stand with daily life, which finds that such things really have to be reckoned with as they occur interwoven in the texture of events.

The only way in which the term reality can ever become more than a blanket denotative term is through recourse to specific events in all their diversity and thatness. Speaking summarily, I find that the retention by philosophy of the notion of a Reality feudally superior to the events of everyday occurrence is the chief source of the increasing isolation of philosophy from common sense and science. For the latter do not operate in any such region. As with them of old, philosophy in dealing with real difficulties finds itself still hampered by reference to realities more real, more ultimate, than those which directly happen.

I have said that identifying the cause of philosophy with the notion of superior reality is the cause of an *increasing* isolation from science and practical life. The phrase reminds us that there was a time when the enterprise of science and the moral interests of men both moved in a universe invidiously distinguished from that of ordinary occurrence. While all that happens is equally real—since it really happens—happenings are not of equal worth. Their respective consequences, their import, varies tremendously. Counterfeit money, although real (or rather *because* real), is really different from valid circulatory medium, just as disease is really different from health; different in specific structure and so different in consequences. In occidental thought, the Greeks were the first to draw the distinction between the genuine and the spurious in a generalized fashion and to formulate and enforce its tremendous significance for the conduct of life. But since they had at command no technique of experimental analysis and no adequate technique of mathematical analysis, they were compelled to treat the difference of the true and the false, the dependable and the deceptive, as signifying two kinds of existence, the truly real and the apparently real.

Two points can hardly be asserted with too much emphasis. The Greeks were wholly right in the feeling that questions of good and ill, as far as they fall within human control, are bound up with discrimination of the genuine from the spurious, of "being" from what only pretends to be. But because they lacked adequate instrumentalities for coping with this difference in specific situations, they were forced to treat the difference as a wholesale and rigid one. Science was concerned with vision of ultimate and true reality; opinion was concerned with getting along with apparent realities. Each had its appropriate region permanently marked off. Matters of opinion could never become matters of science; their intrinsic nature forbade. When the practice of science went on under such conditions, science and philosophy were one and the same thing. Both had to do with ultimate reality in its rigid and insuperable difference from ordinary occurrences.

We have only to refer to the way in which medieval life wrought the philosophy of an ultimate and supreme reality into the context of practical life to realize that for centuries political and moral interests were bound up with the distinction between the absolutely real and the relatively real. The difference was no matter of a remote technical philosophy, but one which controlled life from the cradle to the grave, from the grave to the endless life after death. By means of a vast institution, which in effect was state as well as church, the claims of ultimate reality were enforced; means of access to it were provided. Acknowledgment of The Reality brought security in this world and salvation in the next. It is not necessary to report the story of the change which has since taken place. It is enough for our purposes to note that none of the modern philosophies of a superior reality, or *the* real object, idealistic or realistic, holds that its insight makes a difference like that between sin and holiness, eternal condemnation and eternal bliss. While in its own context the philosophy of ultimate reality entered into the vital concerns of men, it now tends to be an ingenious dialectic exercised in professorial corners by a few who have retained ancient premises while rejecting their application to the conduct of life.

The increased isolation from science of any philosophy identified with the problem of *the* real is equally marked. For the growth of science has consisted precisely in the invention of an equipment, a technique of appliances and procedures, which, accepting all occurrences as homogeneously real, proceeds to distinguish the authenticated from the spurious, the true from the false, by specific modes of treatment in specific situations. The procedures of the trained engineer, of the competent physician, of the laboratory expert, have turned out to be the only ways of discriminating the counterfeit from the valid. And they have revealed that the difference is not one of antecedent fixity of existence, but one of mode of treatment and of the consequences thereon attendant. After mankind has learned to put its trust in specific procedures in order to make its discriminations between the false and the true, philosophy arrogates to itself the enforcement of the distinction at its own cost.

More than once, this essay has intimated that the counterpart of the idea of invidiously real reality is the spectator notion of knowledge. If the knower, however defined, is set over against the world to be known, knowing consists in possessing a transcript, more or less accurate but otiose, of real things. Whether this transcript is presentative in character (as realists say) or whether it is by means of states of consciousness which represent things (as subjectivists say), is a matter of great importance in its own context. But, in another regard, this difference is negligible in comparison with the point in which both agree. Knowing is viewing from outside. But if it be true that the self or subject of experience is part and parcel of the course of events, it follows that the self *becomes* a knower. It becomes a mind in virtue of a distinctive way of partaking in the course of events. The significant distinction is no longer between the knower *and* the world; it is between different ways of being in and of the movement of things; between a brute physical way and a purposive, intelligent way.

There is no call to repeat in detail the statements which have been advanced. Their net purport is that the directive presence of future possibilities in dealing with existent conditions is what is meant by knowing; that the self becomes a knower or mind when anticipation of future consequences operates as its stimulus. What we are now concerned with is the effect of this conception upon the nature of philosophic knowing.

As far as I can judge, popular response to pragmatic philosophy was moved by two quite different considerations. By some it was thought to provide a new species of sanctions, a new mode of apologetics, for certain religious ideas whose standing had been threatened. By others, it was welcomed because it was taken as a sign that philosophy was about to surrender its otiose and speculative remoteness; that philosophers were beginning to recognize that philosophy is of account only if, like everyday knowing and like science, it affords guidance to action and thereby makes a difference in the event. It was welcomed as a sign that philosophers were willing to have the worth of their philosophizing measured by responsible tests.

I have not seen this point of view emphasized, or hardly recognized, by professional critics. The difference of attitude can probably be easily explained. The epistemological universe of discourse is so highly technical that only those who have been trained in the history of thought think in terms of it. It did not occur, accordingly, to non-technical readers to interpret the doctrine that the meaning and validity of thought are fixed by differences made in consequences and in satisfactoriness, to mean consequences in personal feelings. Those who were professionally trained, however, took the statement to mean that consciousness or mind in the mere act of looking at things modifies them. It understood the doctrine of test of validity by consequences to mean that apprehensions and conceptions are true if the modifications affected by them were of an emotionally desirable tone.

Prior discussion should have made it reasonably clear that the source of this misunderstanding lies in the neglect of temporal considerations. The change made in things by the self in knowing is not immediate and, so to say, cross-sectional. It is longitudinal—in the redirection given to changes already going on. Its analogue is found in the changes which take place in the development of, say, iron ore into a watch-spring, not in those of the miracle of transubstantiation. For the static, cross-sectional, non-temporal relation of subject and object, the pragmatic hypothesis substitutes apprehension of a thing in terms of the results in other things which it is tending to effect. For the unique epistemological relation, it substitutes a practical relation of a familiar type:—responsive behavior which changes in time the subject-matter to which it applies. The unique thing about the responsive behavior which constitutes knowing is the specific difference which marks it off from other modes of response, namely, the part played in it by anticipation and prediction. Knowing is the act, stimulated by this foresight, of securing and averting consequences. The success of the achievement measures the standing of the foresight by which response is directed. The popular impression that pragmatic philosophy means that philosophy shall develop ideas relevant to the actual crises of life, ideas influential in dealing with them and tested by the assistance they afford, is correct.

Reference to practical response suggests, however, another misapprehension. Many critics have jumped at the obvious association of the word pragmatic with practical. They have assumed that the intent is to limit all knowledge, philosophic included, to promoting "action," understanding by action either just any bodily movement, or those bodily movements which conduce to the preservation and grosser well-being of the body. James' statement, that general conceptions must "cash in" has been taken (especially by European critics) to mean that the end and measure of intelligence lies in the narrow and coarse utilities which it produces. Even an acute American thinker, after first criticizing pragmatism as a kind of idealistic epistemology, goes on to treat it as a doctrine which regards intelligence as a lubricating oil facilitating the workings of the body.

One source of the misunderstanding is suggested by the fact that "cashing in" to James meant that a general idea must always be capable of verification in specific existential cases. The notion of "cashing in" says nothing about the breadth or depth of the specific consequences. As an empirical doctrine, it could not say anything about them in general; the specific cases must speak for themselves. If one conception is verified in terms of eating beefsteak, and another in terms of a favorable credit balance in the bank, that is not because of anything in the theory, but because of the specific nature of the conceptions in question, and because there exist particular events like hunger and trade. If there are also existences in which the most liberal esthetic ideas and the most generous moral conceptions can be verified by specific embodiment, assuredly so much the better. The fact that a strictly empirical philosophy was taken by so many critics to imply an *a priori* dogma about the kind of consequences capable of existence is evidence, I think, of the inability of many philosophers to think in concretely empirical terms. Since the critics were themselves accustomed to get results by manipulating the concepts of "consequences" and of "practice," they assumed that even a would-be empiricist must be doing the same sort of thing. It will, I suppose, remain for a long time incredible to some that a philosopher should really intend to go to specific experiences to determine of what scope and depth practice admits, and what sort of consequences the world permits to come into being. Concepts are so clear; it takes so little time to develop their implications; experiences are so confused, and it requires so much time and energy to lay hold of them. And yet these same critics charge pragmatism with adopting subjective and emotional standards!

As a matter of fact, the pragmatic theory of intelligence means that the function of mind is to project new and more complex ends—to free experience from routine and from caprice. Not the use of thought to accomplish purposes already given either in the mechanism of the body or in that of the existent state of society, but the use of intelligence to liberate and liberalize action, is the pragmatic lesson. Action restricted to given and fixed ends may attain great technical efficiency; but efficiency is the only quality to which it can lay claim. Such action is mechanical (or becomes so), no matter what the scope of the preformed end, be it the Will of God or *Kultur*. But the doctrine that intelligence develops within the sphere of action for the sake of possibilities not yet given is the opposite of a doctrine of mechanical efficiency. Intelligence *as* intelligence is inherently forward-looking; only by ignoring its primary function does it become a mere means for an end already given. The latter *is* servile, even when the end is labeled moral, religious, or esthetic. But action directed to ends to which the agent has not previously been attached inevitably carries with it a quickened and enlarged spirit. A pragmatic intelligence is a creative intelligence, not a routine mechanic.

All this may read like a defense of pragmatism by one concerned to make out for it the best case possible. Such is not, however, the intention. The purpose is to indicate the extent to which intelligence frees action from a mechanically instrumental character. Intelligence is, indeed, instrumental *through* action to the determination of the qualities of future experience. But the very fact that the concern of intelligence is with the future, with the as-yet-unrealized (and with the given and the established only as conditions of the realization of possibilities), makes the action in which it takes effect generous and liberal; free of spirit. Just that action which extends and approves intelligence has an intrinsic value of its own in being instrumental:—the intrinsic value of being informed with intelligence in behalf of the enrichment of life. By the same stroke, intelligence becomes truly liberal: knowing is a human undertaking, not an esthetic appreciation carried on by a refined class or a capitalistic possession of a few learned specialists, whether men of science or of philosophy.

More emphasis has been put upon what philosophy is not than upon what it may become. But it is not necessary, it is not even desirable, to set forth philosophy as a scheduled program. There are human difficulties of an urgent, deep-seated kind which may be clarified by trained reflection, and whose solution may be forwarded by the careful development of hypotheses. When it is understood that philosophic thinking is caught up in the actual course of events, having the office of guiding them towards a prosperous issue, problems will abundantly present themselves.

Philosophy will not solve these problems; philosophy is vision, imagination, reflection—and these functions, apart from action, modify nothing and hence resolve nothing. But in a complicated and perverse world, action which is not informed with vision, imagination, and reflection, is more likely to increase confusion and conflict than to straighten things out. It is not easy for generous and sustained reflection to become a guiding and illuminating method in action. Until it frees itself from identification with problems which are supposed to depend upon Reality as such, or its distinction from a world of Appearance, or its relation to a Knower as such, the hands of philosophy are tied. Having no chance to link its fortunes with a responsible career by suggesting things to be tried, it cannot identify itself with questions which actually arise in the vicissitudes of life. Philosophy recovers itself when it ceases to be a device for dealing with the problems of philosophers and becomes a method, cultivated by philosophers, for dealing with the problems of men.

Emphasis must vary with the stress and special impact of the troubles which perplex men. Each age knows its own ills, and seeks its own remedies. One does not have to forecast a particular program to note that the central need of any program at the present day is an adequate conception of the nature of intelligence and its place in action. Philosophy cannot disavow responsibility for many misconceptions of the nature of intelligence which now hamper its efficacious operation. It has at least a negative task imposed upon it. It must take away the burdens which it has laid upon the intelligence of the common man in struggling with his difficulties. It must deny and eject that intelligence which is naught but a distant eye, registering in a remote and alien medium the spectacle of nature and life. To enforce the fact that the emergence of imagination and thought is relative to the connexion of the sufferings of men with their doings is of itself to illuminate those sufferings and to instruct those doings. To catch mind in its connexion with the entrance of the novel into the course of the world is to be on the road to see that intelligence is itself the most promising of all novelties, the revelation of the meaning of that transformation of past into future which is the reality of every present. To reveal intelligence as the organ for the guidance of this transformation, the sole director of its quality, is to make a declaration of present untold significance for action. To elaborate these convictions of the connexion of intelligence with what men undergo because of their doings and with the emergence and direction of the creative, the novel, in the world is of itself a program which will keep philosophers busy until something more worth while is forced upon them. For the elaboration has to be made through application to all the disciplines which have an intimate connexion with human conduct:—to logic, ethics, esthetics, economics, and the procedure of the sciences formal and natural.

I also believe that there is a genuine sense in which the enforcement of the pivotal position of intelligence in the world and thereby in control of human fortunes (so far as they are manageable) is the peculiar problem in the problems of life which come home most closely to ourselves—to ourselves living not merely in the early twentieth century but in the United States. It is easy to be foolish about the connexion of thought with national life. But I do not see how any one can question the distinctively national color of English, or French, or German philosophies. And if of late the history of thought has come under the domination of the German dogma of an inner evolution of ideas, it requires but a little inquiry to convince oneself that that dogma itself testifies to a particularly nationalistic need and origin. I believe that philosophy in America will be lost between chewing a historic cud long since reduced to woody fiber, or an apologetics for lost causes (lost to natural science), or a scholastic, schematic formalism, unless it can somehow bring to consciousness America's own needs and its own implicit principle of successful action.

This need and principle, I am convinced, is the necessity of a deliberate control of policies by the method of intelligence, an intelligence which is not the faculty of intellect honored in text-books and neglected elsewhere, but which is the sum-total of impulses, habits, emotions, records, and discoveries which forecast what is desirable and undesirable in future possibilities, and which contrive ingeniously in behalf of imagined good. Our life has no background of sanctified categories upon which we may fall back; we rely upon precedent as authority only to our own undoing— for with us there is such a continuously novel situation that final reliance upon precedent entails some class interest guiding us by the nose whither it will. British empiricism, with its appeal to what has been in the past, is, after all, only a kind of *a priorism*. For it lays down a fixed rule for future intelligence to follow; and only the immersion of philosophy in technical learning prevents our seeing that this is the essence of *a priorism*.

We pride ourselves upon being realistic, desiring a hardheaded cognizance of facts, and devoted to mastering the means of life. We pride ourselves upon a practical idealism, a lively and easily moved faith in possibilities as yet unrealized, in willingness to make sacrifice for their realization. Idealism easily becomes a sanction of waste and carefulness, and realism a sanction of legal formalism in behalf of things as they are—the rights of the possessor. We thus tend to combine a loose and ineffective optimism with assent to the doctrine of take who take can: a deification of power. All peoples at all times have been narrowly realistic in practice and have then employed idealization to cover up in sentiment and theory their brutalities. But never, perhaps, has the tendency been so dangerous and so tempting as with ourselves. Faith in the power of intelligence to imagine a future which is the projection of the desirable in the present, and to invent the instrumentalities of its realization, is our salvation. And it is a faith which must be nurtured and made articulate: surely a sufficiently large task for our philosophy.

REFORMATION OF LOGIC

ADDISON W. MOORE

I

In a general survey of the development of logical theory one is struck by the similarity, not to say identity, of the indictments which reformers, since the days of Aristotle, have brought against it. The most fundamental of these charges are: first, that the theory of logic has left it formal and with little significance for the advancement of science and the conduct of society; second, that it has great difficulty in avoiding the predicament of logical operations that are merely labored reproductions of non-logical activities and therefore tautologous and trifling, or of logical operations that are so far removed from immediate, non-logical experience that they are irrelevant; third, that logical theory has had trouble in finding room in its own household for both truth and error; each crowds out the other.

The identity of these indictments regardless of the general philosophical faith, empiricism, or rationalism, realism, or idealism to which the reformer or the logic to be reformed has belonged, suggests that whatever the differences in the doctrines of these various philosophic traditions, they possess a common ground from which these common difficulties spring.

It is the conviction of a number who are at present attempting to rid logic of these ancient disabilities that their common source is to be found in a lack of continuity between the acts of intelligence (or to avoid the dangers of hypostasis, intelligent acts) and other acts; between logical conduct and other conduct. So wide, indeed, is this breach, that often little remains of the act of knowing but the name. It may still be called an act, but it has no describable instruments nor technique of operation. It is an indefinable and often mystical performance of which only the results can be stated. In recent logical discussion this techniqueless act of knowing has been properly enough transformed into an indefinable "external relation" in which an entity called a knower stands to another entity called the known.

For many centuries this breach between the operations of intelligence and other operations has been closed by various metaphysical devices with the result that logic has been a hybrid science,—half logic, half metaphysics and epistemology. So great has been the momentum of the metaphysical tradition that long after we have begun to discover the connection between logical and non-logical operations its methods remain to plague us. Efforts to heal the breach without a direct appeal to metaphysical agencies have been made by attempting a complete logicizing of all operations. But besides requiring additional metaphysics to effect it, the procedure is as fatal to continuity as is an impassable disjunction. Continuity demands distinction as well as connection. It requires the development, the *growth* of old material and functions into new forms.

Driven by the difficulties of this complete logicization, which are as serious as those of isolation, logical theory was obliged to reinstate some sort of distinction. This it did by resorting to the categories of "explicit" and "implicit." All so-called non-logical operations were regarded as "implicitly" logical. And, paradoxically, logical operations had for their task the transformation of the implicit into the explicit.

An adequate account of the origin and continuance of this isolation of the conduct of intelligence from other conduct is too long a story to be told here. Suffice it to recall that in the society in which the distinction between immediate and reflective experience, between opinion and science, between percepts and universals was first made, intelligence was largely the possession of a special and privileged class removed in great measure from hand-to-hand contact with nature and with much of society. Because it did not fully participate in the operations of nature and society intelligence could not become fully domesticated, i.e., fully naturalized and socialized in its world. It was a charmed spectator of the cosmic and social drama. Doubtless when Greek intelligence discovered the distinction between immediate and reflective experience—possibly the most momentous discovery in history—"the world," as Kant says of the speculations of Thales, "must suddenly have appeared in a new light." But not recognizing the full significance of this discovery, ideas, universals, became but a wondrous spectacle for the eye of reason. They brought, to be sure, blessed relief from the bewildering and baffling flux of perception. But it was the relief of sanctuary, not of victory.

That the brilliant speculations of Greek intelligence were barren because there was no technique for testing and applying them in detail is an old story. But it is merely a restatement, not a solution, of the pertinent question. This is: why did not Greek intelligence develop such a technique? The answer lies in the fact that the technique of intelligence is to be found precisely in the details of the operations of nature and of human conduct from which an aristocratic intelligence is always in large measure shut off. Intelligence cannot operate fruitfully in a vacuum. It must be incarnate. It must, as Hegel said, have "hands and feet." When we turn to the history of modern science the one thing that stands out is that it was not until the point was reached where intelligence was ready (continuing the Hegelian figure) to thrust its hands into the vitals of nature and society that it began to acquire a real control over its operations.

In default of such controlling technique there was nothing to be done with this newly found instrument of intelligence—the universal—but to retain it as an object of contemplation and of worshipful adoration. This involved, of course, its hypostasis as the metaphysical reality of supreme importance. With this, the only difference between "opinion" and "science" became one of the kind of objects known. That universals were known by reason and particulars by sense was of little more logical significance than that sounds are known by the ear and smells by the nose. Particulars and universals were equally given. If the latter required some abstraction this was regarded as merely auxiliary to the immediate vision, as sniffing is to the perception of odor. That universals should or could be conceived as experimental, as hypotheses, was, when translated into later theology, the sin against the Holy Ghost.

However, the fact that the particulars in the world of opinion were the stimuli to the "recollection" of universals and that the latter in turn were the patterns, the forms, for the particulars, opened the way in actual practice for the exercise of a great deal of the controlling function of the universals. But the failure to recognize this control value of the universal as fundamental, made it necessary for the universal to exercise its function surreptitiously, in the disguise of a pattern and in the clumsy garb of imitation and participation.

With perceptions, desires, and impulses relegated to the world of opinion and shadows, and with the newly discovered instrument of knowledge turned into an object, the knower was stripped of all his knowing apparatus and was left an empty, scuttled entity definable and describable only as "a knower." The knower must know, even if he had nothing to know with. Hence the mystical almost indefinable character of the knowing act or relation. I say "almost indefinable"; for as an act it had, of course, to have some sort of conceptualized form. And this form vision naturally furnished. "Naturally," because intelligence was so largely contemplative, and vision so largely immediate, unanalyzed, and diaphanous. There was, to be sure, the concept of effluxes. But this was a statement of the fact of vision in terms of its results, not of the process itself. Thus it was that the whole terminology of knowing which we still use was moulded and fixed upon a very crude conception of one of the constituents of its process. There can be no doubt that this terminology has added much to the inertia against which the advance of logical theory has worked. It would be interesting to see what would be the effect upon logical theory of the substitution of an auditory or olfactory terminology for visual; or of a visual terminology revised to agree with modern scientific analysis of the *act* of vision as determined by its connections with other functions.

With the act of knowing stripped of its technique and left a bare, unique, indescribable act or relation, the foundations for epistemological and metaphysical logic were laid. That Greek logic escaped the ravages of epistemology was due to the saving materialism in its metaphysical conception of mind and to the steadfastness of the aristocratic régime. But when medieval theology and Cartesian metaphysics had destroyed the last remnant of metaphysical connection between the knowing mind and nature, and when revolutions had torn the individual from his social moorings, the stage for epistemological logic was fully set. I do not mean to identify the epistemological situation with the Cartesian disjunction. That disjunction was but the metaphysical expression of the one which constitutes the real foundation of epistemology—the disjunction, namely, between the act of knowing and other acts.

From this point logic has followed one of two general courses. It has sought continuity by attempting to reduce non-logical things and operations to terms of logical operations, i.e., to sensations or universals or both; or it has attempted to exclude entirely the act of knowing from logic and to transfer logical distinctions and operations, and even the attributes of truth and error to objects which, significantly enough, are still composed of these same hypostatized logical processes. The first course results in an epistemological logic of some form of the idealistic tradition, rationalism, sensationalism, or transcendentalism, depending upon whether universals, or sensations, or a combination of both, is made fundamental in the constitution of the object. The second course yields an epistemological logic of the realistic type,—again, sensational or rationalistic (mathematical), or a combination of the two—a sort of realistic transcendentalism. Each type has essentially the same difficulties with the processes of inference, with the problem of change, with truth and error, and, on the ethical side, with good and evil.

With the processes of knowing converted into objects, and with the act of knowing reduced to a unique and external relation between the despoiled knower and the objects made from its own hypostatized processes, all knowing becomes in the end immediate. All attempts at an inference that is anything more than an elaborated and often confused restatement of non-logical operations break down. The associational inference of empiricism, the subsumptive inference of rationalism, the transcendental inference of objective idealism, the analytical inference of neo-realism—all alike face the dilemma of an inference that is trifling or miraculous, tautologous or false. Where the knower and its object are so constituted that the only relation in which the latter can stand to the former is that of presence or absence, and if to be present is to be known, how, as Plato asked, can there be any false knowing?

For those who accept the foregoing general diagnosis the prescription is obvious. The present task of logical theory is the restoration of the continuity of the act and agent of knowing with other acts and agents. But this is not to be done by merely furnishing the act of knowing with a body and a nervous system. If the nervous system be regarded as only an onlooking, beholding nervous system, if no connection be made between the logical operations of a nervous system and its other operations a nervous system has no logical advantage over a purely psychical mind.

It was to be expected that this movement toward restoration of continuity made in the name of "instrumental" or "experimental" logic would be regarded, alike, by the logics of rationalism and empiricism, of idealism and of realism, as an attempt to rob intelligence of its own unique and proper character; to reduce it to a merely "psychological" and "existential" affair; to leave no place for genuine intellectual interest and activity; and to make science a series of more or less respectable adventures. The counter thesis is, that this restoration is truly a restoration—not a despoliation of the character and rights of intelligence; that only such a restoration can preserve the unique function of intelligence, can prevent it from becoming merely "existential," and can provide a distinct place for intellectual and scientific interest and activity. It does not, however, promise to remove the stigma of "adventure" from science. Every experiment is an adventure; and it is precisely the experimental character of scientific logic that distinguishes it from scholasticism, medieval or modern.

II

First it is clear that a reform of logic based upon the restoration of knowing to its connections with other acts will begin with a chapter containing an account of these other operations and the general character of this connection.13 Logical theory has been truncated. It has tried to begin and end in the middle, with the result that it has ended in the air. Logic presents the curious anachronism of a science which attempts to deal with its subject-matter apart from what it comes from and what comes from it.

The objection that such a chapter on the conditions and genesis of the operations of knowing belongs to psychology, only shows how firmly fixed is the discontinuity we are trying to escape. As we have seen, the original motive for leaving this account of genesis to psychology was that the act of knowing was supposed to originate in a purely psychical mind. Such an origin was of course embarrassing to logic, which aimed to be scientific. The old opposition between origin and validity was due to the kind of origin assumed and the kind of validity necessitated by the origin. One may well be excused for evading the question of how ideas, originated in a purely psychical mind, can, in Kant's phrase, "have objective validity," by throwing out the question of origin altogether. Whatever difficulties remain for validity after this expulsion could not be greater than those of the task of combining the objective validity of ideas with their subjective origin.

The whole of this chapter on the connection between logical and non-logical operations cannot be written here. But its central point would be that these other acts with which the act of knowing must have continuity are just the operations of our unreflective conduct. Note that it is "unreflective," not "unconscious," nor yet merely "instinctive" conduct. It is our perceptive, remembering, imagining, desiring, loving, hating conduct. Note also that we do not say "psychical" or "physical," nor "psycho-physical" conduct. These terms stand for certain distinctions in logical conduct,14 and we are here concerned with the character of non-logical conduct which is to be distinguished from, and yet kept in closest continuity with, logical conduct.

If, here, the metaphysical logician should ask: "Are you not in this assumption of a world of reflective and unreflective conduct and affection, and of a world of beings in interaction, begging a whole system of metaphysics?" the reply is that if it is a metaphysics bad for logic, it will keep turning up in the course of logical theory as a constant source of trouble. On the other hand, if logic encounters grave difficulties when it attempts to get on without it, its assumption, for the purposes of logic, has all the justification possible.

Again it will be urged that this alleged non-logical conduct, in so far as it involves perception, memory, and anticipation, is already cognitive and logical; or if the act of knowing is to be entirely excluded from logic, then, in so far as what is left involves objective "terms and relations," it, also, is already logical. And it may be thought strange that a logic based upon the restoration of continuity between the act of knowing and other acts should here be insisting on distinction and separation. The point is fundamental; and must be disposed of before we go on. First, we must observe that the unity secured by making all conscious conduct logical turns out, on examination, to be more nominal than real. As we have already seen, this attempt at a complete logicizing of all conduct is forced at once to introduce the distinction of "explicit" and "implicit," of "conscious and unconscious" or "subconscious" logic. Some cynics have found that this suggests dividing triangles into explicit and implicit triangles, or into triangles and sub-triangles.

Doubtless the attempt to make all perceptions, memories, and anticipations, and even instincts and habits, into implicit or subconscious inference is an awkward effort to restore the continuity of logical and non-logical conduct. Its awkwardness consists in attempting to secure this continuity by the method of subsumptive identity, instead of finding it in a transitive continuity of function;—instead of seeing that perception, memory, and anticipation *become* logical processes when they are employed in a process of inquiry, whose purpose is to relieve the difficulties into which these operations in their function as direct stimuli have fallen. Logical conduct is constituted by the coöperation of these processes for the improvement of their further operation. To regard perception, memory, and imagination as implicit forms or as sub-species of logical operation is much like conceiving the movements of our fingers and arms as implicit or imperfect species of painting, or swimming.

Moreover, this doctrine of universal logicism teaches that when that which is perfect is come, imperfection shall be done away. This should mean that when painting becomes completely "explicit" and perfect, fingers and hands shall disappear. Perfect painting will be the pure essence of painting. And this interpretation is not strained; for this logic expressly teaches that in the perfected real system all temporal elements are unessential to logical operations. They are, of course, *psychologically* necessary for finite beings, who can never have perfectly logical experiences. But, from the standpoint of a completely logicized experience, all finite, temporal processes are accidents, not essentials, of logical operations.

The fact that the processes of perception, memory, and anticipation are transformed in their logical operation into sensations and universals, terms, and relations, and, as such, become the subject-matter of logical theory, does not mean that they have lost their mediating character, and have become merely objects of logical contemplation at large. Sensations or sense-data, and ideas, terms and relations, are the subject-matter of logical theory for the reason that they sometimes succeed and sometimes fail in their logical operations. And it is the business of logical theory to diagnose the conditions of this success and failure. If, in writing, my pen becomes defective and is made an object of inquiry, it does not therefore lose all its character as a pen and become merely an object at large. It is *as* an instrument of writing that it is investigated. So, sense-data, universals, terms, and relations as subject-matter of logic are investigated in their character *as* mediators of the ambiguities and conflicts, of non-logical experience.

If the operations of habit, instinct, perceptions, memory, and anticipation *become* logical, when, instead of operating as direct stimuli, they are employed in a process of inquiry, we must next ask: (1) under what conditions do they pass over into this process of inquiry? (2) what modifications of operation do they undergo, what new forms do they take, and what new results do they produce in their logical operations?

If the act of inquiry be not superimposed, it must arise out of some specific condition in the course of non-logical conduct. Once more, if the alarm be sounded at this proposal to find the origin of logical in non-logical operations it must be summarily answered by asking if the one who raises the cry finds it impossible to imagine that one who is not hungry, or angry, or patriotic, or wise may become so. Non-logical conduct is not the abstract formal contradictory of logical conduct any more than present satiety or foolishness is the contradictory of later hunger or wisdom, or than anger at one person contradicts cordiality to another, or to the same person, later. The old bogie of the logical irrelevance of origin was due to the inability to conceive continuity except in the form of identity in which there was no place for the notion of *growth*.

The conditions under which non-logical conduct *becomes* logical are familiar to those who have followed the doctrines of experimental logic as expounded in the discussions of the past few years. The transformation begins at the point where non-logical processes instead of operating as direct unambiguous stimuli and response become ambiguous with consequent inhibition of conduct. But again this does not mean that at this juncture the non-logical processes quit the field and give place to a totally new faculty and process called reason. They stay on the job. But there is a change in the job, which now is to get rid of this ambiguity.

This modification of the task requires, of course, corresponding modification and adaptation of these operations. They take on the form of sensations and universals, terms and relations, data and hypotheses. This modification of function and form constitutes "reason" or, better, reasoning.

Here some one will ask, "Whence comes this ambiguity? How can a mere perception or memory as such be ambiguous? Must it not be ambiguous to, or for, something, or some one?" The point is well taken. But it should not be taken to imply that the ambiguity is for a merely onlooking, beholding psychical mind—especially when the perception is itself regarded as an act of beholding. Nor are we any better off if we suppose the beholding mind to be equipped with a faculty of reason in the form of the principle of "contradiction." For this throws no light on the origin and meaning of ambiguity. And if we seek to make all perceptions as such ambiguous and contradictory, in order to make room for, and justify, the operations of reason, other difficulties at once beset us. When we attempt to remove this specific ambiguity of perceptive conduct we shall be forced, before we are through, to appeal back to perception, which we have condemned as inherently contradictory, both for data and for verification.

However, the insistence that perception must be ambiguous to, or for, something beyond itself is well grounded. And this was recognized in the statement that it is equivocal as a stimulus in conduct. There need be no mystery as to how such equivocation arises. That there is such a thing as a conduct at all means that there are certain beings who have acquired definite ways of responding to one another. It is important to observe that these forms of interaction—instinct and habit, perception, memory, etc.—are not to be located in either of the interacting beings but are functions of both. The conception of these operations as the private functions of an organism is the forerunner of the epistemological predicament. It results in a conception of knowing as wholly the act of a knower apart from the known. This is the beginning of epistemology.

But to whatever extent interacting beings have acquired definite and specific ways of behavior toward one another it is equally plain—the theory of external relations notwithstanding—that in this process of interaction these ways of behavior, of stimulus and response, undergo modification. If the world consisted of two interacting beings, it is conceivable that the modifications of behavior might occur in such close continuity of relation to each of the interacting beings that the adjustment would be very continuous, and there might be little or no ambiguity and conflict. But in a world where any two interacting beings have innumerable interactions with innumerable other beings and in all these interactions modifications are effected, it is to be expected that changes in the behavior of each or both will occur, so marked that they are bound to result in breaks in the continuity of stimulus and response—even to the point of tragedy. However, the tragedy is seldom so great that the ambiguity extends to the whole field of conduct. Except in extreme pathological cases (and in epistemology), complete skepticism and aboulia do not occur. Ambiguity always falls within a field or direction of conduct, and though it may extend much further, and must extend some further than the point at which equivocation occurs, yet it is never ubiquitous. An ambiguity concerning the action of gravitation is no less specific than one regarding color or sound; indeed, the one may be found to involve the other.

Logical conduct is, then, conduct which aims to remove ambiguity and inhibition in unreflective conduct. The instruments of its operation are forged from the processes of unreflective conduct by such modification and adaptation as is required to enable them to accomplish this end. Since these logical operations sometimes fail and sometimes succeed they become the subject-matter of logical theory. But the technique of this second involution of reflection is not supplied by some new and unique entity. It also is derived from modifications of previous operations of both reflective and non-reflective conduct.

While emphasizing the continuity between non-logical and logical operations, we must keep in mind that their distinction is of equal importance. Confusion at this point is fatal. A case in point is the confusion between non-logical and logical observation. The results of non-logical observation, e.g., looking and listening, are direct stimuli to further conduct. But the purpose and result of *logical* observation are to secure data, not as direct stimuli to immediate conduct but as stimuli to the construction or verification of hypotheses which are the responses of the *logical* operation of imagination to the data. Hypotheses are anticipatory. But they differ from non-logical anticipation in that they are tentatively, experimentally, i.e., logically anticipatory. The non-logical operations of memory and anticipation lack just this tentative, experimental character. When we confuse the logical and non-logical operations of these processes the result is either that logical processes will merely repeat non-logical operations in which case we have inference that is tautologous and trifling; or the non-logical will attempt to perform logical operations, and our inference is miraculous. If we seek to escape by an appeal to habit, as in empiricism, or to an objective universal, as in idealism and neo-realism, we are merely disguising, not removing the miracle.

It may be thought that this confusion would be most likely to occur in a theory which teaches that non-logical processes are carried over into logical operations. But this overlooks the fact that the theory recognizes at the same time that these non-logical operations undergo modification and adaptation to the demands of the logical enterprise. On the other hand, those who make all perceptions, memory, and anticipation, not to speak of habit and instinct, logical, have no basis for the distinction between logical and non-logical results; while those who refuse to give the operations of perception, memory, etc., any place in logic can make no connections between logical and non-logical conduct. Nor are they able to distinguish in a specific case truth from error.

In all logics that fail to make this connection and distinction between logical and non-logical operations there is no criterion for data. If ultimate simplicity is demanded of the data, there is no standard for simplicity except the *minimum sensibile* or the *minimum intelligibile* which have recently been resurrected. On the other hand, where simplicity is waived, as in the logic of objective idealism, there is still no criterion of logical adequacy. But if we understand by *logical* data not anything that happens to be given, but something *sought* as material for an hypothesis, i.e., a proposed solution (proposition) of an ambiguous object of conduct and affection, then whatever results of observation meet this requirement are logical data. And whenever data are found from which an hypothesis is constructed that succeeds in abolishing the ambiguity, they are simple, adequate, and true data.

No scientist, not even the mathematician, in the specific investigations of his field, seeks for ultimate and irreducible data at large. And if he found them he could not use them. It is only in his metaphysical personality that he longs for such data. The data which the scientist in any specific inquiry seeks are the data which suggest a solution of the question in which the investigation starts. When these data are found they are the "irreducibles" of that problem. But they are relative to the question and answer of the investigation. Their simplicity consists in the fact that they are the data from which a conclusion can be made. The term "simple data" is tautologous. That one is in need of data more "simple" means that one is in need of new data from which an hypothesis can be formed.

It is true that the actual working elements with which the scientist operates are always complex in the sense that they are always something more than elements in any specific investigation. They have other connections and alliances. And this complexity is at once the despair and the hope of the scientist; his despair, because he cannot be sure when these other connections will interfere with the allegiance of his elements to his particular undertaking; his hope, because when these alliances are revealed they often make the elements more efficient or exhibit capacities which will make them elements in some other undertaking for which elements have not been found. A general resolves his army into so many marching, eating, shooting units; but these elements are something more than marching, shooting units. They are husbands and fathers, brothers and lovers, protestants and catholics, artists and artisans, etc. And the militarist can never be sure at what point these other activities—I do not say merely external relationships—may upset his calculations. If he could find units whose whole and sole nature is to march and shoot, his problem would be, in some respects, simpler, though in others more complex. As it is, he is constantly required to ask how far these other functions will support and at what point they will rebel at the marching and shooting.

Such, in principle, is the situation in every scientific inquiry. When the failure of the old elements occurs it is common to say that "simpler" elements are needed. And doubtless in his perplexity the scientist may long for elements which have no entangling alliances, whose sole nature and character is to be elements. But what in fact he actually seeks in every specific investigation are elements whose nature and functions *will not interfere* with their serving as units in the enterprise in hand. But from some other standpoint these new elements may be vastly more complex than the old, as is the case with the modern as compared with the ancient atom. When the elements are secured which operate successfully, the non-interfering connections can be ignored and the elements can be treated as if they did not have them,—as if they were metaphysically simple. But there is no criterion for metaphysical simplicity except operative simplicity. To be simple is to serve as an element, and to serve as an element is to be simple.

It is scarcely necessary in view of the foregoing to add that the data of science are not "sense-data," if by sense-data be meant data which are the result of the operations of sense organs alone. Data are as much or more the result of operations, first, of the motor system of the scientist's own organism, and second, of all of the machinery of his laboratory which he calls to his aid.

Whether named after the way they are obtained, or after the way they are used, data are quite as much "motor" as "sense." Nor, on the other hand, are there any purely intellectual data—not even for the mathematician. Some mathematicians may insist that their symbols and diagrams are merely stimuli to the platonic operation of pure and given universals. But until mathematics can get on without these symbols or any substitutes the intuitionist in mathematics will continue to have his say.

Wherever the discontinuity between logical operations and their acts persists, all the difficulties with data have their correlative difficulties with hypotheses. In Mill's logic the account of the origin of hypotheses oscillates between the view that they are happy guesses of a mind composed of states of consciousness, and the view that they are "found in the facts" or are "impressed on the mind by the facts." The miracle of relevancy required in the first position drives the theory to the second. And the tautologous, useless nature of the hypothesis in the second forces the theory back to the first view. In this predicament, little wonder Mill finds that the easiest way out is to make hypotheses "auxiliary" and not indigenous to inference. But this exclusion of hypotheses as essential leaves his account of inference to oscillate between the association of particulars of nominalism and scholastic formalism, from both of which Mill, with the dignified zeal of a prophet, set out to rescue logic.

Mill's rejection of hypotheses formed by a mind whose operations have no discoverable continuity with the operations of things, or by things whose actions are independent of the operations of ideas, is forever sound. But his acceptance of the discontinuity between the acts of knowing and the operation of things, and the conclusion that these two conceptions of the origin and nature of hypotheses are the only alternatives, were the source of most of his difficulties.

III

The efforts of classic empiricism at the reform of logic have long been an easy mark for idealistic reformers. But it is interesting to observe that the idealistic logic from the beginning finds itself in precisely the same predicament regarding hypotheses;—they are trifling or false. And in the end they are made, as in Mill, "accidents" of inference.

The part played by Kant's sense-material and the categories is almost the reverse of those of data and hypothesis in science. Sense material and the categories are the given elements from which objects are somehow made; in scientific procedure data and hypothesis are derived through logical observation and imagination from the content and operations of immediate experience. In Kant's account of the process by which objects are constructed we are nowhere in sight of any experimental procedure. Indeed, the real act of knowing, the selection and application of the category to the sense matter, is, as Kant in the end had to confess, "hidden away in the depths of the soul." Made in the presence of the elaborate machinery of knowing which Kant had constructed, this confession is almost tragic; and the tragic aspect grows when we find that the result of the "hidden" operation is merely a phenomenal object. That this should be the case, however, is not strange. A phenomenal object is the inevitable correlate of the "hidden" act of knowing whether in a "transcendental" or in an "empirical" logic. In vain do we call the act of knowing "constructive" and "synthetic" if its method of synthesis is hidden. A transcendental unity whose method is indefinable has no advantage over empirical association.

It was the dream of Kant as of Mill to replace the logics of sensationalism and rationalism with a "logic of things" and of "truth." But as Mill's things turned to states of consciousness, so Kant's are phenomenal. Their common fate proclaims their common failure—the failure to reëstablish continuity between the conduct of intelligence and other conduct.

One of the chief counts in Hegel's indictment of Kant's logic is that "it had no influence on the methods of science."[15] Hegel's explanation is that Kant's categories have no genesis; they are not constructed in and as part of logical operations. As given, ready-made, their relevance is a miracle. But if categories be "generated" in the process of knowing, says Hegel, they are indigenous, and their fitness is inevitable. In such statements Hegel raises expectations that we are at last to have a logic which squares with the procedure of science. But when we discover that instead of being "generated" out of all the material involved in the scientific problem Hegel's categories are derived from each other, misgivings arise. And when we further learn that this "genesis" is timeless, which means that, after all, the categories stand related to each other in a closed, eternal system of implication, we abandon hope of a scientific—i.e., experimental—logic.

Hegel also says it is the business of philosophy "to substitute categories or in more precise language adequate notions for the several modes of feeling, perception, desire, and will." The word "substitute" reveals the point at issue. If "to substitute" means that philosophy is a complete exchange of the modes of feeling, perception, desire, and will for a world of categories or notions, then, saying nothing of the range of values in such a world, the problem of the meaning of "adequate" is on our hands. What is the notion to be adequate to? But if "to substitute" means that the modes of feeling, perception, desire, and will, when in a specific situation of ambiguity and inhibition, go over into, take on, the modes of data and hypothesis in the effort to get rid of inhibiting conflict that is quite another matter. Here the "notion," as the scientific hypothesis, has a criterion for its adequacy. But if the notion usurps the place of feeling, perception, desire, and will, as many find, in the end, it does in Hegel's logic, it thereby loses all tests for the adequacy of its function and character as a notion.

In the development of the logical doctrines of Kant and Hegel by Lotze, Green, Sigwart, Bradley, Bosanquet, Royce, and others, there are indeed differences. But these differences only throw their common ground into bolder relief. This common ground is that, procedure by hypotheses, by induction, is, in the language of Professor Bosanquet, "a transient and external characteristic of inference."16 And the ground of this verdict is essentially the same as Mill's, when he rejects hypotheses "made by the mind," namely, that such hypotheses are too subjective in their origin and nature to have objective validity. "Objective" idealism is trying, like Mill, to escape the subjectivism of the purely individual and "psychical" knower. But, being unable to reconstruct the finite knower, and being too sophisticated to make what it regards as Mill's naïve appeal to "hypotheses found in things," it transfers the real process of inference to the "objective universal," and the process of all thought, including inference, is now defined as "*the reproduction, by a universal presented in a content, of contents distinguished from the presented content which also are differences of the same universal.*"17

It need scarcely be said that in inference thus defined there is scant room for hypotheses. There is nothing "hypothetical," "experimental," or "tentative" in this process of reproduction by the objective universal as such. As little is there any possibility of error. If there is anything hypothetical, or any possibility of error, in inference, it is due to the temporal, finite human being in which, paradoxically enough, this process of "reproduction" goes on and to whom, at times, is given an "infinitesimal" part in the operation, while at other times he is said merely to "witness" it. But the real inference does not "proceed by hypotheses"; it is only the finite mind in witnessing the real logical spectacle or in its "infinitesimal" contribution to it that lamely proceeds in this manner.

Here, again, we have the same break in continuity between the finite, human act of knowing and the operations that constitute the real world. When the logic of the objective universal rejects imputations of harboring a despoiled psychical knower it has in mind, of course, the objective universal as knower, not the finite, human act. But, if the participations of the latter are all accidents of inference, as they are said to be, its advantage over a purely psychical knower, or "states of consciousness," is difficult to see. The rejection of metaphysical dualism is of no consequence if the logical operations of the finite, human being are only "accidents" of the real logical process. As already remarked, the metaphysical disjunction is merely a schematism of the more fundamental, logical disjunction.

As for tautology and miracle, the follower of Mill might well ask: how an association of particulars, whether mental states or things, could be more tautologous than a universal reproducing its own differences? And if the transition from particular to particular is a miracle in which the grace of God is disguised as "habit," why is not habit as good a disguise for Providence as universals? Moreover, by what miracle does the one all-inclusive universal become *a* universal? And since perception always presents a number of universals, what determines which one shall perform the reproduction? Finally, since there are infinite differences of the universal that might be reproduced, what determines just which differences shall be reproduced? In this wise the controversy has gone on ever since the challenge of the old rationalistic logic by the nominalists launched the issue of empiricism and rationalism. All the charges which each makes against the other are easily retorted upon itself. Each side is resistless in attack, but helpless in defense.

In a conception of inference in which both data and hypothesis are regarded as the tentative, experimental results of the processes of perception, memory, and constructive imagination engaged in the special task of removing conflict, ambiguity, and inhibition, and in which these processes are not conceived as the functions of a private mind nor of an equally private brain and nervous system, but as functions of interacting beings,—in such a conception there is no ground for anxiety concerning the simplicity of data, nor the objectivity of hypotheses. Simplicity and objectivity do not have to be secured through elaborate and labored metaphysical construction. The data are simple and the hypothesis objective in so far as they accomplish the work where unto they are called—the removal of conflict, ambiguity, and inhibition in conduct and affection.

In the experimental conception of inference it is clear that the principles of formal logic must play their rôle wholly inside the course of logical operations. They do not apply to relations *between* these operations and "reality"; nor to "reality" itself. Formal identity and non-contradiction signify, in experimental logic, the complete correlativity of data and hypothesis. They mean that *in* the logical procedure data must not be shifted without a corresponding change in the hypothesis and conversely. The doctrine that "theoretically" there may be any number of hypotheses for "the same facts" is, when these multiple hypotheses are anything more than different names or symbols, nothing less than the very essence of formal contradiction. It doubtless makes little difference whether a disease be attributed to big or little, black or red, demons or whether the cause be represented by a, b, or c, etc. But where data and hypotheses are such as are capable of verification, i.e., of mutually checking up each other, a change in one without a corresponding modification of the other is the principle of all formal fallacies.18

With this conception of the origin, nature, and functions of logical operations little remains to be said of their truth and falsity. If the whole enterprise of logical operation, of the construction and verification of hypothesis, is in the interest of the removal of ambiguity, and inhibition in conduct, the only relevant truth or falsity they can possess must be determined by their success or failure in that undertaking. The acceptance of this view of truth and error, be it said again, depends on holding steadfastly to the conception of the operations of knowing as *real acts*, which, though having a distinct character and function, are yet in closest continuity with other acts of which indeed they are but modifications and adaptations in order to meet the logical demand.

Here, perhaps, is the place for a word on truth and satisfaction. The satisfaction which marks the truth of logical operations—"intellectual satisfaction"—is the satisfaction which attends the accomplishment of their task, viz., the removal of ambiguity in conduct, i.e., in our interaction with other beings. It does not mean that this satisfaction is bound to be followed by wholly blissful consequences. All our troubles are not over when the distress of ambiguity is removed. It may be indeed that the verdict of the logical operation is that we must face certain death. Very well, we must have felt it to be "good to know the worst," or no inquiry would have been started. We should have deemed ignorance bliss and sat with closed eyes waiting for fate to overtake us instead of going forward to meet it and in some measure determine it. Death anticipated and accepted is *realiter* very different from death that falls upon us unawares, however we may estimate that difference. If this distinction in the *foci* of satisfaction is kept clear it must do away with a large amount of the hedonistic interpretations of satisfaction in which many critics have indulged.

But hereupon some one may exclaim, as did a colleague recently: "Welcome to the ranks of the intellectualists!" If so, the experimentalist is bound to reply that he is as willing, and as unwilling, to be welcomed to the ranks of intellectualism as to those of anti-intellectualism. He wonders, however, how long the welcome would last in either. Among the intellectualists the welcome would begin to cool as soon as it should be discovered that the ambiguity to which logical operations are the response is not regarded by the experimentalist as a purely intellectual affair. It is an ambiguity in conduct with all the attendant affectional values that may be at stake.19 It is, to be sure, the fact of ambiguity, and the effort to resolve it, that adds the intellectual, logical character to conduct and to affectional values. But if the logical interest attempts entirely to detach itself it will soon be without either subject-matter or criterion. And if it sets itself up as supreme, we shall be forced to say that our quandaries of affection, our problems of life and death are merely to furnish occasions and material for logical operations.

On the other hand, the welcome of the anti-intellectualists is equally sure to wane when the experimentalist asserts that the doctrine that logical operations mutilate the wholeness of immediate experience overlooks the palpable fact that it is precisely these immediate experiences—the experiences of intuition and instinct—that get into conflict and inhibit and mutilate one another, and as a consequence are obliged to go into logical session to patch up the mutilation and provide new and better methods of coöperation.

At this point the weakness in Bergson's view of logical operations appears. Bergson, too, is impressed by the break in continuity between logical operations and the rest of experience. But with Mr. Bradley he believes this breach to be essentially incurable, because the mutilations and disjunctions are due to and introduced by logical operations. Just why the latter are introduced remains in the end a mystery. Both, to be sure, believe that logical operations are valuable for "practical" purposes,—for action. But, aside from the question of *how* operations essentially mutilative can be valuable for action, immediate intuitional experience being already in unity with Reality, why should there be any practical need for logical operations—least of all such as introduce disjunction and mutilation?

The admission of a demand for logical operations, whether charged to matter, the devil, or any other metaphysical adversary, is, of course, a confession that conflict and ambiguity are as fundamental in experience as unity and immediacy and that logical operations are therefore no less indigenous. The failure to see this implication is responsible for the paradox that in the logic of Creative Evolution the operations of intelligence are neither creative nor evolutional. They not only have no constructive part but are positively destructive and devolutional.

Since, moreover, these logical operations, like those of the objective universal, and like Mill's association of particulars, can only reproduce in fragmentary form what has already been done, it is difficult to see how they can meet the demands of action. For here no more than in Mill, or in the logic of idealism, is there any place for constructive hypotheses or any technique by which they can become effective. Whatever "Creative Evolution" may be, there is no place in its logic for "Creative Intelligence."

The prominence in current discussion of the logical reforms proposed by the "analytic logic" of the neo-realistic movement and the enthusiastic optimism of its representatives over the prospective results of these reforms for logic, science, and practical life are the warrant for devoting a special section to their discussion.

There are indeed some marked differences of opinion among the expounders of the "new logic" concerning the results which it is expected to achieve. Some find that it clears away incredible accumulations of metaphysical lumber; others rejoice that it is to restore metaphysics, "once the queen of the sciences, to her ancient throne."

But whatever the difference among the representatives of analytical logic all seem agreed at the outset on two fundamental reforms which the "new logic" makes. These are: first, that analytic logic gets rid entirely of the *act* of knowing, the retention of which has been the bane of all other logics; second, in its discovery of "terms and relations," "sense-data and universals" as the simple elements not only of logic but of the world, it furnishes science at last with the simple neutral elements at large which it is supposed science so long has sought, and "mourned because it found them not."

Taking these in order, we are told that "realism frees logic as a study of objective fact from all accounts of the states and operations of mind." ... "Logic and mathematics are sciences which can be pursued quite independently of the study of knowing."[20] "The new logic believes that it deals with no such entities as thoughts, ideas, or minds, but with entities that merely are."[20]

The motive for the banishment of the act of knowing from logic is that as an *act* knowing is "mental," "psychological," and "subjective."[21] All other logics have indeed realized this subjective character of the *act* of knowing, but have neither dared completely to discard it nor been able sufficiently to counteract its effects even with such agencies as the objective universal to prevent it from infecting logic with its subjectivity. Because logic has tolerated and attempted to compromise with this subjective act of knowing, say these reformers, it has been forced constantly into epistemology and has become a hybrid science. Had logic possessed the courage long ago to throw overboard this subjective Jonah it would have been spared the storms of epistemology and the reefs of metaphysics.

Analytic logic is the first attempt in the history of modern logical theory at a deliberate, sophisticated exclusion of the act of knowing from logic. Other logics, to be sure, have tried to neutralize the effects of its presence, but none has had the temerity to cast it bodily overboard. The experiment, therefore, is highly interesting.

We should note at the outset that in regarding the act of knowing as incurably "psychical" and "subjective" analytic logic accepts a fundamental premise of the logics of rationalism, empiricism, and idealism which it seeks to reform. It is true that it is the bold proposal of analytic logic to keep logic out of the pit of epistemology by excluding the act of knowing from logic. Nevertheless analytic logic still accepts the subjective character of this act; and if it excludes it from its logic it welcomes it in its psychology. This is a dangerous situation. Can the analytic logician prevent all osmosis between his logic and his psychology?22· If not, and if the psychological act is subjective, woe then to his logic. Had the new logic begun with a bold challenge of the psychical character of the act of knowing, the prospect of a logic free from epistemology would have been much brighter.

With the desire to rid logic of the epistemological taint the "experimental logic" of the pragmatic movement has the strongest sympathy. But the proposal to effect this by the excision of the act of knowing appears to experimental logic to be a case of heroic but fatal surgery. *Prima facie* a logic with no act of knowing presents an uncanny appearance. What sort of logical operations are possible in such a logic and of what kind of truth and falsity are they capable?

Before taking up these questions in detail it is worth while to note the character of the entities that "merely are" with which analytic logic proposes exclusively to deal. In their general form they are "terms" and "propositions," "sense-data" and universals. We are struck at once by the fact that these entities bear the names of logical operations. They are, to be sure, disguised as entities and have been baptised in a highly dilute solution of objectivity called "subsistence." But this does not conceal their origin, nor does it obscure the fact that if it is possible for any entities that "merely are" to have logical character those made from hypostatized processes of logical operations should be the most promising. They might be expected to retain some vestiges of logical character even after they have been torn from the process of inquiry and converted into "entities that merely are." Also it is not surprising that having stripped the act of knowing of its constituent operations analytic logic should feel that it can well dispense with the empty shell called "mind" and, as Professor Dewey says, "wish it on psychology." But if the analytic logician be also a philosopher and perchance a lover of his fellow-man, it is hard to see how he can have a good conscience over this disposition of the case.

Turning now to the character of inference and of truth and falsity which are possible in a logic which excludes the operation of knowing and deals only with "entities that are," all the expounders seem to agree that in such a logic inference must be purely deductive. All alleged induction is either disguised deduction or a lucky guess. This raises apprehension at the start concerning the value of analytic logic for other sciences. But let us observe what deduction in analytic logic is.

We begin at once with a distinction which involves the whole issue.23 We are asked to carefully distinguish "logical" deduction from "psychological" deduction. The latter is the vulgar meaning of the term, and is "the thinker's name for his own act of conforming his thought" to the objective and independent processes that constitute the real logical process. This act of conforming the mind is a purely "psychological" affair. It has no logical function whatever. In what the "conforming" consists is not clear. It seems to be merely the act of turning the "psychological" eye on the objective logical process. "One beholds it (the logical process) as one beholds a star, a river, a character in a play.... The novelist and the dramatist, like the mathematician and logician, are onlookers at the logical spectacle."24 On the other hand, the term "conforming" suggests a task, with the possibilities of success and failure. Have we, then, two wholly independent possibilities of error—one merely "psychological," the other "logical"? The same point may be made even more obviously with reference to the term "beholding." The term is used as if beholding were a perfectly simple act, having no problems and no possibilities of mistakes— as if there could be no mis-beholding.25

But fixing our psychological eye on the "logical spectacle," what does it behold? A universal generating an infinite series of identical instances of itself—i.e., instances which differ only in "logical position." If in a world of entities that "merely are" the term "generation" causes perplexity, the tension is soon relieved; for this turns out to be a merely subsistential non-temporal generation which, like Hegel's generation of the categories, in no way compromises a world of entities that "merely are."

Steering clear of the thicket of metaphysical problems that we here encounter, let us keep to the logical trail. First it is clear that logical operations are of the same reproductive repetitive type that we have found in the associational logic of empiricism, and in the logic of the objective universal. Indeed, after objective idealism has conceded that the finite mind merely "witnesses" or at most contributes only in an "infinitesimal" degree to the logical activity of the objective universal, what remains of the supposed gulf between absolute idealism and analytic realism?

It follows, of course, that there can be no place in analytic logic for "procedure by hypotheses." However, it is to the credit of some analytic logicians that they see this and frankly accept the situation instead of attempting to retain hypotheses by making them "accidents" or mere "auxiliaries" of inference. On the other hand, others find that the chief glory of analytic logic is precisely that it "gives thought wings"26 for the free construction of hypotheses. In his lectures on "Scientific Methods in Philosophy" Mr. Russell calls some of the most elemental and sacred entities of analytic logic "convenient fictions." This retention of hypotheses at the cost of cogency is of course in order to avoid a break with science. Those who see that there is no place in analytic logic for hypotheses are equally anxious to preserve their connections with science. Hence they boldly challenge the "superstition" that science has anything to do with hypotheses. Newton's "*Hypotheses non fingo*" should be the motto of every conscientious scientist who dares "trust his own perceptions and disregard the ukase of idealism." "The theory of mental construction is the child of idealism, now put out to service for the support of its parents." "Theory is no longer regarded in science as an hypothesis added to the observed facts," but a law which is "found in the facts."27 The identity of this with Mill's doctrine of hypotheses as "found in things" is obvious.

As against the conception of hypotheses as "free," "winged," constructions of a psychical, beholding, gossiping mind we may well take our stand with those who would exclude such hypotheses from science. And this doubtless was the sort of mind and sort of hypotheses Newton meant when he said "*Hypotheses non fingo*."28 But had Newton's mind really been of the character which he, as a physicist, had learned from philosophers to suppose it to be, and had he really waited to find his hypotheses ready-made in the facts, there never would have been any dispute about who discovered the calculus, and we should never have been interested in what Newton said about hypotheses or anything else. What Newton did is a much better source of information on the part hypotheses play in scientific method than what he said about them. The former speaks for itself; the latter is the pious repetition of a metaphysical creed made necessary by the very separation of mind from things expressed in the statement quoted.

Logically there is little to choose between hypotheses found ready-made in the facts and those which are the "winged" constructions of a purely psychical mind. Both are equally useless in logic and in science. One makes logic and science "trifling," the other makes them "miraculous." But if hypotheses be conceived not as the output of a cloistered psychical entity but as the joint product of all the beings and operations involved in the specific situation in which logical inquiry originates, and more particularly in all those involved in the operations of the inquiry itself (including all the experimental material and apparatus which the inquiry may require), we shall have sufficient continuity between hypotheses and things to do away with miracle, and sufficient reconstruction to avoid inference that is trifling.

It is, however, the second contribution of analytic logic that is the basis of the enthusiasm over its prospective value for other sciences. This is the discovery that terms and propositions, sense-data, and universals, are not only elements of logical operation but are the simple, neutral elements at large which science is supposed to have been seeking. "As the botanist analyzes the structures of the vegetable organism and finds chemical compounds of which they are built so the ordinary chemist analyzes these compounds into their elements, but does not analyze these. The physical chemist analyzes these elemental atoms, as now appears, into minuter components *which he in turn must leave to the mathematicians and logicians further to analyze.*"29

Again it is worth noting that this mutation of logical into ontological elements seems to differ only "in position" from the universal logicism of absolute idealism.

What are these simple elements into which the mathematician and logician are to analyze the crude elements of the laboratory? And how are these elements to be put into operation in the laboratory? Let us picture an analytic logician meeting a physical scientist at a moment when the latter is distressed over the unmanageable complexity of his elements. Will the logician say to the scientist: "Your difficulty is that you are trusting too much to your mundane apparatus. The kingdom of truth cometh not with such things. Forsake your microscopes, test tubes, refractors and resonators, and follow me, and you shall behold the truly simple elements of which you have dreamed."? And when the moment of revelation arrives and the expectant scientist is solemnly told that the "simple elements" which he has sought so long are "terms and propositions," sense-data and universals, is it surprising that he does not seem impressed? Will he not ask: "What am I to do with these in the specific difficulties of my laboratory? Shall I say to the crude and complex elements of my laboratory operations: 'Be ye resolved into terms and propositions, sense-data and universals'; and will they forthwith obey this incantation and fall apart so that I may locate and remove the hidden source of my difficulty? Are you not mocking me and deceiving yourself with the old ontological argument? Your 'simple' elements—are they anything but the hypostatized process by which elements may be found?"30

The expounders as well as the critics of analytic logic have agreed that it reaches its most critical junction when it faces the problem of truth and error. There is no doubt that the logic of objective idealism, in other respects so similar to analytic logic, has at this point an advantage; for it retains just enough of the finite operation of knowing—an "infinitesimal" part will answer—to furnish the culture germs of error. But analytic logic having completely sterilized itself against this source of infection is in serious difficulty.

Here again it is Professor Holt who has the courage to follow—or shall we say "behold"?—his theory as it "generates" the doctrine that error is a given objective opposition of forces entirely independent of any such thing as a process of inquiry and all that such a process presupposes. "All collisions between bodies, all inference between energies, all process of warming and cooling, of starting and stopping, of combining and separating, all counterbalancings, as in cantilevers and gothic vaultings, are contradictory forces which can be stated only in propositions that manifestly contradict each other."31 But the argument proves too much. For in the world of forces to which we have here appealed there is no force which is not opposed by others and no particle which is not the center of opposing forces. Hence error is ubiquitous. In making error objective we have made all objectivity erroneous. We find ourselves obliged to say that the choir of Westminster Abbey, the Brooklyn bridge, the heads on our shoulders are all supported by logical errors!

Following these illustrations of ontological contradictions there is indeed this interesting statement: "Nature is so full of these mutually negative processes that we are moved to admiration when a few forces coöperate long enough to form what we call an organism."32 The implication is, apparently, that as an "opposition" of forces is error, "coöperation" of forces is truth. But what is to distinguish "opposition" from "coöperation"? In the illustration it is clear that opposing forces—error—do not interfere with coöperative forces—truth. Where should we find more counterbalancing, more starting and stopping, warming and cooling, combining and separating than in an organism? And if these processes can be stated only in propositions that are "manifestly contradictory," are we to understand that truth has errors for its constituent elements? Such paradoxes have always delighted the soul of absolute idealism. But, as we have seen, only the veil of an infinitesimal finitude intervenes between the logic of the objective universal of absolute idealism and the objective logic of analytic realism.

It is, of course, this predicament regarding objective truth and error that has driven most analytic logicians to recall the exiled psychological, "mental" act of knowing. It had to be recalled to provide some basis of distinction between truth and error, but, this act having already been conceived as incurably "subjective," the result is only an exchange of dilemmas. For the reinstatement of this act *ipso facto* reinstates the epistemological predicament to get rid of which it was first banished from logic.

Earnest efforts to escape this outcome have been made by attaching the act of knowing to the nervous system, and this is a move in the right direction. But so far the effort has been fruitless because no connection has been made between the knowing function of the nervous system and its other functions. The result is that the cognitive operation of the nervous system, as of the "psychical" mind, is that of a mere spectator; and the epistemological problem abides. An onlooking nervous system has no advantage over an "onlooking" mind. Onlooking, beholding may indeed be a part of a genuine act of knowing. But in that act it is always a stimulus or response to other acts. It is one of them;—never a mere spectator of them. It is when the act of knowing is cut off from its connection with other acts and finds itself adrift that it seeks metaphysical lodgings. And this it may find either in an empty psychical mind or in an equally empty body.33

If, in reinstating the act of knowing as a function of the nervous system, neo-realism had recognized the logical significance of the fact that the nervous system of which knowing is a function is the same nervous system of which loving and hating, desiring and striving are functions and that the transition from these to the operations of inquiry and knowing is not a capricious jump but a transition motived by the loving and hating, desiring and striving—if this had been recognized the logic of neo-realism would have been spared its embarrassments over the distinction of truth and error. It would have seen that the passage from loving and hating, desiring and striving to inquiry and knowing is made in order to renew and reform specific desires and strivings which, through conflict and consequent equivocation, have become fruitless and vain; and it must have seen that the results of the inquiry are true or false as they succeed or fail in this reformation and renewal.

But once more, it must steadily be kept in view that while the loving and hating, desiring and striving, which the logical operations are reforming and renewing, are functions of the nervous system, they are not functions of the nervous system alone, else the door of subjectivism again closes upon us. Loving and hating, desiring and striving have their "objects." Hence any reformation of these functions involves no less a reformation of their objects. When therefore we say that truth and error are relevant to desires and strivings, this means relevant to them as including their objects, not as entitized processes (such are the pitfalls of language) inclosed in a nervous system or mind. With this before us the relevance of truth and error to desires and strivings can never be made the basis for the charge of subjectivism. The conception of desires as peculiarly individual and subjective is a survival of the very isolation which is the source of the difficulty with truth and error. Hence the appeal to this isolation, made alike by idealism and realism, in charging instrumental logic with subjectivism is an elementary *petitio*.

Doubtless it will be urged again that the act of knowing is motived by an independent desire and striving of its own. This is of course consonant with the neo-realistic atomism, however inconsonant it may be with the conception of implication which it employs. If we take a small enough, isolated segment of experience we can find meaning for this notion, as we may for the idea that the earth is flat and that the sun moves around the earth. But as consequences accrue we find as great difficulties with the one as with the other. If the course of events did not bring us to book, if we could get off with a mere definition of truth and error we might go on piling up subsistential definitional logics world without end. But sublime adventurers, logically unregenerate and uninitiated, will go on sailing westward to the confusion and confounding of all definitional systems that leave them out of account.

The conclusion is plain. If logic is to have room in its household for both truth and error, if it is to avoid the old predicament of knowledge that is trifling or miraculous, tautologous or false, if it is to have no fear of the challenge of other sciences or of practical life, it must be content to take for its subject-matter the operations of intelligence conceived as real acts on the same metaphysical plane and in strictest continuity with other acts. Such a logic will not fear the challenge of science, for it is precisely this continuity that makes possible experimentation, which is the fundamental characteristic of scientific procedure.

Science without experiment is indeed a strange apparition. It is a λόγος with no λέγειν, a science with no *scire*; and this spells dogmatism. How necessary such continuity is to experimentation is apparent when we recall that there is no limit to the range of operations of every sort which scientific experiment calls into play; and that unless there be thoroughgoing continuity between the logical demand of the experiment and all the materials and devices employed in the process of the experiment, the operations of the latter in the experiment will be either miraculous or ruinous.

Finally, if this continuity of the operations of intelligence with other operations be essential to science, its relation to "practical" life is *ipso facto* established. For science is "practical" life aware of its problems and aware of the part that experimental—i.e., creative—intelligence plays in the solution of those problems.

INTELLIGENCE AND MATHEMATICS

HAROLD CHAPMAN BROWN

Herbart is said to have given the deathblow to faculty psychology. Man no longer appears endowed with volition, passion, desire, and reason; and logic, deprived of its hereditary right to elucidate the operations of inherent intelligence, has the new problem of investigating forms of intelligence in the making. This is no inconsequential task. "If man originally possesses only capacities which after a given amount of education will produce ideas and judgments" (Thorndike, *Educational Psychology*, Vol. I, p. 198), and if these ideas and judgments are to be substituted for a mythical intelligence it follows that tracing their development and observing their functioning renders clearer our conception of their nature and value and brings us nearer that exact knowledge of what we are talking about in which the philosopher at least aspires to equal the scientist, however much he may fall below his ideal.

For contemporary thought concerning the mathematical sciences this altered point of view generates peculiarly pressing problems. Mathematicians have weighed the old logic and found it wanting. They have builded themselves a new logic more adequate to their ends. But they have not whole-heartedly recognized the change that has come about in psychology; hence they have retained the faculty of intelligence knit into certain indefinables such as implication, relation, class, term, and the like, and have transported the faculty from the human soul to a mysterious realm of subsistence whence it radiates its ghostly light upon the realm of existence below. But while they reproach the old logic, often bitterly, their new logic merely furnishes a more adequate show-case in which already attained knowledge may be arranged to set off its charms for the observer in the same way that specimens in a museum are displayed before an admiring world. This statement is not a sweeping condemnation, however, for such a setting forth is not useless. It resembles the classificatory stage of science which, although not itself in the highest sense creative, often leads to higher stages by bringing under observation relations and facts that might otherwise have escaped notice. And in the realm of pure mathematics, the new logic has undoubtedly contributed in this manner to such discoveries. Danger appears when the logician attains Cartesian intoxication with the beauty of logico-mathematical form and tries to infer from the form itself the real nature of the formed material. The realm of subsistence too often has armed Indefinables with metaphysical myths whose attack is valiant when the doors of reflection are opened. It may be possible, however, to arrive at an understanding of mathematics without entering the kingdom of these warriors.

It is the essence of science to make prediction possible. The value of prediction lies in the fact that through this function man can control his environment, or, at worst, fortify himself to meet its vagaries. To attain such predictions, however, the world need not be grasped in its full concreteness. Hence arise processes of abstraction. While all other symptoms remain unnoticed, the temperature and pulse may mark a disease, or a barometer-reading the weather. The physicist may work only in terms of quantity in a world which is equally truly qualitative. All that is necessary is to select the elements which are most effective for prediction and control. Such selection gives the principle that dominates all abstractions. Progress is movement from the less abstract to the more abstract, but it is progress only because the more abstract is as genuinely an aspect of the concrete starting-point as anything is. Moreover, the outcome of progress of this sort cannot be definitely foreseen at the beginnings. The simple activities of primitive men have to be spontaneously performed before their value becomes evident. Only afterwards can they be cultivated for the sake of their value, and then only can the self-conscious cultivation of a science begin. The process remains full not only of perplexities, but of surprises; men's activities lead to goals far other than those which appear at the start. These goals, however, never deny the method by which the start is made. Developed intelligence is nothing but skill in using a set of concepts generated in this manner. In this sense the histories of all human endeavors run parallel.

Where the empirical bases of a science are continually in the foreground, as in physics or chemistry, the foregoing formulation of procedure is intelligible and acceptable to most men. Mathematics seem, however, to stand peculiarly apart. Many, with Descartes, have delighted in them "on account of the certitude and evidence of their reasonings" and recognized their contribution to the advancement of mechanical arts. But since the days of Kant even this value has become a problem, and many a young philosophic student has the question laid before him as to why it is that mathematics, "a purely conceptual science," can tell us anything about the character of a world which is, apparently at least, free from the idiosyncrasies of individual mind. It may be that mathematics began in empirical practice, such philosophers admit, but they add that, somehow, in its later career, it has escaped its lowly origin. Now it moves in the higher circles of postulated relations and arbitrarily defined entities to which its humble progenitors and relatives are denied the entrée. Parvenus, however, usually bear with them the mark of history, and in the case of this one, at least, we may hope that the history will be sufficient to drag it from the affectations of its newly acquired set and reinstate it in its proper place in the workaday world. For the sake of this hope, we shall take the risk of being tedious by citing certain striking moments of mathematical progress; and then we shall try to interpret its genuine status in the world of working truths.

I

Beginnings of Arithmetic and Geometry

The most primitive mathematical activity of man is counting, but here his first efforts are lost in the obscurity of the past. The lower races, however, yield us evidence that is not without value. Although the savage mind is not identical with the mind of primitive man, there is much in the activities of undeveloped races that can throw light upon the behavior of peoples more advanced. We must be careful in our inferences, however. Among the Australians and South Americans there are peoples whose numerical systems go little, or not at all, beyond the first two or three numbers. "It has been inferred from this," writes Professor Boas (*Mind of Primitive Man*, pp. 152-53), "that the people speaking these languages are not capable of forming the concept of higher numbers.... People like the South American Indians, ... or like the Esquimo ... are presumably not in need of higher numerical expressions, because there are not many objects that they have to count. On the other hand, just as soon as these same people find themselves in contact with civilization, and when they acquire standards of value that have to be counted, they adopt with perfect ease higher numerals from other languages, and develop a more or less perfect system of counting.... It must be borne in mind that counting does not become necessary until objects are considered in such generalized form that their individualities are entirely lost sight of. For this reason it is possible that even a person who owns a herd of domesticated animals may know them by name and by their characteristics, without even desiring to count them."

And there is one other false interpretation to be avoided. Man does not feel the need of counting and then develop a system of numerals to meet the need. Such an assumption is as ridiculous as to assume prehistoric man thinking to himself: "I must speak," and then inventing voice culture and grammar to make speaking pleasant and possible. Rather, when powers of communication are once attained, presumably in their beginnings also without forethought, man being still more animal than man, there were gradually dissociated communications of a kind approaching what numbers mean to us. But the number is not yet a symbol apart from that of the things numbered. Picture writing, re-representing the things meant, preceded developmentally any kind of symbolization representing the number by mere one-one correspondence with non-particularized symbols. It is plausible, although I have no anthropological authority for the statement, that the prevalence of finger words as number symbols (cf. infra) is originally a consequence of the fact that our organization makes the hand the natural instrument of pointing.

The difficulty of passing from concrete representations to abstract symbols has been keenly stated by Conant (*The Number Concept*, pp. 72-73), although his terminology is that of an old psychology and the limitations implied for the primitive mind are limitations of practice rather than of capacity as Mr. Conant seems to believe. "An abstract conception is something quite foreign to the essentially primitive mind, as missionaries and explorers have found to their chagrin. The savage can form no mental concept of what civilized man means by such a word as *soul*; nor would his idea of the abstract number 5 be much clearer. When he says *five*, he uses, in many cases at least, the same word that serves him when he wishes to say *hand*; and his mental concept when he says *five* is a hand. The concrete idea of a closed fist, of an open hand with outstretched fingers, is what is uppermost in his mind. He knows no more and cares no more about the pure number 5 than he does about the law of conservation of energy. He sees in his mental picture only the real, material image, and his only comprehension of the number is, "these objects are as many as the fingers on my hand." Then, in the lapse of the long interval of centuries which intervene between lowest barbarism and highest civilization, the abstract and concrete become slowly dissociated, the one from the other. First the actual hand picture fades away, and the number is recognized without the original assistance furnished by the derivation of the word. But the number is still for a long time a certain number *of objects*, and not an independent concept."

An excellent fur trader's story, reported to me by Mr. Dewey, suggests a further impulse to count besides that given by the need of keeping a tally, namely, the need of making one thing correspond to another in a business transaction. The Indian laid down one skin and the trader two dollars; if he proposed to count several skins at once and pay for all together, the former replied "too much cheatem." The result, however, demanded a tally either by the fingers, a pebble, or a mark made in the sand, and as the magnitude of such transactions grows the need of a specific number symbol becomes ever more acute.

The first obstacle, then, to overcome—and it has already been successfully passed by many primitive peoples—is the need of fortuitous attainment of a numerical symbol, which is not the mere repeated symbol of the things numbered. Significantly, this symbol is usually derived from the hand, suggesting gestures of tallying, and not from the words of already developed language. Consequently, number words relate themselves for the most part to the hand, and written number symbols, which are among the earliest writings of most peoples, tend to depict it as soon as they have passed beyond the stage mentioned above of merely repeating the symbol of the things numbered. W. C. Eells, in writing of the Number Systems of the North American Indians (*Am. Math. Mo.*, Nov., 1913; pp. 263-72), finds clear linguistic evidence for a digital origin in about 40% of the languages examined. Of the non-digital instances, I was sometimes connected with the first personal pronoun, 2 with roots meaning separation, 3, rarely, meaning more, or plural as distinguished from the dual, just as the Greek uses a plural as well as a dual in nouns and verbs, 4 is often the perfect, complete right. It is often a sacred number and the base of a quaternary system. Conant (*loc. cit.* p. 98) also gives a classification of the meanings of simple number words for more advanced languages; and even in them the hand is constantly in evidence, as in 5, the hand; 10, two hands, half a man, when fingers and toes are both considered, or a man, when the hands alone are considered; 20, one man, two feet. The other meanings hang upon the ideas of existence, piece, group, beginning, for I; and repetition, division, and collection for higher numerals.

A peculiar difficulty lies in the fact that when once numbering has become a self-conscious effort, the collection of things to be numbered frequently tends to exceed the number of names that have become available. Sometimes the difficulty is met by using a second man when the fingers and toes of the first are used up, sometimes by a method of repetition with the record of the number of the repetition itself added to the numerical significance of the whole process. Hence arise the various systems of bases that occur in developed mathematics. But the inertia to be overcome in the recognition of the base idea is nowhere more obvious than in the retention by the comparatively developed Babylonian system of a second base of 60 to supplement the decimal one for smaller numbers. Among the American Indians (Eells, *loc. cit.*) the system of bases used varies from the cumbersome binary scale, that exercised such a fascination over Leibniz (*Opera, III*, p. 346), through the rare ternary, and the more common quarternary to the "natural" quinary, decimal, and vigesimal systems derived from the use of the fingers and toes in counting. The achievement of a number base and number words, however, does not always open the way to further mathematical development. Only too often a complexity of expression is involved that almost immediately cuts off further progress. Thus the Youcos of the Amazon cannot get beyond the number three, for the simplest expression for the idea in their language is "pzettarrarorincoaroac" (Conant, *loc. cit.*, pp. 145, 83, 53). Such names as "99, tongo solo manani nun solo manani" (i.e., 10, understood, 5 plus 4 times, and 5 plus 4) of the Soussous of Sierra Leone; "399, caxtolli onnauh poalli ipan caxtolli onnaui" (15 plus 4 times 20 plus 15 plus 4) of the Aztec; "29, wick a chimen ne nompah sam pah nep e chu wink a" (Sioux), make it easy to understand the proverb of the Yorubas of Abeokuta, "You may be very clever, but you can't tell 9 times 9."

Almost contemporaneously with the beginnings of counting various auxiliary devices were introduced to help out the difficult task. In place of many men, notched sticks, knotted strings, pebbles, or finger pantomime were used. In the best form, these devices resulted in the abacus; indeed, it was not until after the introduction of arabic numerals and well into the Renaissance period that instrumental arithmetic gave way to graphical in Europe (D. E. Smith, *Rara Arithmetica*, under "Counters"). "In eastern Europe," say Smith and Mikami (*Japanese Mathematics*, pp. 18-19), "it"—the abacus—"has never been replaced, for the tschotü is used everywhere in Russia to-day, and when one passes over into Persia the same type of abacus is common in all the bazaars. In China the swan-pan is universally used for the purposes of computation, and in Japan the soroban is as strongly entrenched as it was before the invasion of western ideas."

Given, then, the idea of counting, and a mechanical device to aid computation, it still remains necessary to obtain some notation in which to record results. At the early dawn of history the Egyptians seem to have been already possessed of number signs (cf. Cantor, *Gesch. de. Math.*, p. 44) and the Phœnicians either wrote out their number words or used a few simple signs, vertical, horizontal, and oblique lines, a process which the Arabians perpetuated up to the beginning of the eleventh century (Fink, p. 15); the Greeks, as early as 600 B. C., used the initial letters of words for numbers. But speaking generally, historical beginnings of European number signs are too obscure to furnish us good material.

Our Indians have few number symbols other than words, but when they occur (cf. Eells, *loc. cit.*) they usually take the form of pictorial presentation of some counting device such as strokes, lines dotted to suggest a knotted cord, etc. Indeed, the smaller Roman numerals were probably but a pictorial representation of finger symbols. However, a beautiful concrete instance is furnished us in the Japanese mathematics (cf. Smith and Mikami, Ch. III). The earliest instrument of reckoning in Japan seems to have been the rod, Ch'eou, adapted from the Chinese under the name of Chikusaku (bamboo rods) about 600 A. D. At first relatively large (measuring rods?), they became reduced to about 12 cm., but from their tendency to roll were quickly replaced by the sangi (square prisms, about 7 mm. thick and 5 cm. long) and the number symbols were evidently derived from the use of these rods:

I, II, III, IIII, IIIII, T, TT, TTT, TTTT.

For the sake of clearness, tens, hundreds, etc., were expressed in the even place by horizontal instead of vertical lines and vice versa; thus 1267 would be formed

— II ⊥ TT.

The rods were arranged on a sort of chessboard called the swan-pan. Much later the lines were transferred to paper, and a circle used to denote the vacant square. The use of squares, however, rendered it unnecessary to arrange the even places differently from the odd, so numbers like 38057 came to be written

instead of

as in the earlier notation.

Somewhere in the course of these early mathematical activities the process has changed from the more or less spontaneous operating that led primitive man to the first enunciation of arithmetical ideas, and has become a self-conscious striving for the solution of problems. This change had already taken place before the historical origins of arithmetic are met. Thus, the treatise of Ahmes (2000 B. C.) contains the curious problem: 7 persons each have 7 cats; each cat eats 7 mice; each mouse eats 7 ears of barley; from each ear 7 measures of corn may grow; how much grain has been saved? Such problems are, however, half play, as appears in a Leonardo of Pisa version some 3000 years later: 7 old women go to Rome; each woman has 7 mules; each mule, 7 sacks; each sack contains 7 loaves; with each loaf are 7 knives; each knife is in 7 sheaths. Similarly in Diophantus' epitaph (330 A. D.): "Diophantus passed 1/6 of his life in childhood, 1/12 in youth, and 1/7 more as a bachelor; 5 years after his marriage, was born a son who died 4 years before his father at 1/2 his age." Often among peoples such puzzles were a favorite social amusement. Thus Braymagupta (628 A. D.) reads, "These problems are proposed simply for pleasure; the wise man can invent a thousand others, or he can solve the problems of others by the rules given here. As the sun eclipses the stars by its brilliancy, so the man of knowledge will eclipse the fame of others in assemblies of the people if he proposes algebraic problems, and still more if he solves them" (Cajori, *Hist. of Math.*, p. 92).

The limitation of these early methods is that the notation merely records and does not aid computation. And this is true even of such a highly developed system as was in use among the Romans. If the reader is unconvinced, let him attempt some such problem as the multiplication of CCCXVI by CCCCLXVIII, expressing it and carrying it through in Roman numerals, and he will long for the abacus to assist his labors. It was the positional arithmetic of the Arabians, of which the origins are obscure, that made possible the development of modern technique. Of this discovery, or rediscovery from the Hindoos, together with the zero symbol, Cajori (*Hist. of Math.*, p. 11) has said "of all mathematical discoveries, no one has contributed more to the general progress of intelligence than this." The notation no longer merely records results, but now assists in performing operations.

The origins of geometry are even more obscure than those of arithmetic. Not only is geometry as highly developed as arithmetic when it first appears in occidental civilization, but, in addition, the problems of primitive peoples seem to have been such that they have developed no geometrical formulæ striking enough to be recorded by investigators, so far as I have been able to discover. But just as the commercial life of the Phœnicians early forced them self-consciously to develop arithmetical calculation, so environmental conditions seem to have forced upon the Egyptians a need for geometrical considerations.

It is almost platitudinous to quote Herodotus' remark that the invention of geometry was necessary because of the floods of the Nile, which washed away the boundaries and changed the contours of the fields. And as Proclus Diadochus adds (*Procli Diadochi, in primum Euclidis elementorum librum commentarii*—quoted Cantor, I, p. 125): "It is not surprising that the discovery of this as well as other sciences has sprung from need, because everything in the process of beginning proceeds from the incomplete to the complete. There takes place a suitable transition from sensible perception to thoughtful consideration and rational knowledge. Just as with the Phœnicians, for the sake of business and commerce, an exact knowledge of numbers had its beginning, so with the Egyptians, for the above-mentioned reasons, was geometry contrived."

The earliest Egyptian mathematical writing that we know is that of Ahmes (2000 B. C.), but long before this the mural decorations of the temple wall involved many figures, the construction of which involved a certain amount of working knowledge of such operations as may be performed with the aid of a ruler and compass. The fact that these operations did not earlier lead to geometry, as ruler and compass work seems to have done in Japan in the nineteenth century (Smith and Mikami, index, "Geometry"), is probably due to the stage at which the development of Egyptian intelligence had arrived, feebly advanced on the road to higher abstract thinking. It is everywhere characteristic of Egyptian genius that little purely intellectual curiosity is shown. Even astronomical knowledge was limited to those determinations which had religious or magically practical significance, and its arithmetic and geometry never escaped these bounds as with the more imaginative Pythagoreans, where mystical interpretation seems to have been a consequence of rather than a stimulus to investigation. An old Egyptian treatise reads (Cantor, p. 63): "I hold the wooden pin (Nebi) and the handle of the mallet (semes), I hold the line in concurrence with the Goddess Safech. My glance follows the course of the stars. When my eye comes to the constellation of the great bear and the time of the number of the hour determined by me is fulfilled, I place the corner of the temple." This incantation method could hardly advance intelligence; but the methods of practical measuring were more effective. Here the rather happy device of using knotted cords, carried about by the Harpedonapts, or cord stretchers, was of some moment. Especially, the fact that the lengths 3, 4, and 5, brought into triangular form, served for an interesting connection between arithmetic and the right triangle, was not a little gain, later making possible the discovery of the Pythagorean theorem, although in Egypt the theoretical properties of the triangle were never developed. The triangle obviously must have been practically considered by the decorators of the temple and its builders, but the cord stretchers rendered clear its arithmetical significance. However, Ahmes' "Rules for attaining the knowledge of all dark things ... all secrets that are contained in objects" (Cantor, *loc. cit.*, p. 22) contains merely a mixture of all sorts of mathematical information of a practical nature,—"rules for making a round fruit house," "rules for measuring fields," "rules for making an ornament," etc., but hardly a word of arithmetical and geometrical processes in themselves, unless it be certain devices for writing fractions and the like.

II

The Progress of Self-conscious Theory

A characteristic of Greek social life is responsible both for the next phase of the development of mathematical thought and for the misapprehension of its nature by so many moderns. "When Archytas and Menaechmus employed mechanical instruments for solving certain geometrical problems, 'Plato,' says Plutarch, 'inveighed against them with great indignation and persistence as destroying and perverting all the good that there is in geometry; for the method absconds from incorporeal and intellectual or sensible things, and besides employs again such bodies as require much vulgar handicraft: in this way mechanics was dissimilated and expelled from geometry, and being for a long time looked down upon by philosophy, became one of the arts of war.' In fact, manual labor was looked down upon by the Greeks, and a sharp distinction was drawn between the slaves who performed bodily work and really observed nature, and the leisured upper classes who speculated, and often only knew nature by hearsay. This explains much of the naïve dreamy and hazy character of ancient natural science. Only seldom did the impulse to make experiments for oneself break through; but when it did, a great progress resulted, as was the case of Archytas and Archimedes. Archimedes, like Plato, held that it was undesirable for a philosopher to seek to apply the results of science to any practical use; but, whatever might have been his view of what ought to be in the case, he did actually introduce a large number of new inventions" (Jourdain, *The Nature of Mathematics*, pp. 18-19). Following the Greek lead, certain empirically minded modern thinkers construe geometry wholly from an intellectual point of view. History is read by them as establishing indubitably the proposition that mathematics is a matter of purely intellectual operations. But by so construing it, they have, in geometry, remembered solely the measuring and forgotten the land, and, in arithmetic, remembered the counting and forgotten the things counted.

Arithmetic experienced little immediate gain from its new association with geometry, which was destined to be of momentous import in its latter history, beyond the discovery of irrationals (which, however, were for centuries not accepted as numbers), and the establishment of the problem of root-taking by its association with the square, and interest in negative numbers.

The Greeks had only subtracted smaller numbers from larger, but the Arabs began to generalize the process and had some acquaintance with negative results, but it was difficult for them to see that these results might really have significance. N. Chuquet, in the fifteenth century, seems to have been the first to interpret the negative numbers, but he remained a long time without imitators. Michael Stifel, in the sixteenth century, still calls them "Numeri absurdi" as over against the "Numeri veri."

However, their geometrical interpretation was not difficult, and they soon won their way into good standing. But the case of the imaginary is more striking. The need for it was first felt when it was seen that negative numbers have no square roots. Chuquet had dealt with second-degree equations involving the roots of negative numbers in 1484, but says these numbers are "impossible," and Descartes (*Geom.*, 1637) first uses the word "imaginary" to denote them. Their introduction is due to the Italian algebrists of the sixteenth century. They knew that the real roots of certain algebraic equations of the third degree are represented as results of operations effected upon "impossible" numbers of the form $a + b\sqrt{-1}$ (where a and b are real numbers) without it being possible in general to find an algebraic expression for the roots containing only real numbers. Cardan calculated with these "impossibles," using them to get real results $[(5 + \sqrt{-15})(5 - \sqrt{-15}) = 25 - (-15) = 40]$, but adds that it is a "quantitas quae vere est sophistica" and that the calculus itself "adeo est subtilis ut est inutilis." In 1629, Girard announced the theorem that every complete algebraic equation admits of as many roots, real or imaginary, as there are units in its degree, but Gauss first proved this in 1799, and finally, in his *Theory of Complex Quantity*, in 1831.

Geometry, however, among the Greeks passed into a stage of abstraction in which lines, planes, etc., in the sense in which they are understood in our elementary texts, took the place of actually measured surfaces, and also took on the deductive form of presentation that has served as a model for all mathematical presentation since Euclid. Mensuration smacked too much of the exchange, and before the time of Archimedes is practically wholly absent. Even such theorems as "that the area of a triangle equals half the product of its base and its altitude" is foreign to Euclid (cf. Cajori, p. 39). Lines were merely directions, and points limitations from which one worked. But there was still dependence upon the things that one measures. Euclid's elements, "when examined in the light of strict mathematical logic, ... has been pronounced by C. S. Peirce to be 'Riddled with fallacies'"

(Cajori, p. 37). Not logic, but observation of the figures drawn, that is, concrete symbolization of the processes indicated, saves Euclid from error.

Roman practical geometry seems to have come from the Etruscans, but the Roman here is as little inventive as in his arithmetical ventures, although the latter were stimulated somewhat by problems of inheritance and interest reckoning. Indeed, before the entrance of Arabic learning into Europe and the translation of Euclid from the Arabic in 1120, there is little or no advance over the Egyptian geometry of 600 B. C. Even the universities neglected mathematics. At Paris "in 1336 a rule was introduced that no student should take a degree without attending lectures on mathematics, and from a commentary on the first six books of Euclid, dated 1536, it appears that candidates for the degree of A. M. had to give an oath that they had attended lectures on these books. Examinations, when held at all, probably did not extend beyond the first book, as is shown by the nickname 'magister matheseos' applied to the *Theorem of Pythagoras*, the last in the first book.... At Oxford, in the middle of the fifteenth century, the first two books of Euclid were read" (Cajori, *loc. cit.*, p. 136). But later geometry dropped out and not till 1619 was a professorship of geometry instituted at Oxford. Roger Bacon speaks of Euclid's fifth proposition as "elefuga," and it also gets the name of "pons asinorum" from its point of transition to higher learning. As late as the fourteenth century an English manuscript begins "Nowe sues here a Tretis of Geometri whereby you may knowe the hegte, depnes, and the brede of most what erthely thynges."

The first significant turning-point lies in the geometry of Descartes. Viete (1540-1603) and others had already applied algebra to geometry, but Descartes, by means of coördinate representation, established the idea of motion in geometry in a fashion destined to react most fruitfully on algebra, and through this, on arithmetic, as well as enormously to increase the scope of geometry. These discoveries are not, however, of first moment for our problem, for the ideas of mathematical entities remain throughout them the generalized processes that had appeared in Greece. It is worth noting, however, that in England mechanics has always been taught as an experimental science, while on the Continent it has been expanded deductively, as a development of *a priori* principles.

III

Contemporary Thought in Arithmetic and Geometry

To develop the complete history of arithmetic and geometry would be a task quite beyond the limits of this paper, and of the writer's knowledge. In arithmetic we were able to observe a stage in which spontaneous behavior led to the invention of number names and methods of counting. Then, by certain speculative and "play" impulses, there arose elementary arithmetical problems which began to be of interest in themselves. Geometry here also comes into consideration, and, in connection with positional number symbols, begin those interactions between arithmetic and geometry that result in the forms of our contemporary mathematics. The complex quantities represented by number symbols are no longer merely the necessary results of analyzing commercial relations or practical measurements, and geometry is no longer directly based upon the intuitively given line, point, and plane. If number relations are to be expressed in terms of empirical spatial positions, it is necessary to construct many imaginary surfaces, as is done by Riemann in his theory of functions, a construction representing the type of imagination which Poincaré has called the intuitional in contradistinction to the logical (*Value of Science*, Ch. I). And geometry has not only been led to the construction of many non-Euclidian spaces, but has even, with Peano and his school, been freed from the bonds of any necessary spatial interpretation whatsoever.

To trace in concrete detail the attainment of modern refinements of number theory would likewise exhibit nothing new in the building up of mathematical intelligence. We should find, here, a process carried out without thought of the consequences, there, an analogy suggesting an operation that might lead us beyond a difficulty that had blocked progress; here, a play interest leading to a combination of symbols out of which a new idea has sprung; there, a painstaking and methodical effort to overcome a difficulty recognized from the start. It is rather for us now to ask what it is that has been attained by these means, to inquire finally what are those things called "number" and "line" in the broad sense in which the terms are now used.

In so far as the cardinal number at least is concerned, the answer generally accepted by Dedekind, Peano, Russell, and such writers is this: the number is a "class of similar classes" (Whitehead and Russell, *Prin. Math.*, Vol. II, p. 4). To the interpretation of this answer, Mr. Russell, the most self-consciously philosophical of these mathematicians, has devoted his full dialectic skill. The definition has at least the merit of being free from certain arbitrary psychologizing that has vitiated many earlier attempts at the problem. Mr. Russell claims for it "(1) that the formal properties which we expect cardinal numbers to have result from it; (2) that unless we adopt this definition or some more complicated and practically equivalent definition, it is necessary to regard the cardinal number of a class as indefinable" (*loc. cit.*, p. 4). That the definition's terms, however, are not without obscurity appears in Mr. Russell's struggles with the zigzag theory, the no-class theory, etc., and finally in his taking refuge in the theory of "logical types" (*loc. cit.*, Vol. III, Part V. E.), whereby the contradiction that subverted Frege and drove Mr. Russell from the standpoint of the *Principles of Mathematics* is finally overcome.

The second of Mr. Russell's claims for his definition adds nothing to the first, for it merely asserts that unless we adopt some definition of the cardinal number from which its formal properties result, number is undefined. Any such definition would be, *ipso facto*, a practical equivalent of the first. We need only consider whether or not the formal properties of numbers clearly follow from this definition.

Mr. Russell's own experience makes us hesitate. When he first adopted this definition from Frege, he was led to make the inference that the class of all possible classes might furnish a type for a greatest cardinal number. But this led to nothing but paradox and contradiction. The obvious conclusion was that something was wrong with the concept of class, and the obvious way out was to deny the possibility of any such all-inclusive class. Just why there should be such limitation, except that it enables one to escape the contradiction, is not clear from Mr. Russell's analysis (cf. Brown, "The Logic of Mr. Russell," *Journ. of Phil., Psych., and Sci. Meth.*, Vol. VIII, No. 4, pp. 85-89). Furthermore, to pass to the theory of types on this ground is to give up the value of the first claim for the definition (quoted above), since the formal properties of numbers now merely follow from the definition because the terms of the definition are reinterpreted from the properties of number, so that these properties will follow from it. The definition has become circular.

The real difficulty lies in the concept of the class. Dogmatic realism is prone to find here an entity for which, as it is obviously not a physical thing, a home must be provided in some region of "being." Hence arises the realm of subsistence, as for Plato the world of facts duplicated itself in a world of ideas. But the subsistent realm of the mathematician is even more astounding than the ideal realm of Plato, for the latter world is a prototype of the world of things, while the world of the mathematician is peopled by all sorts of entities that never were on land or sea. The transfinite numbers of Cantor have, without doubt, a definite mathematical meaning, but they have no known representatives in the world of things, nor in the imagination of man, and in spite of the efforts of philosophers it may even be doubted whether an entity correlative to the mathematical infinite has ever been or can ever be specified.

Mr. Russell now teaches that "classes are merely symbolic" (*Sci. Meth. in Phil.*, p. 208), but this expression still needs elucidation. It does, to be sure, avoid the earlier difficulty of admitting "new and mysterious metaphysical entities" (*loc. cit.*, p.

204), but the "feeling of oddity" that accompanies it seems not without significance. What can be meant by a merely symbolic class of similar classes themselves merely symbolical? I do not know, unless it is that we are to throw overboard the effort aimed at arbitrary and creative definition and proceed in simple inductive and interpretative fashion. With classes as entities abandoned, we are left, until we have passed to a new point of view as to arithmetical entities, in the position of the intelligent ignoramus who defined a stock market operation as buying what you can't get with money you never had, and selling what you never owned for more than it was ever worth.

The situation seems to be that we are now face to face with new generalizations. Just as number symbols arose to denote operations gone through in counting things when attention is diverted from the particular characteristics of the things counted, and remained a symbol for those operations with things, so now we are becoming self-conscious of the character of the operations we have been performing and are developing new symbols to express possible operations with operations. The infinity of the number series expresses the fact that it is possible to continue the enumerating process indefinitely, and when we are asked by certain mathematicians to practise ourselves in such thoughts as that for infinite series a proper part can be the equal of the whole, where equality is defined through the establishment of one-one correspondence, we are really merely informed that among the group of symbols used to denote the concrete steps of an ever open counting process are groups of symbols that can be used to indicate operations that are of the same type as the given one in so far as the characteristic of being an open series is concerned. If there were anywhere an infinity of things to count, an unintelligible supposition, it would by no means be true that any selection of things from that series would be the equivalent of all things in the series, except in so far as equivalence meant that they could be arranged in the same type of series as that from which they were drawn.

Similarly the mathematical conception of the continuum is nothing but a formulation of the manner in which the cuts of a line or the numbers of a continuous series must be chosen so that there shall remain no possible cut or number of which the choice is not indicated. Correspondence is reached between elements of such series when the corresponding elements can be reached by an identical process. It seems to me, however, a mistake to *identify* the number continuum with the linear continuum, for the latter must include the irrational numbers, whereas the irrational number can never represent a spatial position in a series. For example, the $\sqrt{2}$ is by nature a decimal involving an infinite, i. e., an ever increasing, number of digits to express it and, by virtue of the infinity of these digits, they can never be looked upon as all given. It is then truly a number, for it expresses a genuine numerical operation, but it is not a position, for it cannot be a determinate magnitude but merely a quantity approaching a determinate magnitude as closely as one may please. That is, without its complete expression, which would be analogous to the self-contradictory task of finding a greatest cardinal number, there can be no cut in the line which is symbolized by it. But the operations of translating algebraic expressions into geometrical ones and vice versa (operations which are so important in physical investigations) are facilitated by the notion of a one to one correspondence between number and space.

When we pass to the transfinite numbers, we have nothing in the Alephs but the symbols of certain groupings of operations expressible in ordinary number series. And the many forms of numbers are all simply the result of recognizing value in naming definite groups of operations of a lower level, which may itself be a complication of processes indicated by the simple numerical signs. To create such symbols is by no means illegitimate and no paradox results in any forms as long as we remember that our numbers are not things but are signs of operations that may be performed directly upon things or upon other operations.

For example, let us consider such a symbol as   -5. -5 signifies the totality of a counting process carried on in an opposite sense from that denoted by $+5$. To take the square root is to symbolize a number, the totality of an operation, such that when the operation denoted by multiplying it by itself is performed the result is 5. Consequently the -5 is merely the symbol of these processes combined in such a way that the whole operation is to be considered as opposite in some sense to that denoted by $\sqrt{5}$. Hence, an easy method for the representation of such imaginaries is based on the principle of analytic geometry and a system of co-ordinates.

The nature of this last generalization of mathematics is well shown by Mr. Whitehead in his monumental *Universal Algebra*. The work begins with the definition of a calculus as "The art of manipulating substitutive signs according to fixed rules, and the deduction therefrom of true propositions" (*loc. cit.*, p. 4). The deduction itself is really a manipulation according to rules, and the truth consists essentially in the results being actually derived from the premises according to rule. Following Stout, substitutive signs are characterized thus: "a word is an instrument for thinking about the meaning which it expresses; a substitutive sign is a means of not thinking about the meaning which it symbolizes." Mathematical symbols have, then, become substitutive signs. But this is only possible because they were at an early stage of their history expressive signs, and the laws which connected them were derived from the relations of the things for which they stood. First it became possible to forget the things in their concreteness, and now they have become mere terms for the relations that had been generalized between them. Consequently, the things forgotten and the terms treated as mere elements of a relational complex, it is possible to state such relational complexes with the utmost freedom. But this does not mean that mathematics can be created in a purely arbitrary fashion. The mark of its origin is upon it in the need of exhibiting some existing situation through which the non-contradictory character of its postulates can be verified. The real advantage of the generalization is that of all generalizations in science, namely, that by looking away from practical applications (as appears in a historical survey) results are frequently obtained that would never have been attained if our labor had been consciously limited merely to those problems where the advantages of a solution were obvious. So the most fantastic forms of mathematics, which themselves seem to bear no relation to actual phenomena, just because the relations involved in them are the relations that have been derived from dealing with an actual world, may contribute to the solutions of problems in other forms of calculus, or even to the creation of new forms of mathematics. And these new forms may stand in a more intimate connection with aspects of the real world than the original mathematics.

In 1836-39 there appeared in the *Gelehrte Schriften der Universität Kasan*, Lobatchewsky's epoch-making "New Elements of Geometry, with a Complete Theory of Parallels." After proving that "if a straight line falling on two other straight lines make the alternate angles equal to one another, the two straight lines shall be parallel to one another," Euclid, finding himself unable to prove that in every other case they were not parallel, assumed it in an axiom. But it had never seemed obvious. Lobatchewsky's system amounted merely to developing a geometry on the basis of the contradictory axiom, that through a point outside a line an indefinite number of lines can be drawn, no one of which shall cut a given line in that plane. In 1832-33, similar results were attained by Johann Bolyai in an appendix to his father's "*Tentamen juventutem studiosam in elementa matheseosos puræ ... introducendi*" entitled "The Science of Absolute Space." In 1824 the dissertation of Riemann, under Gauss, introduced the idea of an n-ply extended magnitude, or a study of n-dimensional manifolds and a new road was opened for mathematical intelligence.

At first this new knowledge suggested all sorts of metaphysical hypotheses. If it is possible to build geometries of n-dimensions or geometries in which the axiom of parallels is no longer true, why may it not be that the space in which we make our measurements and on which we base our mechanics is some one of these "non-Euclidian" spaces? And indeed many experiments were conducted in search of some clue that this might be the case. Such experiments in relation to "curved spaces" seemed particularly alluring, but all have turned out to be fruitless in results. Failure leads to investigation of the causes of failure. If our space had been some one of these spaces how would it have been possible for us to know this fact? The traditional definition of a straight line has never been satisfactory from a physical point of view. To define it as the shortest distance between two points is to introduce the idea of distance, and the idea of distance itself has no meaning without the idea of straight line, and so the definition moves in a vicious circle. On the metaphysical side, Lotze (*Metaphysik*, p. 249) and others (Merz, *History of European Thought in the Nineteenth Century*, Vol. II, p. 716) criticized these attempts, on the whole justly, but the best interpretation of the situation has been given by Poincaré.

Two lines of thought now lead to a recasting of our conceptions of the fundamental notions of geometry. On the one hand, that very investigation of postulates that had led to the discovery of the apparently strange non-Euclidian geometries was easily continued to an investigation of the simplest basis on which a geometry could be founded. Then by reaction it was continued with similar methods in dealing with algebra, and other forms of analysis, with the result that conceptions of mathematical entities have gradually emerged that represent a new stage of abstraction in the evolution of mathematics, soon to be discussed as the dominating conceptions in contemporary thought. On the other hand, there also developed the problem of the relations of these geometrical worlds to one another, which has been primarily significant in helping to clear up the relations of mathematics in its "pure" and "applied" forms.

Geometry passed through a stage of abstraction like that examined in connection with arithmetic. Beginning with the discovery of non-Euclidian geometry, it has been becoming more and more evident that a line need not be a name for an aspect of a physical object such as the ridge-pole line of a house and the like, nor even for the more abstract mechanical characteristic of direction of movement;—although the persistency with which intuitionally minded geometers have sought to adapt such illustrations to their needs has somewhat obscured this fact. However, even a cursory examination of a modern treatise on geometry makes clear what has taken place. For example, Professor Hilbert begins his *Grundlagen der Geometrie*, not with definition of points, lines, and planes, but with the assumption of three different systems of things (Dinge) of which the first, called points, are denoted A, B, C, etc., second, called straight lines (Gerade), are denoted a, b, c, etc., and the third, called planes, are denoted by α, β, γ, etc. The relations between these things then receive "genaue und vollständige Beschreibung" through the axioms of the geometry. And the fact that these "things" are called points, lines, and planes is not to give to them any of the connotations ordinarily associated with these words further than are determined by the axiom groups that follow. Indeed, other geometers are even more explicit on this point. Thus for Peano (*I Principii di Geometria*, 1889) the line is a mere class of entities, the relations amongst which are no longer concrete relations but types of relations. The plane is a class of classes of entities, etc. And an almost unlimited number of examples, about which the theorems of the geometry will express truths, can be exhibited, not one of which has any close resemblance to spatial facts in the ordinary sense.

Philosophers, it seems to me, have been slow to recognize the significance of the step involved in this last phase of mathematical thought. We have been so schooled in an arbitrary distinction between relations and concepts, that while long familiar with general ideas of concepts, we are not familiar with generalized ideas of relations. Yet this is exactly what mathematics is everywhere presenting. A transition has been made from relations to types of relations, so that instead of speaking in terms of quantitative, spatial and temporal relations, mathematicians can now talk in terms of symmetrical, asymmetrical, transitive, intransitive relational types and the like. These present, however, nothing but the empirical character that is common to such relations as that of father and son; debtor and creditor; master and servant; a is to the left of b, b of c; c of d; a is older than b, b than c, c than d, etc. Hence this is not abandonment of experience but a generalization of it, which results in a calculus potentially applicable not only to it but also to other subject-matter of thought. Indeed, if it were not for the possibility of this generalization, the almost unlimited applicability of diagrams, so useful in the classroom, to illustrate everything from the nature of reality to the categorical imperative, as well as to the more technical usages of the psychological and social sciences, would not be understandable.

It would be a paradox, however, if starting out from processes of counting and measuring, generalizations had been attained that no longer had significance for counting or measuring, and the non-Euclidian hyper-dimensional geometries seem at first to present this paradox. But, as the outcome of our second line of thought proves, this is not the case. The investigation of the relations of different geometrical systems to each other has shown (cf. Brown, "The Work of H. Poincaré," *Journ. of Phil., Psy., and Sci. Meth.*, Vol. XI, No. 9, p. 229) that these different systems have a correspondence with one another so that for any theorem stated in one of them there is a corresponding theorem that can be stated in another. In other words, given any factual situation that can be stated in Euclidian geometry, the aspect treated as a straight line in the Euclidian exposition will be treated as a curve in the non-Euclidian, and a situation treated as three-dimensional by Euclid's methods can be treated as of any number of dimensions when the proper fundamental element is chosen, and vice versa, although of course the element will not be the line or plane in our empirical usage of the term. This is what Poincaré means by saying that our geometry is a free choice, but not arbitrary (*The Value of Science*, Pt. III, Ch. X, Sec. 3), for there are many limitations imposed by fact upon the choice, and usually there is some clear indication of convenience as to the system chosen, based on the fundamental ideal of simplicity.

It is evident, then, that geometry and arithmetic have been drawing closer together, and that to-day the distinction between them is somewhat hard to maintain. The older arithmetic had limited itself largely to the study of the relations involved in serial orders as suggested by counting, whereas geometry had concerned itself primarily with the relations of groups of such series to each other when the series, or groups of series, are represented as lines or planes. But partly by interaction in analytic geometry, and partly in the generalization of their own methods, both have come to recognize the fundamental character of the relations involved in their thought, and arithmetic, through the complex number and the algebraic unknown quantities, has come to consider more complex serial types, while geometry has approached the analysis of its series through interaction with number theory. For both, the content of their entities and the relations involved have been brought to a minimum. And this is true even of such apparently essentially intuitional fields as projective geometry, where entities can be substituted for directional lines and the axioms be turned into relational postulates governing their configurations.

Nevertheless, geometry like arithmetic, has remained true to the need that gave it initial impulse. As in the beginning it was only a method of dealing with a concrete situation, so in the end it is nothing but such a method, although, as in the case of arithmetic, from ever closer contact with the situation in question, it has been led, by refinements that thoughtful and continual contact bring, to dissect that situation and give heed to aspects of it which were undreamed of at the initial moment. In a sense, then, there are no such things as mathematical entities, as scholastic realism would conceive them. And yet, mathematics is not dealing with unrealities, for it is everywhere concerned with real rational types and systems where such types may be exemplified. Or we can say in a purely practical way that mathematical entities are constituted by their relations, but this phrase cannot here be interpreted in the Hegelian ontological sense in which it has played so great and so pernicious a part in contemporary philosophy. Such metaphysical interpretation and its consequences are the basis of paradoxical absolutisms, such as that arrived at by Professor Royce (*World and the Individual*, Vol. II, Supplementary Essay). The peculiar character of abstract or pure mathematics seems to be that its own operations on a lower level constitute material which serves for the subject-matter with which its later investigations deal. But mathematics is, after all, not fundamentally different from the other sciences. The concepts of all sciences alike constitute a special language peculiarly adapted for dealing with certain experience adjustments, and the differences in the development of the different sciences merely express different degrees of success with which such languages have been formulated with respect to making it possible to predict concerning not yet realized situations. Some sciences are still seeking their terms and fundamental concepts, others are formulating their first "grammar," and mathematics, still inadequate, yearly gains both in vocabulary and flexibility.

But if we are to conceive mathematical entities as mere terminal points in a relational system, it is necessary that we should become clear as to just what is meant by relation, and what is the connection between relations and quantities. Modern thought has shown a strong tendency to insist, somewhat arbitrarily, on the "internal" or "external" character of relations. The former emphasis has been primarily associated with idealistic ontology, and has often brought with it complex dialectic questions as to the identity of an individual thing in passing from one relational situation to another. The latter insistence has meant primarily that things do not change with changing relations to other things. It has, however, often implied the independent existence, in some curiously metaphysical state, of relations that are not relating anything, and is hardly less paradoxical than the older view. In the field of physical phenomena, it seems to triumph, while the facts of social life, on the other hand, lend some countenance to the view of the "internalists." Like many such discussions, the best way around them is to forget their arguments, and turn to a fresh and independent investigation of the facts in question.

IV

Things, Relations, and Quantities

As I write, the way is paved for me by Professor Cohen (*Journ. of Phil., Psy., and Sci. Meth.*, Vol. XI, No. 23, Nov. 5, 1914, pp. 623-24), who outlines a theory of relations closely allied to that which I have in mind. Professor Cohen writes: "Like the distinction between primary and secondary qualities, the distinction between qualities and relations seems to me a shifting one because the 'nature' of a thing changes as the thing shifts from one context to another.... To Professors Montague and Lovejoy the 'thing' is like an old-fashioned landowner and the qualities are its immemorial private possessions. A thing may enter into commercial relations with others, but these relations are extrinsic. It never parts with its patrimony. To me, the 'nature' of a thing seems not to be so private or fixed. It may consist entirely of bonds, stocks, franchises, and other ways in which public credit or the right to certain transactions is represented.... At any rate, relations or transactions may be regarded as wider or more primary than qualities or possessions. The latter may be defined as internal relations, that is, relations *within* the system that constitutes the 'thing.' The nature of a thing contains an essence, i.e., a group of characteristics which, in any given system or context, remain invariant, so that if these are changed the things drop out of our system ... but the same thing may present different essences in different contexts. As a thing shifts from one context to another, it acquires new relations and drops old ones, and in all transformations there is a change or readjustment of the line between the internal relations which constitute the essence and the external relations which are outside the inner circle...."

Before continuing, however, I wish to make certain interpretations of these statements for which, of course, Professor Cohen is not responsible, and with which he would not be wholly in agreement. My general attitude will be shown by the first comment. Concepts are only means of denoting fragments of experience directly or indirectly given. If we then try to speak of a "nature of a thing" two interpretations of this expression are possible. The "thing" as such is only a bit of reality which some motive, that without undue extension of the term can be called practical, has led us to treat as more or less isolable from the rest of reality. Its nature, then, may consist of either its relations to other practically isolated realities or things, its actual effective value in its environment (and hence shift with the environment as Professor Cohen points out), or may consist of its essence, the "relations within the system," considered from the point of view of the potentialities implied by these for various environments. In the first sense the nature may easily change with change in environment, but if it changes in the second sense, as Professor Cohen remarks, it "drops out of our system." This I should interpret as meaning that we no longer have that thing, but some other thing selected from reality by a different purpose and point of view. I should not say with Professor Cohen that "the same thing may present different essences in different contexts." Every reality is more than one thing—man is an aggregate of atoms, a living being, an animal, and a thinker, and all of these are different things in essence, although having certain common characteristics. All attribution of "thingship" is abstraction, and all particular things may be said to participate in higher, i.e., more abstract, levels of thingship. Hence the effort to retain a thingship through a changing of essence seems to me but the echo of the motive that has so long deduced ontological monism from the logical fact that to conceive any two things is at least to throw them into a common universe of discourse. Consequently I should part company from Professor Cohen on this one point (which is perhaps largely a matter of definition, though here not unimportant) and distinguish merely the nature of a thing as *actual* and as *potential*. Of these the former alone changes with the environment, while the latter changes only as the thing ceases to be by passing into some other thing. In other words, if the example does not do violence to Professor Cohen's thought, I can quite understand this paper as a stimulator of criticism, or as a means of kindling a fire. Professor Cohen would, I suspect, take this to mean that the same thing—this paper—must be looked upon as having two different essences in two different contexts, for "the same thing may possess two different essences in different contexts," whereas I should prefer to interpret the situation as meaning that there are before me three (and as many more as may be) different things having three different essences: first, the paper as a physical object having a considerable number of definite properties; second, written words, which are undoubtedly in one sense mere structural modifications of the physical object paper (i.e., coloring on it by ink, etc.), but whose reality for my purpose lies in the power of evoking ideas acquired by things as symbols (things, indeed, but things whose essence lies in the effects they produce upon a reader rather than in their physical character); and third, the chemical and combustion producing properties of the paper. Now it is simpler for me to consider the situation as one in which three things have a common point in thingship, i.e., an abstract element in common, than to think of "a thing" shifting contexts and thereby changing its essence.

But now my divergence from Professor Cohen becomes more marked. He continues with the following example (p. 622): "Our neighbor M. is tall, modest, cheerful, and we understand a banker. His tallness, modesty, cheerfulness, and the fact that he is a banker we usually regard as his qualities; the fact that he is our neighbor is a relation which he seems to bear to us. He may move his residence, cease to be our neighbor, and yet remain the same person with the same qualities. If, however, I become his tailor, his tallness becomes translated into certain relations of measurement; if I become his social companion, his modesty means that he will stand in certain social relations with me, etc." In other words, we are illustrating the doctrine that "qualities are reducible to relations" (cf. p. 623). This doctrine I cannot quite accept without modification, for I cannot tell what it means.

Without any presuppositions as to subjectivity or consciousness (cf. p. 623, (a).) there are in the world as I know it certain colored objects—let the expression be taken naïvely to avoid idealistico-realistic discussion which is here irrelevant. Now it is as unintelligible to me that the red flowers and green leaves of the geraniums before my windows should be reducible to mere relations in any existential sense, as it would be to ask for the square root of their odor, though of course it is quite intelligible that the physical theory and predictions concerning green and red surfaces (or odors) should be stated in terms of atomic distances and ether vibrations of specific lengths. The scientific conception is, after all, nothing more than an indication of how to take hold of things and manipulate them to get foreseen results, and its entities are real things only in the sense that they are the practically effective keynotes of the complex reality. Accordingly, instead of reducing qualities to relations, it seems to me a much more intelligible view to consider relations as abstract ways of taking qualities in general, as qualities thought of in their function of bridging a gap or making a transition between two bits of reality that have previously been taken as separate things. Indeed, it is just because things are not ontologically independent beings (but rather selections from genuinely concatenated existence) that relations become important as indications of the practical significance of qualitative continuities which have been neglected in the prior isolation of the thing. Thus, instead of an existential world that is "a network of relations whose intersections are called terms" (p. 622), I find more intelligible a qualitatively heterogeneous reality that can be variously partitioned into things, and that can he abstractly replaced by systems of terms and relations that are adequate to symbolize their effective nature in particular respects. There is a tendency for certain attributes to maintain their concreteness (qualitativeness) in things, and for others to suggest the connection of things with other things, and so to emphasize a more abstract aspect of experience. Thus then arises a temporary and practical distinction that tends to be taken as opposition between qualities and relations. As spatial and temporal characteristics possess their chief practical value in the connection of things, so they, like Professor Cohen's neighbor-character, are ordinarily assumed abstractly as mere relations, while shapes, colors, etc., and Professor Cohen's "modesty, tallness, cheerfulness," may be thought of more easily without emphasis on other things and so tend to be accepted in their concreteness as qualities, but how slender is the dividing-line Professor Cohen's easy translation of these things into relations makes clear.

Taken purely intellectualistically, there would be first a fiction of separation in what is really already continuous and then another fiction to bridge the gap thus made. This would, of course, be the falsification against which Bergson inveighs. But this interpretation is to misunderstand the nature of abstraction. Abstraction does not substitute an unreal for a real, but selects from reality a genuine characteristic of it which is adequate for a particular purpose. Thus to conceive time as a succession of moments is not to falsify time, but to select from processes going on in time a characteristic of them through which predictions can be made, which may be verified and turned into an instrument for the control of life or environment. A similar misunderstanding of abstraction, coupled with a fuller appreciation than Bergson evinces of the value of its results, has led to the neo-realistic insistence on turning abstractions into existent entities of which the real world is taken to be an organized composite aggregate.

The practice of turning qualities into merely conscious entities has done much to obscure the status of scientific knowing, for it has left mere quantity as the only real character of the actual world. But once take a realistic standpoint, and quantity is no more real than quality. For primitive man, the qualitative aspect of reality is probably the first to which he gives heed, and it is only through efforts to get along with the world in its qualitative character that its quantitative side is forced upon the attention. Then so-called "exact" science is born, but it does not follow that qualities henceforth become insignificant. They are still the basis of all relations, even of those that are most directly construed as quantitative. Quality and quantity are only different aspects of the world which the status of our practical life leads us to take separately or abstractly. "Thing" is no less an abstraction, in which we disregard certain continuities with the rest of the world because we are so constituted that the demands of living make it expedient to do so. Things once given, further abstractions become possible, among which are those leading to mathematical thinking, in which higher abstractions are made, guided always by the "generating problem" (cf. Karl Schmidt, *Jour. of Phil., Psy., and Sci. Meth.*, Vol. X, No. 3, 1913, pp. 64-75).

V

The Function of Theory in Science

The controlling factors for the progress of scientific thought are inventions that lead the scientist into closer contact with his data, and direct attention to complexities which would otherwise have escaped observation. This end is best fulfilled by conceiving entities that under some point of view are practically isolable from the context in which they occur. Only too often philosophic thought has confused this practical segregation with ontological separation, and so been obliged to introduce metaphysical and external relations to bring these entities together again in a real world, when in reality they have never been separated from one another and hence not from the real world. Furthermore, the conceptual model, built on the lines of a calculus of mathematics, is often considered the truth *par excellence* after the analogy of a camera's portrait. Progress in science, however, shows that these models have to be continually rebuilt. Each seems to lead to further knowledge that necessitates its reconstruction, so that truth takes on an ideal value as an ultimate but unattained, if not unattainable, goal, while existing science becomes reduced to working hypotheses. From a positivistic point of view, however, the goal is not only practically unattainable, but it is irrational, for there seems to be every evidence that it expresses something contrary to the nature of the real. Yet scientific theory is not wholly arbitrary. We cannot construe nature as constituted of any sorts of entities that may suit our whim. And this is because science itself recognizes that its entities are not really isolated, but are endowed with all sorts of properties that serve to connect them with other entities. They are only symbols of critical points of reality which, conceived in a certain way, make the behavior of the whole intelligible. Indeed, the only significant sense in which they are true for the scientist is that they indicate real connections that might otherwise have been overlooked, and this is only possible from the fact that reality has the characteristics that they present and that, with their relations, they give an approximate presentation of what is actually presented just as a successful portrait painter considers the individuality of the eyes, nose, mouth, etc., although he does not imply that a face is compounded of these separate features as a house is built of boards.

The atomic theory, for example, has undoubtedly been of the greatest service to chemistry, and atoms undoubtedly denote a significant resting-place in the analysis of the physical world. Yet in the light of electron theories, it is becoming more and more evident that atoms are not ultimate particles, and are not even all alike (Becker, "Isostasy and Radioactivity," *Sci.,* Jan. 29, 1915) when they represent a single substance. Again, while there is as yet no evidence to suggest that the electron must itself be considered as divisible (unless it be the distinction between the positive and negative electron), there are suggestions that electrons may themselves arise and pass away (cf. Moore, *Origin, and Nature of Life,* p. 39). "A wisely positivistic mind," writes Enriques (*Problems of Science,* p. 34), "can see in the atomic hypothesis only a subjective representation,"[34] and, we might add, "in any other hypothesis." He continues (pp. 34-36): "robbing the atom of the concrete attributes inherent in its image, we find ourselves regarding it as a mere symbol. The logical value of the atomic theory depends, then, upon the establishment of a proper correspondence between the symbols which it contains and the reality which we are trying to represent.

"Now, if we go back to the time when the atomic theory was accepted by modern chemistry, we see that the plain atomic formulæ contain only the representation of the invariable relations in the combination of simple bodies, in weight and volume; these last being taken in relation to a well-defined gaseous state.

"But, once introduced into science, the atomic phraseology suggested the extension of the meaning of the symbols, and the search in reality for facts in correspondence with its more extended conception.

"The theory advances, urged on, as it were, by its metaphysical nature, or, if you wish, by the association of ideas which the concrete image of the atom carries with it.

"Thus for the plain formulæ we have substituted, in the chemistry of carbon compounds, structural formulæ, which come to represent, thanks to the disposition or grouping of atoms in a molecule, structural relations of the second degree, that is to say, relations inherent in certain chemical transformations with respect to which some groups of elements have in some way an invariant character. And here, because the image of a simple molecule upon a plane does not suffice to explain, for example, the facts of isomerism, we must resort to the stereo-chemical representation of Van't Hoff.

"Must we further recall the kinetic theory of gases, the facts explained by the breaking up of molecules into ions, the hypothesis suggested, for example, by Van der Waals by the view that an atom has an actual bulk? Must we point to a physical phenomenon of quite a different class, for example, to the coloring of the thin film forming the soap-bubbles which W. Thomson has taken as the measure of the size of a molecule?

"Such a résumé of results shows plainly that we cannot help the progress of science by blocking the path of theory and looking only at its positive aspects, that is to say, at the collection of facts that it explains. The value of a theory lies rather in the hypothesis which it can suggest, by means of the psychological representation of the symbols.

"We shall not draw from all this the conclusion that the atomic hypothesis ought to correspond to the extremely subtle sensations of a being resembling a perfected man. We shall not even reason about the possibility of those imaginary sensations, in so far as they are conceived simply as an extension of our own. But we shall repeat, in regard to the atomic theory, what an illustrious master is said to have remarked as to the unity of matter: if on first examination a fact seems possible which contradicts the atomic view of things, there is a strong probability that such a fact will be disproved by experience.

"Does not such a capacity for adaptation to facts, thus furnishing a model for them, perhaps denote the *positive* reality of a theory?"

And the above principles are as true of mathematical concepts as of chemical. Everywhere it is "capacity of adaptation to facts" that is the criterion of a branch of mathematics, except, of course, that in mathematics the facts are not always physical facts. Mathematics has successfully accomplished a generalization whereby its own methods furnish the material for higher generalizations. The imaginary number and the hyper-dimensional or non-Euclidian geometries may be absurd if measured by the standard of physical reality, but they nevertheless have something real about them in relation to certain mathematical processes on a lower level. There is no philosophic paradox about modern arithmetic or geometry, once it is recognized that they are merely abstractions of genuine features of simpler and more obviously practical manipulations that are clearly derived from the dealing of a human being with genuine realities.

In the light of these considerations, I cannot help feeling that the frequent attempts of mathematicians with a philosophical turn of mind, and philosophers who are dipping into mathematics, to derive geometrical entities from psychological considerations are quite mistaken, and are but another example of those traditional presuppositions of psychology which, Professor Dewey has pointed out (*Jour. of Phil., Psy., and Sci. Meth.*, XI, No. 19, p. 508), were "bequeathed by seventeenth-century philosophy to psychology, instead of originating within psychology" ... that "were wished upon it by philosophy when it was as yet too immature to defend itself."

Henri Poincaré (*Science and Hypothesis*, Ch. IV, *The Value of Science*, Ch. IV) and Enriques (*Problems of Science*, Ch. IV, esp. B—*The Psychological Acquisition of Geometrical Concepts*) furnish two of the most familiar examples of this sort of philosophizing. Each isolates special senses, sight, touch, or motion, and tries to show how a being merely equipped with one or the other of these senses might arrive at geometrical conceptions which differ, of course, from space as represented by our familiar Euclidian geometry. Then comes the question of fusing these different sorts of experience into a single experience of which geometry may be an intelligible transcription. Enriques finds a parallel between the historical development and the psycho-genetic development of the postulates of geometry (*loc. cit.*, p. 214 *seq.*). "The three groups of ideas that are connected with the concepts that serve as the basis for the theory of continuum (*Analysis situs*), of metrical, and of projective geometry, may be connected, as to their psychological origin, with three groups of sensations: with the general tactile-muscular sensations, with those of special touch, and of sight, respectively." Poincaré even evokes ancestral experience to make good his case (*Sci. and Hyp.*, Ch. V, end). "It has often been said that if individual experience could not create geometry, the same is not true of ancestral experience. But what does that mean? Is it meant that we could not experimentally demonstrate Euclid's postulate, but that our ancestors have been able to do it? Not in the least. It is meant that by natural selection our mind has *adapted* itself to the conditions of the external world, that it has adopted the geometry *most advantageous* to the species: or in other words, the *most convenient*."

Now undoubtedly there may be a certain modicum of truth in these statements. As implied by the last quotation from Poincaré, the modern scientist can hardly doubt that the fact of the adaptation of our thinking to the world we live in is due to the fact that it is in that world that we evolved. As is implied by both writers, if one could limit human contact with the world to a particular form of sense response, thought about that world would take place in different terms from what it now does and would presumably be less efficient. But these admissions do not imply that any light is thrown upon the nature of mathematical entities by such abstractions. Russell (*Scientific Method in Philosophy*) is in the curious position of raising arithmetic to a purely logical status, but playing with geometry and sensation after the manner of Poincaré, to whom he gives somewhat grudging praise on this account.

The psychological methods upon which all such investigations are based are open to all sorts of criticisms. Chiefly, the conceptions on which they are based, even if correct, are only abstractions. There is not the least evidence for the existence of organisms with a single differentiated sense organ, nor the least evidence that there ever was such an organism. Indeed, according to modern accounts of the evolution of the nervous system (cf. G. H. Parker, *Pop. Sci. Month.*, Feb., 1914) different senses have arisen through a gradual differentiation of a more general form of stimulus receptor, and consequently, the possibility of the detachment of special senses is the latter end of the series and not the first. But, however this may be, the mathematical concepts that we are studying have only been grasped by a highly developed organism, man, but they had already begun to be grasped by him in an early stage of his career before he had analyzed his experience and connected it with specific sense organs. It may of course be a pleasant exercise, if one likes that sort of thing, to assume with most psychologists certain elementary sensations, and then examine the amount of information each can give in the light of possible mathematical interpretations, but to do so is not to show that a being so scantily endowed would ever have acquired a geometry of the type in question, or any geometry at all. Inferences of the sort are in the same category with those from hypothetical children, that used to justify all theories of the pedagogue and psychologist, or from the economic man, that still, I fear, play too great a part in the world of social science.

VI

Mathematical Intelligence

The real nature of intelligence as it appears in the development of mathematics is something quite other than that of sensory analysis. Intelligence is fundamentally skill, and although skill may be acquired in connection with some sort of sensory contact of an organism and environment, it is only determined by that contact in the sense that if the sensory conditions were different the needs of the organism might be different, and the kind and degree of skill it could attain would be other than under the conditions at first assumed. Whenever the beginnings of mathematics appear with primitive people, we find a stage of development that calls for the exercise of skill in dealing with certain practical situations. Hence we found early in our investigations that it was impossible to affirm a weak intelligence from limited achievements in counting, just as it would be absurd to assume the feeble intelligence of a philosopher from his inability to manipulate a boomerang. The instance merely suggests a kind of skill that he has never been led to acquire.

Yet it is possible to distinguish intellectual skill, or better skills, from physical or athletic prowess. Primarily, it is directed at the formation and use of concepts, and the concept is only a symbol that can be substituted for experiences. A well-built concept is a part of a system of concepts where relations have taken the place of real connections in such a fashion that, forgetting the actuality, it is possible to present situations that have never occurred or at least are not immediately given at the time and place of the presentation, and to substitute them for actual situations in such a fashion that these may be expediently met, if or when such situations present themselves. An isolated concept, that is, one not a part of any system, is as mythical an entity as any savage ever dreamed. Indeed, it would add much to the clearness of our thinking if we could limit the use of "intelligence" to skill in constructing and using different systems of concepts, and speak concretely of mathematical intelligence, philosophical intelligence, economic intelligence, historic intelligence, and the like. The problem of creative intelligence is, after all, the problem of the acquisition of certain forms of skill, and while the general lines are the same for all knowledge (because the instruments are everywhere symbolic presentations, or concepts), in each field the situation studied makes different types of difficulties to be overcome and suggest different methods of attaining the object.

In mathematics, the formal impulse to reduce the content of fundamental concepts to a minimum, and to stress merely relations has been most successful. We saw its results in such geometries as Hilbert's and Peano's, where the empty name "entity" supplants the more concrete "point," and the "I" of arithmetic has the same character. In the social sciences, however, such examples as the "political" and the "economic" man are signal failures, while, perhaps, the "atom" and the "electron" approach the ideal in physics and chemistry. In mathematics, all further concepts can be defined by collections of these fundamental entities constituted in certain specified ways. And it is worth noting that both factually and logically a collection of entities so defined is not a mere aggregate, but possesses a differentiated character of its own which, although the resultant of its constitution, is not a property of any of its elements. A whole number is thus a collection of Is, but the properties of the whole number are something quite different from that of the elements through which it is constituted, just as an atom may be composed of electrons and yet, in valency, possess a property that is not the direct analogue of any property possessed by electrons not so organized.

Natural science, however, considers such building up of its fundamental entities into new entities as a process taking place in time rather than as consequent upon change of form of the whole rendering new analytic forms expedient. Hence it points to the occurrence of genuine novelties in the realm of objective reality. Mathematics, on the other hand, has generalized its concepts beyond the facts implied in spatial and temporal observations, so that while significant in both fields by virtue of the nature of its abstractions, its novelties are the novelties of new conceptual formations, a distinguishing of previously unnoted generalizations of relations existent in the realm of facts. But the fact that time has thus passed beyond its empirical meaning in the mathematical realm is no ground for giving mathematics an elevated position as a science of eternal realities, of subsistent beings, or the like. The generalization of concepts to cover both spatial and temporal facts does not create new entities for which a home must be provided in the partition of realities. Metaphysicians should not be the "needy knife grinders" of M. Anatole France (cf. *Garden of Epicurus*, Ch. "The Language of the Metaphysicians"). Nevertheless, the success of abstraction for mathematical intelligence has been immense.

No significant thinking is wholly the work of an individual man. Ideas are a product of social coöperation in which some have wrested crude concepts from nature, others have refined them through usage, and still others have built them into an effective system. The first steps were undoubtedly taken in an effort to communicate, and progress has been in part the progress of language. The original nature of man may have as a part those reactions which we call curiosity, but, as Auguste Comte long ago pointed out (Lévy-Bruhl, *A. Comte*, p. 67), these reactions are among the feeblest of our nature and without the pressure of practical affairs could hardly have advanced the race beyond barbarism. Science was the plaything of the Greek, the consolation of the Middle Ages, and only for the modern has it become an instrument in such fashion as to mark an epoch in the still dawning discovery of mind.

Man is, after all, rational only because through his nervous system he can hold his immediate responses in check and finally react as a being that has had experiences and profited by them. Concepts are the medium through which these experiences are in effect preserved; they express not merely a fact recorded but also the significance of a fact, not merely a contact with the world but also an attitude toward the future. It may be that the mere judgment of fact, a citation of resemblances and differences, is the basis of scientific knowledge, but before knowledge is worthy of the name, these facts have undergone an ideal transformation controlled by the needs of successful prediction and motivated by that self-conscious realization of the value of control which has raised man above the beasts of the field.

The realm of mathematics, which we have been examining, is but one aspect of the growth of intelligence. But in theory, at least, it is among the most interesting, since in it are reached the highest abstractions of science, while its empirical beginnings are not lost. But its processes and their significance are in no way different in essence from those of the other sciences. It marks one road of specialization in the discovery of mind. And in these terms we may read all history. To quote Professor Woodbridge (*Columbia University Quarterly*, Dec., 1912, p. 10): "We may see man rising from the ground, startled by the first dim intimation175 that the things and forces about him are convertible and controllable. Curiosity excites him, but he is subdued by an untrained imagination. The things that frighten him, he tries to frighten in return. The things that bless him, he blesses. He would scare the earth's shadow from the moon and sacrifice his dearest to a propitious sky. It avails not. But the little things teach him and discipline his imagination. He has kicked the stone that bruised him only to be bruised again. So he converts the stone into a weapon and begins the subjugation of the world, singing a song of triumph by the way. Such is his history in epitome—a blunder, a conversion, a conquest, and a song. That sequence he will repeat in greater things. He will repeat it yet and rejoice where he now despairs, converting the chaos of his social, political, industrial, and emotional life into wholesome force. He will sing again. But the discovery of mind comes first, and then, the song."

SCIENTIFIC METHOD AND INDIVIDUAL THINKER

GEORGE H. MEAD

The scientist in the ancient world found his test of reality in the evidence of the presence of the essence of the object. This evidence came by way of observation, even to the Platonist. Plato could treat this evidence as the awaking of memories of the ideal essence of the object seen in a world beyond the heavens during a former stage of the existence of the soul. In the language of Theatetus it was the agreement of fluctuating sensual content with the thought-content imprinted in or viewed by the soul. In Aristotle it is again the agreement of the organized sensuous experience with the vision which the mind gets of the essence of the object through the perceptual experience of a number of instances. That which gives the stamp of reality is the coincidence of the percept with a rational content which must in some sense be in the mind to insure knowledge, as it must be in the cosmos to insure existence, of the object. The relation of this test of reality to an analytical method is evident. Our perceptual world is always more crowded and confused than the ideal contents by which the reality of its meaning is to be tested. The aim of the analysis varies with the character of the science. In the case of Aristotle's theoretical sciences, such as mathematics and metaphysics, where one proceeds by demonstration from the given existences, analysis isolates such elements as numbers, points, lines, surfaces, and solids, essences and essential accidents. Aristotle approaches nature, however, as he approaches the works of human art. Indeed, he speaks of nature as the artificer par excellence. In the study of nature, then, as in the study of the practical and productive arts, it is of the first importance that the observer should have the idea—the final cause—as the means of deciphering the nature of living forms. Here analysis proceeds to isolate characters which are already present in forms whose functions are assumed to be known. By analogy such identities as that of fish fins with limbs of other vertebrates are assumed, and some very striking anticipations of modern biological conceptions and discoveries are reached. Aristotle recognizes that the theory of the nature of the form or essence must be supported by observation of the actual individual. What is lacking is any body of observation which has value apart from some theory. He tests his theory by the observed individual which is already an embodied theory, rather than by what we are wont to call the facts. He refers to other observers to disagree with them. He does not present their observations apart from their theories as material which has existential value, independent for the time being of any hypothesis. And it is consistent with this attitude that he never presents the observations of others in support of his own doctrine. His analysis within this field of biological observation does not bring him back to what, in modern science, are the data, but to general characters which make up the definition of the form. His induction involves a gathering of individuals rather than of data. Thus analysis in the theoretical, the natural, the practical, and the productive sciences, leads back to universals. This is quite consistent with Aristotle's metaphysical position that since the matter of natural objects has reality through its realization in the form, whatever appears without such meaning can be accounted for only as the expression of the resistance which matter offers to this realization. This is the field of a blind necessity, not that of a constructive science.

Continuous advance in science has been possible only when analysis of the object of knowledge has supplied not elements of meanings as the objects have been conceived but elements abstracted from those meanings. That is, scientific advance implies a willingness to remain on terms of tolerant acceptance of the reality of what cannot be stated in the accepted doctrine of the time, but what must be stated in the form of contradiction with these accepted doctrines. The domain of what is usually connoted by the term facts or data belongs to the field lying between the old doctrine and the new. This field is not inhabited by the Aristotelian individual, for the individual is but the realization of the form or universal essence. When the new theory has displaced the old, the new individual appears in the place of its predecessor, but during the period within which the old theory is being dislodged and the new is arising, a consciously growing science finds itself occupied with what is on the one hand the débris of the old and on the other the building material of the new. Obviously, this must find its immediate *raison d'être* in something other than the meaning that is gone or the meaning that is not yet here. It is true that the barest facts do not lack meaning, though a meaning which has been theirs in the past is lost. The meaning, however, that is still theirs is confessedly inadequate, otherwise there would be no scientific problem to be solved. Thus, when older theories of the spread of infectious diseases lost their validity because of instances where these explanations could not be applied, the diagnoses and accounts which could still be given of the cases of the sickness themselves were no explanation of the spread of the infection. The facts of the spread of the infection could be brought neither under a doctrine of contagion which was shattered by actual events nor under a doctrine of the germ theory of disease, which was as yet unborn. The logical import of the dependence of these facts upon observation, and hence upon the individual experience of the scientist, I shall have occasion to discuss later; what I am referring to here is that the conscious growth of science is accompanied by the appearance of this sort of material.

There were two fields of ancient science, those of mathematics and of astronomy, within which very considerable advance was achieved, a fact which would seem therefore to offer exception to the statement just made. The theory of the growth of mathematics is a disputed territory, but whether mathematical discovery and invention take place by steps which can be identified with those which mark the advance in the experimental sciences or not, the individual processes in which the discoveries and inventions have arisen are almost uniformly lost to view in the demonstration which presents the results. It would be improper to state that no new data have arisen in the development of mathematics, in the face of such innovations as the minus quantity, the irrational, the imaginary, the infinitesimal, or the transfinite number, and yet the innovations appear as the recasting of the mathematical theories rather than as new facts. It is of course true that these advances have depended upon problems such as those which in the researches of Kepler and Galileo led to the early concepts of the infinitesimal procedure, and upon such undertakings as bringing the combined theories of geometry and algebra to bear upon the experiences of continuous change. For a century after the formulation of the infinitesimal method men were occupied in carrying the new tool of analysis into every field where its use promised advance. The conceptions of the method were uncritical. Its applications were the center of attention. The next century undertook to bring order into the concepts, consistency into the doctrine, and rigor into the reasoning. The dominating trend of this movement was logical rather than methodological. The development was in the interest of the foundations of mathematics rather than in the use of mathematics as a method for solving scientific problems. Of course this has in no way interfered with the freedom of application of mathematical technique to the problems of physical science. On the contrary, it was on account of the richness and variety of the contents which the use of mathematical methods in the physical sciences imported into the doctrine that this logical housecleaning became necessary in mathematics. The movement has been not only logical as distinguished from methodological but logical as distinguished from metaphysical as well. It has abandoned a Euclidean space with its axioms as a metaphysical presupposition, and it has abandoned an Aristotelian subsumptive logic for which definition is a necessary presupposition. It recognizes that everything cannot be proved, but it does not undertake to state what the axiomata shall be; and it also recognizes that not everything can be defined, and does not undertake to determine what shall be defined implicitly and what explicitly. Its constants are logical constants, as the proposition, the class and the relation.

With these and their like and with relatively few primitive ideas, which are represented by symbols, and used according to certain given postulates, it becomes possible to bring the whole body of mathematics within a single treatment. The development of this pure mathematics, which comes to be a logic of the mathematical sciences, has been made possible by such a generalization of number theory and theories of the elements of space and time that the rigor of mathematical reasoning is secured, while the physical scientist is left the widest freedom in the choice and construction of concepts and imagery for his hypotheses. The only compulsion is a logical compulsion. The metaphysical compulsion has disappeared from mathematics and the sciences whose techniques it provides.

It was just this compulsion which confined ancient science. Euclidian geometry defined the limits of mathematics. Even mechanics was cultivated largely as a geometrical field. The metaphysical doctrine according to which physical objects had their own places and their own motions determined the limits within which astronomical speculations could be carried on. Within these limits Greek mathematical genius achieved marvelous results. The achievements of any period will be limited by two variables: the type of problem against which science formulates its methods, and the materials which analysis puts at the scientist's disposal in attacking the problems. The technical problems of the trisection of an angle and the duplication of a cube are illustrations of the problems which characterize a geometrical doctrine that was finding its technique. There appears also the method of analysis of the problem into simpler problems, the assumption of the truth of the conclusion to be proved and the process of arguing from this to a known truth. The more fundamental problem which appears first as the squaring of the circle, which becomes that of the determination of the relation of the circle to its diameter and development of the method of exhaustion, leads up to the sphere, the regular polyhedra, to conic sections and the beginnings of trigonometry. Number was not freed from the relations of geometrical magnitudes, though

Archimedes could conceive of a number greater or smaller than any assignable magnitude. With the method of exhaustion, with the conceptions of number found in writings of Archimedes and others, with the beginnings of spherical geometry and trigonometry, and with the slow growth of algebra finding its highest expression in that last flaring up of Greek mathematical creation, the work of Diophantes; there were present all the conceptions which were necessary for attack upon the problems of velocities and changing velocities, and the development of the method of analysis which has been the revolutionary tool of Europe since the Renaissance. But the problems of a relation between the time and space of a motion that should change just as a motion, without reference to the essence of the object in motion, were problems which did not, perhaps could not, arise to confront the Greek mind. In any case its mathematics was firmly embedded in a Euclidian space. Though there are indications of some distrust, even in Greek times, of the parallel axiom, the suggestion that mathematical reasoning could be made rigorous and comprehensive independently of the specific content of axiom and definition was an impossible one for the Greek, because such a suggestion could be made only on the presupposition of a number theory and an algebra capable of stating a continuum in terms which are independent of the sensuous intuition of space and time and of the motion that takes place within space and time. In the same fashion mechanics came back to fundamental generalizations of experience with reference to motions which served as axioms of mechanics, both celestial and terrestrial: the assumptions of the natural motion of earthly substances to their own places in straight lines, and of celestial bodies in circles and uniform velocities, of an equilibrium where equal weights operate at equal distances from the fulcrum.

The incommensurable of Pythagoras and the paradoxes of Zeno present the "no thoroughfares" of ancient mathematical thought. Neither the continuum of space nor of motion could be broken up into ultimate units, when incommensurable ratios existed which could not be expressed, and when motion refused to be divided into positions of space or time since these are functions of motion. It was not until an algebraic theory of number led mathematicians to the use of expressions for the irrational, the minus, and the imaginary numbers through the logical development of generalized expressions, that problems could be formulated in which these irrational ratios and quantities were involved, though it is also true that the effort to deal with problems of this character was in no small degree responsible for the development of the algebra. Fixed metaphysical assumptions in regard to number, space, time, motion, and the nature of physical objects determined the limits within which scientific investigation could take place. Thus though the hypothesis of Copernicus and in all probability of Tycho Brahe were formulated by Greek astronomers, their physical doctrine was unable to use them because they were in flagrant contradiction with the definitions the ancient world gave to earthly and celestial bodies and their natural motions. The atomic doctrine with Democritus' thoroughgoing undertaking to substitute a quantitative for a qualitative conception of matter with the location of the qualitative aspects of the world in the experience of the soul appealed only to the Epicurean who used the theory as an exorcism to drive out of the universe the spirits which disturbed the calm of the philosopher.

There was only one field in which ancient science seemed to break away from the fixed assumptions of its metaphysics and from the definitions of natural objects which were the bases for their scientific inferences, this was the field of astronomy in the period after Eudoxus. Up to and including the theories of Eudoxus, physical and mathematical astronomy went hand in hand. Eudoxus' nests of spheres within spheres hung on different axes revolving in different uniform periods was the last attempt of the mathematician philosopher to state the anomalies of the heavens, and to account for the stations, the retrogressions, and varying velocities of planetary bodies by a theory resolving all phenomena of these bodies into motions of uniform velocities in perfect circles, and also placing these phenomena within a physical theory consistent with the prevailing conceptions of the science and philosophy of the time. As a physicist Aristotle felt the necessity of introducing further spheres between the nests of spheres assigned by Eudoxus to the planetary bodies, spheres whose peculiar motions should correct the tendency of the different groups of spheres to pass their motions on to each other. Since the form of the orbits of heavenly bodies and their velocities could not be considered to be the results of their masses and of their relative positions with reference to one another; since it was not possible to calculate the velocities and orbits from the physical characters of the bodies, since in a word these physical characters did not enter into the problem of calculating the positions of the bodies nor offer explanations for the anomalies which the mathematical astronomer had to explain, it was not strange that he disinterested himself from the metaphysical celestial mechanics of his time and concentrated his attention upon the geometrical hypotheses by means of which he could hope to resolve into uniform revolutions in circular orbits the anomalous motions of the planetary bodies. The introduction of the epicycle with the deferent and the eccentric as working hypotheses to solve the anomalies of the heavens is to be comprehended largely in view of the isolation of the mathematical as distinguished from the physical problem of astronomy. In no sense were these conceptions working hypotheses of a celestial mechanics. They were the only means of an age whose mathematics was almost entirely geometrical for accomplishing what a later generation could accomplish by an algebraic theory of functions. As has been pointed out, the undertaking of the ancient mathematical astronomer to resolve the motions of planetary bodies into circular, uniform, continuous, symmetrical movements is comparable to the theorem of Fourier which allows the mathematician to replace any one periodic function by a sum of circular functions. In other words, the astronomy of the Alexandrian period is a somewhat cumbrous development of the mathematical technique of the time to enable the astronomer to bring the anomalies of the planetary bodies, as they increased under observation, within the axioms of a metaphysical physics. The genius exhibited in the development of the mathematical technique places the names of Apollonius of Perga, Hipparchus of Nicaea, and Ptolemy among the great mathematicians of the world, but they never felt themselves free to attack by their hypotheses the fundamental assumptions of the ancient metaphysical doctrine of the universe. Thus it was said of Hipparchus by Adrastus, a philosopher of the first century A. D., in explaining his preference for the epicycle to the eccentric as a means of analyzing the motions of the planetary bodies: "He preferred and adopted the principle of the epicycle as more probable to his mind, because it ordered the system of the heavens with more symmetry and with a more intimate dependence with reference to the center of the universe. Although he guarded himself from assuming the rôle of the physicist in devoting himself to the investigations of the real movements of the stars, and in undertaking to distinguish between the motions which nature has adopted from those which the appearances present to our eyes, he assumed that every planet revolved along an epicycle, the center of which describes a circumference concentric with the earth." Even mathematical astronomy does not offer an exception to the scientific method of the ancient world, that of bringing to consciousness the concepts involved in their world of experience, organizing these concepts with reference to each, analyzing and restating them within the limits of their essential accidents, and assimilating the concrete objects of experience to these typical forms as more or less complete realizations.

At the beginning of the process of Greek self-conscious reflection and analysis, the mind ran riot among the concepts and their characters until the contradictions which arose from these unsystematized speculations brought the Greek mind up to the problems of criticism and scientific method. Criticism led to the separation of the many from the one, the imperfect copy from the perfect type, the sensuous and passionate from the rational and the intrinsically good, the impermanent particular from the incorruptible universal. The line of demarcation ran between the lasting reality that answered to critical objective thought and the realm of perishing imperfect instances, of partially realized forms full of unmeaning differences due to distortion and imperfection, the realm answering to a sensuous passionate unreflective experience. It would be a quite inexcusable mistake to put all that falls on the wrong side of the line into a subjective experience, for these characters belonged not alone to the experience, but also to the passing show, to the world of imperfectly developed matter which belonged to the perceptual passionate experience. While it may not then be classed as subjective, the Greeks of the Sophistic period felt that this phase of existence was an experience which belongs to the man in his individual life, that life in which he revolts from the conventions of society, in which he questions accepted doctrine, in which he differentiates himself from his fellows. Protagoras seems even to have undertaken to make this experience of the individual, the stuff of the known world. It is difficult adequately to assess Protagoras' undertaking. He seems to be insisting both that the man's experience as his own must be the measure of reality as known and on the other hand that these experiences present norms which offer a choice in conduct. If this is true Protagoras conceived of the individual's experience in its atypical and revolutionary form as not only real but the possible source of fuller realities than the world of convention. The undertaking failed both in philosophic doctrine and in practical politics. It failed in both fields because the subjectivist, both in theory and practice, did not succeed in finding a place for the universal character of the object, its meaning, in the mind of the individual and thus in finding in this experience the hypothesis for the reconstruction of the real world. In the ancient world the atypical individual, the revolutionist, the non-conformist was a self-seeking adventurer or an anarchist, not an innovator or reformer, and subjectivism in ancient philosophy remained a skeptical attitude which could destroy but could not build up.

Hippocrates and his school came nearer consciously using the experience of the individual as the actual material of the object of knowledge. In the skeptical period in which they flourished they rejected on the one hand the magic of traditional medicine and on the other the empty theorizing that had been called out among the physicians by the philosophers. Their practical tasks held them to immediate experience. Their functions in the gymnasia gave their medicine an interest in health as well as in disease, and directed their attention largely toward diet, exercise, and climate in the treatment even of disease. In its study they have left the most admirable sets of observations, including even accounts of acknowledged errors and the results of different treatments of cases, which ancient science can present. It was the misfortune of their science that it dealt with a complicated subject-matter dependent for its successful treatment upon the whole body of physical, chemical, and biological disciplines as well as the discovery and invention of complicated techniques. They were forced after all to adopt a hopelessly inadequate physiological theory—that of the four humors—with the corresponding doctrine of health and disease as the proper and improper mixture of these fluids. Their marvelously fine observation of symptoms led only to the definition of types and a medical practice which was capable of no consistent progress outside of certain fields of surgery. Thus even Greek medicine was unable to develop a different type of scientific method except in so far as it kept alive an empiricism which played a not unimportant part in post-Aristotelian philosophy. Within the field of astronomy in explaining the anomalies of the heavens involved in their metaphysical assumptions, they built up a marvelously perfect Euclidian geometry, for here refined and exhaustive definition of all the elements was possible. The problems involved in propositions to be proved appeared in the individual experience of the geometrician, but this experience in space was uniform with that of every one else and took on a universal not an individual form. The test of the solution was given in a demonstration which holds for every one living in the same Euclidian space. When the mathematician found himself carried by his mathematical technique beyond the assumptions of a metaphysical physics he abandoned the field of physical astronomy and confined himself to the development of his mathematical expressions.

In other fields Greek science analyzed with varying success and critical skill only the conceptions found in the experience of their time and world. Nor did Greek thought succeed in formulating any adequate method by which the ultimate concepts in any field of science were to be determined. It is in Aristotle's statement of induction and the process of definition that we appreciate most clearly the inadequacy of their method. This inadequacy lies fundamentally in Aristotle's conception of observation which, as I have already noted, implies the recognition of an individual, that is, an object which is an embodied form or idea. The function of knowledge is to bring out this essence. The mind sees through the individuals the universal nature. The value of the observation lies, then, not in the controlled perception of certain data as observed facts, but in the insight with which he recognizes the nature of the object. When this nature has been seen it is to be analyzed into essential characters and thus formulated into the definition. In Aristotle's methodology there is no procedure by which the mind can deliberately question the experience of the community and by a controlled method reconstruct its received world. Thus the natural sciences were as really fixed by the conceptions of the community as were the exact sciences by the conceptions of a Euclidian geometry and the mathematics which the Greeks formulated within it. The individual within whose peculiar experience arises a contradiction to the prevailing conceptions of the community and in whose creative intelligence appears the new hypothesis which makes possible a new heaven and a new earth could utilize his individual experience only in destructive skepticism. Subjectivism served in ancient thought to invalidate knowledge not to enlarge it.

Zeller has sketched a parallelism between the ideal state of Plato and the social structure of the medieval world. The philosopher-king is represented by the Pope, below him answering to the warrior class in the Platonic state stands the warrior class of the Holy Roman Empire, who in theory enforce the dictates of the Roman curia, while at the bottom in both communities stand the mass of the people bound to obedience to the powers above. There is, however, one profound difference between the two, and that is to be found in the relative positions of the ideal worlds that dominate each. Plato's ideal world beyond the heavens gives what reality it has to this through the participation by the world of becoming in the ideas. Opinion dimly sensed the ideas in the evanescent objects about it, and though Plato's memory theory of knowledge assumed that the ideas had been seen in former existence and men could thus recognize the copies here, the ideal world was not within the mind but without. In a real sense the Kingdom of Heaven was within men in the medieval world, as was the Holy Roman Empire. They were ideal communities that ought to exist on earth, and it was due to the depravity of men that they did not exist. From time to time men undertook in various upheavals to realize in some part these spiritual and political ideals which they carried within them. And men not only carried within them the ideas of a New Jerusalem in which the interest of one was the interest of all and of an earthly state ordered by a divine decree to fulfil this Christian ideal, but the determining causes of the present condition and the future realization depended also upon the inner attitudes and experiences of the individuals themselves.

Without carrying the analogy here too far, this relation between the experience of the individual and the world which may arise through the realization of his ideas is the basis of the most profound distinction between the ancient world and the modern. Before the logic of this attitude could appear in science a long period of intellectual and social growth was necessary. The most essential part of this growth was the slow but steady development of psychological doctrine which placed the objective world in the experience of the individual. It is not of interest here to bring out the modern epistemological problem that grew out of this, or to present this in the world of Leibnitzian monads that had no windows or in the Berkeleyan subjective idealism. What is of interest is to point out that this attitude established a functional relationship between even the subjective experience of the individual and the object of knowledge. A skepticism based upon subjectivism might thereafter question the justification of the reference of experience beyond itself; it could not question knowledge and its immediate object.

Kant formalizes the relation of what was subjective and what was objective by identifying the former with the sensuous content of experience and the latter with the application of the forms of sensibility and understanding to this content. The relationship was formal and dead. Kant recognized no functional relationship between the nature of the *Mannigfaltigkeit* of sensuous experience and the forms into which it was poured. The forms remained external to the content, but the relationship was one which existed within experience, not without it, and within this experience could be found the necessity and universality which had been located in the world independent of experience. The melting of these fixed Kantian categories came with the spring floods of the romantic idealism that followed Kant.

The starting-point of this idealism was Kantian. Within experience lay the object of knowledge. The Idealist's principal undertaking was to overcome the skepticism that attached to the object of knowledge because of its reference to what lies outside itself. If, as Kant had undertaken to prove, the reality which knowledge implies must reach beyond experience, then, on the Kantian doctrine that knowledge lies within experience, knowledge itself is infected with skepticism. Kant's practical bridge from the world of experience to the world of things-in-themselves, which he walked by faith and not by sight, was found in the postulates of the conduct of the self as a moral being, as a personality. The romantic idealists advance by the same road, though as romanticists not critical philosophers, they fashioned the world of reality, that transcends experience, out of experience itself, by centering the self in the absolute self and conceiving the whole infinite universe as the experience of the absolute self. The interesting phase of this development is that the form which experience takes in becoming objective is found in the nature and thought of the individual, and that this process of epistemological experience becomes thus a process of nature, if the objective is the natural. In Kant's terms our minds give laws to nature. But this nature constantly exhibits its dependence upon underlying noumena that must therefore transcend the laws given by the understanding. The Romanticist insists that this other reality must be the same stuff as that of experience, that in experience arise forms which transcend those which bound the experience in its earlier phase. If in experience the forms of the objective world are themselves involved, the process of knowledge sets no limits to itself, which it may not, does not, by implication transcend. As further indication of the shift by which thought had passed into possession of the world of things in themselves stands the antinomy which in Kantian experience marks the limit of our knowledge while in post-Kantian idealism it becomes the antithesis that leads to the synthesis upon the higher plane. Contradiction marks the phase at which the spirit becomes creative, not simply giving an empty formal law to nature, but creating the concrete universe in which content and form merge in true actuality. The relation of the sensuous content to the conceptual form is not dead, as in Kant's doctrine. It is fused as perception into concept and carries its immediacy and concreteness of detail into the concrete universal as the complete organization of stimulation and response pass into the flexible habit. And yet in the Hegelian logic, the movement is always away from the perceptual experience toward the higher realm of the *Idee.* Thought is creative in the movement, but in its ultimate reality it transcends spatial and temporal experience, the experience with which the natural and mathematical sciences deal. Thought is not a means of solving the problems of this world as they arise, but a great process of realization in which this world is forever transcended. Its abstract particularities of sensuous detail belong only to the finite experience of the partial self. This world is, therefore, always incomplete in its reality and, in so far, always untrue. Truth and full reality belong not to the field of scientific investigation.

In its metaphysics Romantic Idealism, though it finds a place for scientific discovery and reconstruction, leaves these disdainfully behind, as incomplete phases of the ultimate process of reality, as infected with untruth and deceptive unwarranted claims. The world is still too much with us. We recognize here three striking results of the development of reflective consciousness in the modern world:—first, it is assumed that the objective world of knowledge can be placed within the experience of the individual without losing thereby its nature as an object, that all characters of that object can be presented as belonging to that experience, whether adequately or not is another question; and second, it is assumed that the contradictions in its nature which are associated with its inclusion in individual experience, its references beyond itself when so included, may themselves be the starting-point of a reconstruction which at least carries that object beyond the experience within which these contradictions arose; and third, it is assumed that this growth takes place in a world of reality within which the incomplete experience of the individual is an essential part of the process, in which it is not a mere fiction, destroying reality by its representation, but is a growing-point in that reality itself.

These characters of philosophic interpretation, the inclusion of the object of knowledge in the individual experience and the turning of the conflicts in that experience into the occasion for the creation of new objects transcending these contradictions, are the characters in the conscious method, of modern science, which most profoundly distinguish it from the method of ancient science. This, of course, is tantamount to saying that they are those which mark the experimental method in science.

That phase of the method upon which I have touched already has been its occupation with the so-called data or facts as distinguished from Aristotelian individuals.

Whenever we reduce the objects of scientific investigation to facts and undertake to record them as such, they become events, happenings, whose hard factual character lies in the circumstance that they have taken place, and this quite independently of any explanation of their taking place. When they are explained they have ceased to be facts and have become instances of a law, that is, Aristotelian individuals, embodied theories, and their actuality as events is lost in the necessity of their occurrence as expressions of the law; with this change their particularity as events or happenings disappears. They are but the specific values of the equation when constants are substituted for variables. Before the equation is known or the law discovered they have no such ground of existence. Up to this point they find their ground for existence in their mere occurrence, to which the law which is to explain them must accommodate itself.

There are here suggested two points of view from which these facts may be regarded. Considered with reference to a uniformity or law by which they will be ordered and explained they are the phenomena with which the positivist deals; as existencies to be identified and localized before they are placed within such a uniformity they fall within the domain of the psychological philosopher who can at least place them in their relation to the other events in the experience of the individual who observes them. Considered as having a residual meaning apart from the law to which they have become exceptions, they can become the subject-matter of the rationalist. It is important that we recognize that neither the positivist nor the rationalist is able to identify the nature of the fact or datum to which they refer. I refer to such stubborn facts as those of the sporadic appearance of infectious diseases before the germ theory of the disease was discovered. Here was a fact which contradicted the doctrine of the spread of the infection by contact. It appeared not as an instance of a law, but as an exception to a law. As such, its nature is found in its having happened at a given place and time. If the case had appeared in the midst of an epidemic, its nature as a case of the infectious disease would have been cared for in the accepted doctrine, and for its acceptance as an object of knowledge its location in space and time as an event would not have been required. Its geographical and historical traits would have followed from the theory of the infection, as we identify by our calculations the happy fulfilment of Thales' prophecy. The happening of an instance of a law is accounted for by the law. Its happening may and in most instances does escape observation, while as an exception to an accepted law it captures attention. Its nature as an event is, then, found in its appearance in the experience of some individual, whose observation is controlled and recorded as his experience. Without its reference to this individual's experience it could not appear as a fact for further scientific consideration.

Now the attitude of the positivist toward this fact is that induced by its relation to the law which is *subsequently* discovered. It has then fallen into place in a series, and his doctrine is that all laws are but uniformities of such events. He treats the fact when it is an exception to law as an instance of the new law and assumes that the exception to the old law and the instance of the new are identical. And this is a great mistake,—the mistake made also by the neo-realist when he assumes that the object of knowledge is the same within and without the mind, that nothing happens to what is to be known when it by chance strays into the realm of conscious cognition. Any as yet unexplained exception to an old theory can happen only in the experience of an individual, and that which has its existence as an event in some one's biography is a different thing from the future instance which is not beholden to any one for its existence. Yet there are, as I indicated earlier, meanings in this exceptional event which, at least for the time, are unaffected by the exceptional character of the occurrence. For example, certain clinical symptoms by which an infectious disease is identified have remained unchanged in diagnosis since the days of Hippocrates. These characters remain as characters of the instance of the law of germ-origin when this law has been discovered. This may lead us to say that the exception which appears for the time being as a unique incident in a biography is identical with the instance of a germ-induced disease. Indeed, we are likely to go further and, in the assurance of the new doctrine, state that former exceptions can (or with adequate acquaintance with the facts could) be proved to be necessarily an instance of a disease carried by a germ. The positivist is therefore confident that the field of scientific knowledge is made up of events which are instances of uniform series, although under conditions of inadequate information some of them appear as exceptions to the statements of uniformities, in truth the latter being no uniformities at all.

That this is not a true statement of the nature of the exception and of the instance, it is not difficult to show if we are willing to accept the accounts which the scientists themselves give of their own observation, the changing forms which the hypothesis assumes during the effort to reach a solution and the ultimate reconstruction which attends the final tested solution. Wherever we are fortunate enough, as in the biographies of men such as Darwin and Pasteur, to follow a number of the steps by which they recognized problems and worked out tenable hypotheses for their solution, we find that the direction which is given to attention in the early stage of scientific investigation is toward conflicts between current theories and observed phenomena, and that since the form which these observations take is determined by the opposition, it is determined by a statement which itself is later abandoned. We find that the scope and character of the observations change at once when the investigator sets about gathering as much of the material as he can secure, and changes constantly as he formulates tentative hypotheses for the solution of the problem, which, moreover, generally changes its form during the investigation. I am aware that this change in the form of the data will be brushed aside by many as belonging only to the attitude of mind of the investigator, while it is assumed that the "facts" themselves, however selected and organized in his observation and thought, remain identical in their nature throughout. Indeed, the scientist himself carries with him in the whole procedure the confidence that the fact-structure of reality is unchanged, however varied are the forms of the observations which refer to the same entities.35

The analysis of the fact-structure of reality shows in the first place that the scientist undertakes to form such an hypothesis that all the data of observation will find their place in the objective world, and in the second place to bring them into such a structure that future experience will lead to anticipated results. He does not undertake to preserve facts in the form in which they existed in experience before the problem arose nor to construct a world independent of experience or that will not be subject itself to future reconstructions in experience. He merely insists that future reconstructions will take into account the old in re-adjusting it to the new. In such a process it is evident that the change of the form in the data is not due to a subjective attitude of the investigator which can be abstracted from the facts. When Darwin, for instance, found that the marl dressings which farmers spread over their soil did not sink through the soil by the force of gravity as was supposed, but that the earthworm castings were thrown up above these dressings at nearly the same rate at which they disappeared, he did not correct a subjective attitude of mind. He created in experience a humus which took the place of a former soil, and justified itself by fitting it into the whole process of disintegration of the earth's surface. It would be impossible to separate in the earlier experiences certain facts and certain attitudes of mind entertained by men with reference to these facts. Certain objects have replaced other objects. It is only after the process of analysis, which arose out of the conflicting observations, has broken up the old object that what was a part of the object, heavier-things-pushing-their way-through-soil-of-lighter-texture, can become a mere idea. Earlier it was an object. Until it could be tested the earthworm as the cause of the disappearance of the dressings was also Darwin's idea. It became fact. For science at least it is quite impossible to distinguish between what in an object must be fact and what may be idea. The distinction when it is made is dependent upon the form of the problem and is functional to its solution, not metaphysical. So little can a consistent line of cleavage between facts and ideas be indicated, that we can never tell where in our world of observation the problem of science will arise, or what will be regarded as structure of reality or what erroneous idea.

There is a strong temptation to lodge these supposititious fact-structures in a world of conceptual objects, molecules, atoms, electrons, and the like. For these at least lie beyond the range of perception by their very definition. They seem to be in a realm of things-in-themselves. Yet they also are found now in the field of fact and now in that of ideas. Furthermore, a study of their structure as they exist in the world of constructive science shows that their infra-sensible character is due simply to the nature of our sense-processes, not to a different metaphysical nature. They occupy space, have measurable dimensions, mass, and are subject to the same laws of motion as are sensible objects. We even bring them indirectly into the field of vision and photograph their paths of motion.

The ultimate elements referred to above provide a consistent symbolism for the finding and formulating of applied mathematical sciences, within which lies the whole field of physics, including Euclidian geometry as well. However, they have succeeded in providing nothing more than a language and logic pruned of the obstinate contradictions, inaccuracies, and unanalyzed sensuous stuff of earlier mathematical science. Such a rationalistic doctrine can never present in an unchanged form the objects with which natural science deals in any of the stages of its investigation. It can deal only with ultimate elements and forms of propositions. It is compelled to fall back on a theory of analysis which reaches ultimate elements and an assumption of inference as an indefinable. Such an analysis is actually impossible either in the field of the conceptual objects into which physical science reduces physical objects, or in the field of sensuous experience. Atoms can be reduced into positive and negative electrical elements and these may, perhaps do, imply a structure of ether that again invites further analysis and so on ad infinitum. None of the hypothetical constructs carry with themselves the character of being ultimate elements unless they are purely metaphysical. If they are fashioned to meet the actual problems of scientific research they will admit of possible further analysis, because they must be located and defined in the continuity of space and time. They cannot *be* the points and instants of modern mathematical theory. Nor can we reach ultimate elements in sensuous experience, for this lies also within a continuum. Furthermore, our scientific analyses are dependent upon the form that our objects assume. There is no general analysis which research in science has ever used. The assumption that psychology provides us with an analysis of experience which can be carried to ultimate elements or facts, and which thereby provides the elements out of which the objects of our physical world must be constructed, denies to psychology its rights as a natural science of which it is so jealous, turning it into a Berkeleyan metaphysics.

This most modern form of rationalism being unable to find ultimate elements in the field of actual science is compelled to take what it can find there. Now the results of the analysis of the classical English psychological school give the impression of being what Mr. Russell calls "hard facts," i.e., facts which cannot be broken up into others. They seem to be the data of experience. Moreover, the term hard is not so uncompromising as is the term element. A fact can be more or less hard, while an ultimate element cannot be more or less ultimate. Furthermore, the entirely formal character of the logic enables it to deal with equal facility with any content. One can operate with the more or less hard sense-data, putting them in to satisfy the seeming variables of the propositions, and reach conclusions which are formally correct. There is no necessity for scrutinizing the data under these circumstances, if one can only assume that the data are those which science is actually using. The difficulty is that no scientist ever analyzed his objects into such sense-data. They exist only in philosophical text-books. Even the psychologists recognize that these sensations are abstractions which are not the elements out of which objects of sense are constructed. They are abstractions made from those objects whose ground for isolation is found in the peculiar problems of experimental psychology, such as those of color or tone perception. It would be impossible to make anything in terms of Berkeleyan sense-data and of symbolic logic out of any scientific discovery. Research defines its problem by isolating certain facts which appear for the time being not as the sense-data of a solipsistic mind, but as experiences of an individual in a highly organized society, facts which, because they are in conflict with accepted doctrines, must be described so that they can be experienced by others under like conditions. The ground for the analysis which leads to such facts is found in the conflict between the accepted theory and the experience of the individual scientist. The analysis is strictly *ad hoc*. As far as possible the exception is stated in terms of accepted meanings. Only where the meaning is in contradiction with the experience does the fact appear as the happening to an individual and become a paragraph out of his biography. But as such an event, whose existence for science depends upon the acceptance of the description of him to whom it has happened, it must have all the setting of circumstantial evidence. Part of this circumstantial evidence is found in so-called scientific control, that is, the evidence that conditions were such that similar experiences could happen to others and could be described as they are described in the account given. Other parts of this evidence which we call corroborative are found in the statements of others which bear out details of this peculiar event, though it is important to note that these details have to be wrenched from their settings to give this corroborative value. To be most conclusive they must have no intentional connection with the experience of the scientist. In other words, those individuals who corroborate the facts are made, in spite of themselves, experiencers of the same facts. The perfection of this evidence is attained when the fact can happen to others and the observer simply details the conditions under which he made the observation, which can be then so perfectly reproduced that others may repeat the exceptional experience.

This process is not an analysis of a known world into ultimate elements and their relations. Such an analysis never isolates this particular exception which constitutes the scientific problems as an individual experience. The extent to which the analysis is carried depends upon the exigencies of the problem. It is the indefinite variety of the problems which accounts for the indefinite variety of the facts. What constitutes them facts in the sense in which we are using the term is their *exceptional* nature; formally they appear as particular judgments, being denials of universal judgments, whether positive or negative. This exceptional nature robs the events of a reality which would have belonged to them as instances of a universal law. It leaves them, however, with the rest of their meaning. But the value which they have lost is just that which was essential to give them their place in the world as it has existed for thought. Banished from that universally valid structure, their ground for existence is found in the experience of the puzzled observer. Such an observation was that of the moons of Jupiter made possible by the primitive telescope of Galileo. For those who lived in a Ptolemaic cosmos, these could have existence only as observations of individuals. As moons they had distinct meaning, circling Jupiter as our moon circles the earth, but being in contradiction with the Ptolemaic order they could depend for their existence only on the evidence of the senses, until a Copernican order could give them a local habitation and a name. Then they were observed not as the experiences of individuals but as instances of planetary order in a heliocentric system. It would be palpably absurd to refer to them as mere sense-data, mere sensations. They are for the time being inexplicable experiences of certain individuals. They are inexplicable because they have a meaning which is at variance with the structure of the whole world to which they belong. They are the phenomena termed accidental by Aristotle and rejected as full realities by him, but which have become, in the habitat of individual experience, the headstone of the structure of modern research of science.

A rationalism which relegates implication to the indefinables cannot present the process of modern science. Implication is exactly that process by which these events pass from their individual existence into that of universal reality, and the scientist is at pains to define it as the experimental method. It is true that a proposition implies implication. But the proposition is the statement of the result of the process by which an object has arisen for knowledge and merely indicates the structure of the object. In discovery, invention, and research the escape from the exceptional, from the data of early stages of observation, is by way of an hypothesis; and every hypothesis so far as it is tenable and workable in its form is universal. No one would waste his time with a hypothesis which confessedly was not applicable to all instances of the problem. An hypothesis may be again and again abandoned, it may prove to be faulty and contradictory, but in so far as it is an instrument of research it is assumed to be universal and to perfect a system which has broken down at the point indicated by the problem. Implication and more elaborated instances flow from the structure of this hypothesis. The classical illustration which stands at the door of modern experimental science is the hypothesis which Galileo formed of the rate of the velocity of a falling body. He conceived that this was in proportion to the time elapsed during the fall and then elaborated the consequences of this hypothesis by working it into the accepted mathematical doctrines of the physical world, until it led to an anticipated result which would be actually secured and which would be so characteristic an instance of a falling body that it would answer to every other instance as he had defined them. In this fashion he defined his inference as the anticipation of a result because this result was a part of the world as he presented it amended by his hypothesis. It is true that back of the specific implication of this result lay a mass of other implications, many not even presented specifically in thought and many others presented by symbols which generalized innumerable instances. These implications are for the scientist more or less implicit meanings, but they are meanings each of which may be brought into question and tested in the same fashion if it should become an actual problem. Many of them which would not have occurred to Galileo as possible problems have been questioned since his day. What has remained after this period of determined questioning of the foundations of mathematics and the structure of the world of physical science is a method of agreement with one self and others, in (a) the identification of the object of thought, in (b) the accepted values of assent and denial called truth and falsehood, and in (c) referring to meaning, in its relation to what is meant. In any case the achievement of symbolic logic, with its indefinables and axioms has been to reduce this logic to a statement of the most generalized form of possible consistent thought intercourse, with entire abstraction from the content of the object to which it refers. If, however, we abstract from its value in giving a consistent theory of number, continuity, and infinity, this complete abstraction from the content has carried the conditions of thinking in agreement with self and others so far away from the actual problem of science that symbolic logic has never been used as a research method. It has indeed emphasized the fact that thinking deals with problems which have reference to uses to which it can be put, not to a metaphysical world lying beyond experience. Symbolic logic has to do with the world of discourse, not with the world of things.

What Russell pushes to one side as a happy guess is the actual process of implication by which, for example, the minute form in the diseased human system is identified with unicellular life and the history of the disease with the life history of this form. This identification implies reclassification of these forms and a treatment of the disease that answers to their life history. Having made this identification we anticipate the result of this treatment, calling it an inference.

Implication belongs to the reconstruction of the object. As long as no question has arisen, the object is what it means or means what it is. It does not imply any feature of itself. When through conflict with the experience of the individual some feature of the object is divorced from some meaning the relationship between these becomes a false implication. When a hypothetically reconstructed object finds us anticipating a result which accords with the nature of such objects we assert an implication of this meaning. To carry this relation of implication back into objects which are subject to no criticism or question would of course resolve the world into elements connected by external relations, with the added consequence that these elements can have no content, since every content in the face of such an analysis must be subject to further analysis. We reach inevitably symbols such as X, Y, and Z, which can symbolize nothing. Theoretically we can assume an implication between any elements of an object, but in this abstract assumption the symbolic logician overlooks the fact that he is also assuming some content which is not analyzed and which is the ground of the implication. In other words this logician confuses the scientific attitude of being ready to question anything with an attitude of being willing to question everything at once. It is only in an unquestioned objective world that the exceptional instance appears and it is only in such a world that an experimental science tests the implications of the hypothetically reconstructed object.

The guess is happy because it carries with it the consequences which follow from its fitting into the world, and the guess, in other words the hypothesis, takes on this happy form solely because of the material reconstruction which by its nature removes the unhappy contradiction and promises the successful carrying out of the conflicting attitudes in the new objective world. There is no such thing as formal implication.

Where no reconstruction of the world is involved in our identification of objects that belong to it and where, therefore, no readjustment of conduct is demanded, such a logic symbolizes what takes place in our direct recognition of objects and our response to them. Then "X is a man implies X is mortal for all values of X" exactly symbolizes the attitude toward a man subject to a disease supposedly mortal. But it fails to symbolize the biological research which starting with inexplicable sporadic cases of an infectious disease carries over from the study of the life history of infusoria a hypothetical reconstruction of the history of disease and then acts upon the result of this assumption. Research-science presents a world whose form is always universal, but this universal form is neither a metaphysical assumption nor a fixed form of the understanding. While the scientist may as a metaphysician assume the existence of realities which lie beyond a possible experience, or be a Kantian or Neo-Kantian, neither of these attitudes is necessary for his research. He may be a positivist—a disciple of Hume or of John Stuart Mill. He may be a pluralist who conceives, with William James, that the order which we detect in parts of the universe is possibly one that is rising out of the chaos and which may never be as universal as our hypothesis demands. None of these attitudes has any bearing upon his scientific method. This simplifies his thinking, enables him to identify the object in which he is interested wherever he finds it, and to abstract in the world as he conceives it those features which carry with them the occurrence he is endeavoring to place. Especially it enables him to make his thought a part of the socially accepted and socially organized science to which his thought belongs. He is far too modest to demand that the world be as his inference demands.

He asks that his view of the world be cogent and convincing to all those whose thinking has made his own possible, and be an acceptable premise for the conduct of that society to which he belongs. The hypothesis has no universal and necessary characters except those that belong to the thought which preserves the same meanings to the same objects, the same relations between the same relata, the same attributes of assent and dissent under the same conditions, the same results of the same combinations of the same things. For scientific research the meanings, the relations with the relata, the assent and dissent, the combinations and the things combined are all in the world of experience. Thinking in its abstractions and identifications and reconstructions undertakes to preserve the values that it finds, and the necessity of its thinking lies in its ability to so identify, preserve, and combine what it has isolated that the thought structure will have an identical import under like conditions for the thinker with all other thinkers to whom these instruments of research conduct are addressed. Whatever conclusions the scientist draws as necessary and universal results from his hypothesis for a world independent of his thought are due, not to the cogency of his logic, but to other considerations. For he knows if he reflects that another problem may arise which will in its solution change the face of the world built upon the present hypothesis. He will defend the inexorableness of his reasoning, but the premises may change. Even the contents of tridimensional space and sensuous time are not essential to the cogency of that reasoning nor can the unbroken web of the argument assure the content of the world as invariable. His universals, when applied to nature, are all hypothetical universals; hence the import of experiment as the test of an hypothesis. Experience does not rule out the possible cropping up of a new problem which may shift the values attained. Experience simply reveals that the new hypothesis fits into the meanings of the world which are not shaken; it shows that, with the reconstruction which the hypothesis offers, it is possible for scientific conduct to proceed.

But if the universal character of the hypothesis and the tested theory belong to the instrumental character of thought in so reconstructing a world that has proved to be imperfect, and inadequate to conduct, the stuff of the world and of the new hypothesis are the same. At least this is true for the scientist who has no interest in an epistemological problem that does not affect his scientific undertakings in one way nor another. I have already pointed out that from the standpoint of logical and psychological analysis the things with which science deals can be neither ultimate elements nor sense-data; but that they must be phases and characters and parts of things in some whole, parts which can only be isolated because of the conflict between an accepted meaning and some experience. I have pointed out that an analysis is guided by the practical demands of a solution of this conflict; that even that which is individual in its most unique sense in the conflict and in attempts at its solution does not enter into the field of psychology—which has its own problems peculiar to its science. Certain psychological problems belong to the problems of other sciences, as, for example, that of the personal equation belongs to astronomy or that of color vision to the theory of light. But they bulk small in these sciences. It cannot be successfully maintained that a scientific observation of the most unique sort, one which is accepted for the time being simply as a happening in this or that scientist's experience, is as such a psychological datum, for the data in psychological text-books have reference to *psychological* problems. Psychology deals with the consciousness of the individual in its dependence upon the physiological organism and upon those contents which detach themselves from the objects outside the individual and which are identified with his inner experience. It deals with the laws and processes and structures of this consciousness in all its experiences, not with *exceptional* experiences. It is necessary to emphasize again that for science these particular experiences arise within a world which is in its logical structure organized and universal. They arise only through the conflict of the individual's experience with such an accepted structure. For science individual experience *presupposes* the organized structure; hence it cannot provide the material out of which the structure is built up. This is the error of both the positivist and of the psychological philosopher, if scientific procedure gives us in any sense a picture of the situation.

A sharp contrast appears between the accepted hypothesis with its universal form and the experiences which invalidate the earlier theory. The reality of these experiences lies in their happening. They were unpredictable. They are not instances of a law. The later theory, the one which explains these occurrences, changes their character and status, making them necessary results of the world as that is conceived under this new doctrine. This new standpoint carries with it a backward view, which explains the erroneous doctrine, and accounts for the observations which invalidated it. Every new theory must take up into itself earlier doctrines and rationalize the earlier exceptions. A generalization of this attitude places the scientist in the position of anticipating later reconstructions. He then must conceive of his world as subject to continuous reconstructions. A familiar interpretation of his attitude is that the hypothesis is thus approaching nearer and nearer toward a reality which would never change if it could be attained, or, from the standpoint of the Hegelian toward a goal at infinity. The Hegelian also undertakes to make this continuous process of reconstruction an organic phase in reality and to identify with nature the process of finding exceptions and of correcting them. The fundamental difference between this position and that of the scientist who looks before and after is that the Hegelian undertakes to make the exception in its exceptional character a part of the reality which transcends it, while the scientist usually relegates the exception to the experience of individuals who were simply caught in an error which later investigation removes.

The error remains as an historical incident explicable perhaps as a result of the conditions under which it occurred, but in so far as it was an error, not a part of reality. It is customary to speak of it as subjective, though this implies that we are putting the man who was unwittingly in error into the position of the one who has corrected it. To entertain that error in the face of its correction would be subjective. A result of this interpretation is that the theories are abstracted from the world and regarded as something outside it. It is assumed that the theories are mental or subjective and change while the facts remain unchanged. Even when it is assumed that theories and facts agree, men speak of a correspondence or parallelism between idea and the reality to which it refers. While this attitude seems to be that of science toward the disproved theories which lie behind it, it is not its attitude to the theories which it accepts. These are not regarded as merely parallel to realities, as abstracted from the structure of things. These meanings go into the makeup of the world. It is true that the scientist who looks before and after realizes that any specific meaning which is now accepted may be questioned and discarded. If he carries his refection far enough he sees that a complete elimination of all the meanings which might conceivably be so discredited would leave nothing but logical constants, a world with no facts in any sense. In this position he may of course take an agnostic attitude and be satisfied with the attitude of Hume or Mill or Russell. But if he does so, he will pass into the camp of the psychological philosophers and will have left the position of the scientist. The scientist always deals with an *actual* problem, and even when he looks before and after he does so in so far as he is facing in inquiry some actual problem. No actual problem could conceivably take on the form of a conflict involving the whole world of meaning. The conflict always arises between an individual experience and certain laws, certain meanings while others are unaffected. These others form the necessary field without which no conflict can arise. They give the man of research his (π ου στω) upon which he can formulate his problem and undertake its solution. The possible calling in question of any content, whatever it may be, means always that there is left a field of unquestioned reality. The attitude of the scientist never contemplates or could contemplate the possibility of a world in which there would be no reality by which to test his hypothetical solution of the problem that arises. Nor does this attitude when applied to past discarded theories necessarily carry with it the implication that these older theories were subjective ideas in men's minds, while the reality lay beside and beyond them unmingled with ideas. It always finds a standpoint from which these ideas in the earlier situation are still recognized as reliable, for there are no scientific data without meanings. There could be no history of science on any other basis. No history of science goes back to ultimate elements or sense-data, or to any combination of bare data on one hand and logical elements on the other. The world of the scientist is always there as one in which reconstruction is taking place with continual shifting of problems, but as a real world within which the problems arise. The errors of the past and present appear as untenable hypotheses which could not bear the test of experiment if the experience were sufficiently enlarged and interpreted. But they are not mere errors to be thrown into the scrap heap. They become a part of a different phase of reality which a fuller history of the past records or a fuller account of the present interprets, giving them thereby their proper place in a real world.36

The completion of this program, however, awaits the solution of the scientific problem of the relation of the psychical and the physical with the attendant problem of the meaning of the so-called origin of consciousness in the history of the world. My own feeling is that these problems must be attacked from the standpoint of the social nature of so-called consciousness. The clear indications of this I find in the reference of our logical constants to the structure of thought as a means of communication, in the explanation of errors in the history of science by their social determination, and in the interpretation of the inner field of experience as the importation of social intercourse into the conscious conduct of the individual. But whatever may be the solution of these problems, it must carry with it such a treatment of the experience of the individual that the latter will never be regarded merely as a subjective state, however inadequate it may have proved itself as a scientific hypothesis. This seems to me to be involved in the conception of psychology as a natural science and in any legitimate carrying out of the Hegelian program of giving reality and creative import to individual experience. The experience of the individual in its exceptional character is the growing-point of science, first of all in the recognition of data upon which the older theories break, and second in the hypothesis which arises in the individual and is tested by the experiment which reconstructs the world. A scientific history and a scientific psychology from which epistemology has been banished must place these observations and hypotheses together with erroneous conceptions and mistaken observations *within* the real world in such a fashion that their reference to the experience of the individual and to the world to which he belongs will be comprehensible. As I have indicated, the scientific theory of the physical and conscious individual in the world implied in this problem has still to be adequately developed. But there is implied in the conception of such a theory such a location of the process of thought in the process of reality as will give it an import both in the meaning of things and in the individual's thinking. We have the beginning of such a doctrine in the conception of a functional value of consciousness in the conduct of living forms, and the development of reflective thought out of such a consciousness which puts it within the act and gives it the function of preparation where adjustment is necessary. Such a process creates the situation with reference to which the form acts. In all adjustment or adaptation the result is that the form which is adjusted finds that by its adjustment it has created an environment. The ancients by their formulation of the Ptolemaic theory committed themselves to the world in which the fixed values of the heavenly over against the earthly obtained. Such a world was the interpretation of the experience involved in their physical and social attitudes. They could not accept the hypothesis of Aristarchus because it conflicted with the world which they had created, with the values which were determining values for them. The same was true of the hypothesis of Democritus. They could not, as they conceived the physical world, accept its purely quantitative character. The conception of a disinterested truth which we have cherished since the Middle Ages is itself a value that has a social basis as really as had the dogma of the church. The earliest statement of it was perhaps that of Francis Bacon. Freeing investigation from the church dogma and its attendant logic meant to him the freedom to find in nature what men needed and could use for the amelioration of their social and physical condition. The full implication of the doctrine has been recognized as that of freedom, freedom to effect not only values already recognized, but freedom to attain as well such complete acquaintance with nature that new and unrecognized uses would be at our disposal; that is, that progress should be one toward any possible use to which increased knowledge might lead. The cult of increasing knowledge, of continually reconstructing the world, took the place both of the ancient conception of adequately organizing the world as presented in thought, and of the medieval conception of a systematic formulation on the basis of the statement in church dogma of social values. This modern conception proceeds from the standpoint not of formulating values, but giving society at the moment the largest possible number of alternatives of conduct, i.e., undertaking to fix from moment to moment the widest possible field of conduct. The purposes of conduct are to be determined in the presence of a field of alternative possibilities of action. The ends of conduct are not to be determined in advance, but in view of the interests that fuller knowledge of conditions awaken. So there appears a conception of determining the field that shall be quite independent of given values. A real world which consists not of an unchanged universe, but of a universe which may be continually readjusted according to the problems arising in the consciousness of the individuals within society. The seemingly fixed character of such a world is found in the generally fixed conditions which underlie the type of problems which we find. We determine the important conditions incident to the working out of the great problems which face us. Our conception of a given universe is formed in the effort to mobilize all the material about us in relation to these problems—the structure of the self, the structure of matter, the physical process of life, the laws of change and the interrelation of changes. With reference to these problems certain conditions appear fixed and become the statement of the world by which we must determine by experimental test the viability of our hypotheses. There arises then the conception of a world which is unquestioned over against any particular problem. While our science continually changes that world, at least it must be always realized as there. On the other hand, these conceptions are after all relative to the ends of social conduct which may be formulated in the presence of any freedom of action.

We postulate freedom of action as the condition of formulating the ends toward which our conduct shall be directed. Ancient thought assured itself of its ends of conduct and allowed these to determine the world which tested its hypothesis. We insist such ends may not be formulated until we know the field of possible action. The formulation of the ends is essentially a social undertaking and seems to follow the statement of the field of possible conduct, while in fact the statement of the possible field of conduct is actually dependent on the push toward action. A moving end which is continually reconstructing itself follows upon the continually enlarging field of opportunities of conduct.

The conception of a world of existence, then, is the result of the determination at the moment of the conditions of the solution of the given problems. These problems constitute the conditions of conduct, and the ends of conduct can only be determined as we realize the possibilities which changing conditions carry with them. Our world of reality thus becomes independent of any special ends or purposes and we reach an entirely disinterested knowledge. And yet the value and import of this knowledge is found in our conduct and in our continually changing conditions. Knowledge for its own sake is the slogan of freedom, for it alone makes possible the continual reconstruction and enlargement of the ends of conduct.

The individual in his experiences is continually creating a world which becomes real through his discovery. In so far as new conduct arises under the conditions made possible by his experience and his hypothesis the world, which may be made the test of reality, has been modified and enlarged.

I have endeavored to present the world which is an implication of the scientific method of discovery with entire abstraction from any epistemological or metaphysical presuppositions or complications. Scientific method is indifferent to a world of things-in-themselves, or to the previous condition of philosophic servitude of those to whom its teachings are addressed. It is a method not of knowing the unchangeable but of determining the form of the world within which we live as it changes from moment to moment. It undertakes to tell us what we may expect to happen when we act in such or such a fashion. It has become a matter of serious consideration for a philosophy which is interested in a world of things-in-themselves, and the epistemological problem. For the cherished structures of the metaphysical world, having ceased to house the values of mankind, provide good working materials in the hypothetical structures of science, on condition of surrendering their metaphysical reality; and the epistemological problem, having seemingly died of inanition, has been found to be at bottom a problem of method or logic. My attempt has been to present what seems to me to be two capital instances of these transformations. Science always has a world of reality by which to test its hypotheses, but this world is not a world independent of scientific experience, but the immediate world surrounding us within which we must act. Our next action may find these conditions seriously changed, and then science will formulate this world so that in view of this problem we may logically construct our next plan of action. The plan of action should be made self-consistent and universal in its form, not that we may thus approach nearer to a self-consistent and universal reality which is independent of our conduct, but because our plan of action needs to be intelligent and generally applicable. Again science advances by the experiences of individuals, experiences which are different from the world in which they have arisen and which refer to a world which is not yet in existence, so far as scientific experience is concerned. But this relation to the old and new is not that of a subjective world to an objective universe, but is a process of logical reconstruction by which out of exceptions the new law arises to replace a structure that has become inadequate.

In both of these processes, that of determining the structure of experience which will test by experiment the legitimacy of the new hypothesis, and that of formulating the problem and the hypothesis for its solution, the individual functions in his full particularity, and yet in organic relationship with the society that is responsible for him. It is the import for scientific method of this relationship that promises most for the interpretation of the philosophic problems involved.

CONSCIOUSNESS AND PSYCHOLOGY

BOYD H. BODE

If it is true that misery loves company, those persons who feel despondent over the present situation in philosophy may console themselves with the reflection that things are not so bad as they might be. Our friends, the psychologists, are afflicted even as we are. The disagreements of experts as to both the subject-matter and the method of psychology are as fundamental as anything that philosophy can show. A spirit of revolt is abroad in the land, and psychology is once more on trial. The compact which provided that psychology should be admitted to the rank of a natural science, on condition that it surrender its pretension to be the science of the soul and confine itself to the study of consciousness, is no longer considered binding. The suspicion is growing that consciousness is nothing more nor less than an attenuated form of the soul that it pretends to displace. Consequently the psychology without a soul to which we have just become accustomed is now attacked on behalf of a psychology without a consciousness, on the ground that this latter standpoint alone can give assurance against entangling alliances between psychology and metaphysics.

From the side of philosophy this situation is interesting, not only to such as may crave the comfort that springs from the spectacle of distress, but also to those who take a more hopeful view of present-day tendencies. The question that is at issue is fundamentally the question of the nature of consciousness, which is quite as important to philosophy as to psychology. On the one hand it is maintained that psychology has to do with consciousness and that its distinctive method is the method of introspection. On the other hand it is urged that psychology is nothing more nor less than a study of behavior, that it is not a science at all, unless the existence of consciousness is denied or at least ignored, and that the method of introspection is a delusion and a snare. The two standpoints are not always clearly formulated, nor can we say that every system of psychology is true to type. It is, in fact, the lack of clearness in the fundamental concepts that makes the status of psychology a matter of so much uncertainty.

The situation presents an apparent anomaly. Both parties profess to deal with facts of observation, yet the claim of the introspectionist that he observes facts of consciousness is met by the assertion of his rival that there is no consciousness to be observed. How can this be, unless we assume that introspection presupposes an esoteric principle, like the principle of grace in religion? It seems evident that we have to do here with some deep-seated misconception regarding the facts that are supposed to constitute the subject-matter for observation and description.

A common procedure on the part of introspectionism is to assert the existence of consciousness as something which is indeed indefinable, but which admits of observation and description. But this procedure is no longer justified. In the first place, the assertion that consciousness exists is not the statement of a fact but the designation of a problem. What is the nature of the fact that we call consciousness? If the common-sense individual, who assents so readily to the proposition that we all know consciousness, be asked to differentiate between consciousness and the objects of consciousness, he is dazed and helpless. And, secondly, the assertion of indefinability involves us in a difficulty. The indefinability of consciousness has sometimes been likened to that of space, but in this latter case we find no such confusion between space and the objects in space. It is clear, however, that if consciousness is not something distinguishable from objects, there is no need to discuss consciousness, and if it is distinguishable, it must be distinguished before we are entitled to proceed with observation and description. Definition is indispensable, at least to the extent of circumscribing the facts that are to be investigated. Moreover, if consciousness cannot be defined, neither can it be described. What is definition, after all, but a form of description? To assert, in effect, that consciousness is indefinable because it is indescribable, and that for this reason we must be content with description, is both a flagrant disregard of consistency and an unwarranted abuse of our good nature.

This difficulty leads on to another, for doubts, like lies, have a singular propensity to breed more of their kind. If consciousness is something that everybody knows, why should it be necessary to look to the psychologist for a description of it? if the study of consciousness brings to light any new fact, that fact by definition is not a conscious fact at all, and consequently is not the kind of thing that we set out to describe. Consciousness, in short, cannot be analyzed; it cannot be resolved into elements or constituents. It is precisely what it is and not some product of our after-thought that we are pleased to substitute for it.

These familiar considerations do not, indeed, decide the issue between the rival theories of psychology, but they serve to suggest that our introspective psychology has been too easily satisfied in the conception of its specific problem or subject-matter. As a matter of fact, the work that has been done in the name of psychology has been peculiarly barren of results, so far as a consciousness *an sich* is concerned, although it has led to a wealth of material pertaining to adaptive behavior. Its solid achievements lie in the domain, not of consciousness, but of instinctive, habitual, and intelligent adaptation. It teaches us little that has to do unequivocally with consciousness as distinct from things, but it teaches us much concerning stimulus and response, attention and habit, conflict and adjustment. The doctrine that psychology is a science of behavior is justified at least to the extent that it emphasizes a factor, the importance of which introspectionism has consistently refused to recognize. Whatever conclusion we may ultimately reach regarding the nature of consciousness, the whole drift of psychological and biological investigation seems to indicate that an adequate conception of consciousness and of the distinctive problem of psychology can be attained only on the basis of a painstaking reflection on the facts of behavior.

I

It is evident that the attempt to ascertain the nature of consciousness and of psychology from the standpoint of behavior is committed to the assumption that the behavior in question is of a distinctive kind. The justification of this assumption will enable us to formulate the definitions which we seek. Discussions of conscious behavior ordinarily emphasize the similarity between conscious and reflex behavior rather than the difference. An attitude of expectancy, for example, is usually conceived as a sort of temporary reflex. Certain nervous connections are organized for the occasion, so that, when a given stimulus arrives, it will induce its appropriate response. This situation is best exemplified, perhaps, in simple reaction-experiments, in which the subject makes a certain predetermined response upon presentation of the stimulus. The process is supposed to be of the reflex type throughout, the only difference being that ordinary reflexes are relatively permanent and unvarying, whereas a prearranged response to a stimulus has to do with a reflex that is made to order so as to meet the exigencies of the moment.

For certain purposes such a description of conscious behavior is no doubt sufficiently accurate. Our present concern, however, is with the differences between these temporary organizations and ordinary reflexes. In order to bring out these differences, let us introduce a slight complication into our reaction-experiment and suppose that the subject is to make one of two alternative responses, according to the nature of the stimulus. His state of expectancy is accompanied by a certain bodily "set" or preparedness for the coming event, although the precise nature of the event is a matter of uncertainty. His nervous system is in readiness to respond this way or that, or rather, it has already started to act in both of the alternative ways. If the subject is to respond with the right hand to one stimulus and with the left hand to the other, both hands are in a state of activity before the stimulus appears. The organization of the temporary reflex through the agency of the cerebral cortex could not be achieved were it not for the fact that all the movements entering into the organization are nascently aroused before the spring is touched which permits the act to unroll itself in orderly sequence.

The various successive movements, then, which make up our temporary reflex achieve their relationship to one another from the fact that they are started simultaneously, and this peculiarity constitutes a distinctive feature. Apparently this feature is absent from true reflexes. An act of swallowing, performed unconsciously, may start the complicated processes of digestion, but it is merely the first act of a series. There is no evidence that the movements of the stomach and of the other organs concerned in digestion must be presupposed before the act of swallowing can take place. The swallowing may start the other processes, but we cannot say that these other processes react back upon the first act and make it one of swallowing rather than something else. Yet this "back stroke" is precisely what is necessary in our reaction-experiment, for it is by virtue of this fact that the organization of the temporary reflex becomes a possibility. The first response cannot take place until the last is provided for. Thus the immediate act of looking has embodied in it the activity that is to follow later. The looking is not simply with the eye, but with the hands that are to complete the response. The optical response is a response which, in the language of Bergson, prefigures or sketches out the act of a later moment. The nervous system is enabled to act as a unit, because the movements that are to occur at a later time are represented in the first stage of the complete act. The first stage, accordingly, does not occur independently, but *as* a preliminary to the second. With an imperfect organization of the entire response, it may happen that the subsequent movements are not suppressed until their proper moment arrives, but appear in advance of their scheduled time. In writing, for example, we frequently omit words or add to a word the final letter of some word that belongs to a subsequent part of the sentence. An error of this sort could hardly occur so readily in the course of an act that belongs to the type of the true reflex.

Lest the reader suspect that this is *a priori* physiology, I may quote the following from a prominent neurologist: "No simple sensory impulse can, under ordinary circumstances, reach the cerebral cortex without first being influenced by subcortical association centers, within which complex reflex combinations may be effected and various automatisms set off in accordance with their preformed structure. These subcortical systems are to some extent modifiable by racial and individual experience, but their reactions are chiefly of the determinate or stereotyped character, with a relatively limited range of possible reaction types for any given stimulus complex.

"It is shown by the lower vertebrates, which lack the cerebral cortex, that these subcortical mechanisms are adequate for all of the ordinary simple processes of life, including some degree of associative memory. But here, when emergencies arise which involve situations too complex to be resolved by these mechanisms, the animal will pay the inevitable penalty of failure—perhaps the loss of his dinner, or even of his life.

"In the higher mammals with well-developed cortex the automatisms and simple associations are likewise performed mainly by the subcortical apparatus, but the inadequacy of this apparatus in any particular situation presents not the certainty of failure, but rather a dilemma. The rapid preformed automatisms fail to give relief, or perhaps the situation presents so many complex sensory excitations as to cause mutual interference and inhibition of all reaction. There is a stasis in the subcortical centers. Meanwhile the higher neural resistance of the cortical pathways has been overcome by summation of stimuli and the cortex is excited to function. Here is a mechanism adapted, not for a limited number of predetermined and immediate responses, but for a much greater range of combination of the afferent impressions with each other and with memory vestiges of previous reactions and a much larger range of possible modes of response to any given set of afferent impressions. By a process of trial and error, perhaps, the elements necessary to effect the adaptive response may be assembled and the problem solved.

"It is evident here that the physiological factors in the dilemma or problem as this is presented to the cortex are by no means simple sensory impressions, but definitely organized systems of neural discharge, each of which is a physiological resultant of the reflexes, automatisms, impulses, and inhibitions characteristic of its appropriate subcortical centers. The precise form which these subcortical combinations will assume in response to any particular excitation is in large measure determined by the structural connections *inter se*....

"From the standpoint of the cerebral cortex considered as an essential part of the mechanism of higher conscious acts, every afferent stimulus, as we have seen, is to some extent affected by its passage through various subcortical association centers (i.e., it carries a quale of central origin). But this same afferent impulse in its passage through the spinal cord and brain stem may, before reaching the cortex, discharge collateral impulses into the lower centers of reflex coördination, from which incipient (or even actually consummated) motor responses are discharged previous to the cortical reaction. These motor discharges may, through the 'back stroke' action, in turn exert an influence upon the slower cortical reaction. Thus the lower reflex response may in a literal physiological sense act *into* the cortical stimulus complex and become an integral part of it."[37]

It seems clear, then, that conscious behavior involves a certain *process* of organization which constitutes a differential. The units entering into this process are "definitely organized systems of neural discharge," the antecedent organization of these several systems being due either to the inherited or to the acquired structure of the nervous system. Given a certain amount of plasticity, the nervous system builds up specific forms of response for certain objects or situations, and these forms of response subsequently become the material from which new organizations or new modes of response are constructed. The achievements of the past, accordingly, become stepping-stones to new achievement. The new organization, moreover, is not determined by a mechanism antecedently provided, but has a peculiar flexibility, so as to meet the demands of a new situation. That is, a new mode of procedure is adopted. Instead of being a purely mechanical reaction, the response that results from the situation is tentative or experimental in character, and "by a process of trial and error, perhaps, the elements necessary to effect the adaptive response may be assembled and the problem solved."

We may add at once that the reorganization which is required to constitute conscious behavior varies a great deal in extent. In an act that is more or less habitual, a comparatively slight modification of the corresponding organized system of neural discharge will suffice to harmonize the conflicting elements, whereas on other occasions a more extensive modification is required. But in any case it appears that there is a certain impropriety in describing conscious behavior in terms of a temporary reflex, since the study of this behavior is concerned with the organization of the discordant elements, not as a result, but primarily as a process. In a reflex act we may suppose that the stimulus which evokes the first stage in the response is like the first in a row of upstanding bricks, which in falling knocks down another. That is, the reflex arc is built up by agencies that are quite independent of the subsequent act. The arc is all set up and ready for use by the time the reflex act appears upon the scene. In the case of conscious activity, on the other hand, we find a very different state of affairs. The arc is not first constructed and then used, but is constructed as the act proceeds; and this progressive organization is, in the end, what is meant by conscious behavior. If the course of a reflex act may be compared with traveling in a railroad train, the progress of a conscious act is more like that of a band of explorers, who hew their path and build their bridges as they go along. The direction of the act is not determined from without but from within; the end is internal to the process.

This process of organization and purposive direction is exemplified in every act of attention. Is that noise, for example, a horse in the street, or is it the rain on the roof? What we find in such a situation is not a paralysis of activity, but a redirection. The incompatibility of responses is purely relative. There is indeed a mutual inhibition of the responses for hoof-beats and rain respectively, in the sense that neither has undisputed possession of the field; but this very inhibition sets free the process of attention, in which the various responses participate and coöperate. There is no static balancing of forces, but rather a process in which the conflict is simply a condition for an activity of a different kind. If I am near a window facing the street, my eye turns thither for a clue; if the appeal to vision be eliminated, the eye becomes unseeing and coöperates with the ear by excluding all that is irrelevant to the matter in hand. In this process the nervous system functions as a unit, with reference to the task of determining the source and character of the sound. This task or problem dominates the situation. A voice in an adjoining room may break in, but only as something to be ignored and shut out; whereas a voice in the street may become all-absorbing as possibly indicating the driver of the hypothetical horse. That is, the reason why the conflict of responses does not end in a deadlock, but in a redirection, is that a certain selectiveness of response comes into play. Out of the mass of more or less inchoate activities a certain response is selected as a rallying-point for the rest, and this selection is of a purposive character. The selection is determined by reference to the task in hand, which is to restore a certain harmony of response. Accordingly, that response is selected which gives promise of forwarding the business of the moment. By virtue of this selective character, one of the constituents of the total activity becomes exalted among its fellows and is entrusted with the function of determining further behavior.

The purpose of the discussion, up to this point, is to put forward this selective or teleological character as the fundamental and differentiating trait of conscious behavior; and our task, accordingly, is to give an account of the nature and *modus operandi* of this purposive control. This control, it is evident, consists in giving direction to behavior with reference to results that are still in the future. The basis for this anticipation of the future is furnished by the nascent responses which foreshadow further activity, even while they are still under the thraldom of the inhibitions which hold them back. These suppressed activities furnish a sort of diagram or sketch of further possible behavior, and the problem of consciousness is the problem of making the result or outcome of these incipient responses effective in the control of behavior. Future results or consequences must be converted into present stimuli; and the accomplishment of this conversion is the miracle of consciousness. To be conscious is to have a future possible result of present behavior embodied as a present existence functioning as a stimulus to further behavior. Thus the qualities of a perceptual experience may be interpreted, without exception, as anticipations of the results of activities which are as yet in an embryonic stage. The results of the activity that is as yet partly suppressed are already expressed or anticipated in the perception. The present experience may, as James says, "shoot its perspective far before it, irradiating in advance the regions in which lie the thoughts as yet unborn."[38] A baseball player, for example, who is all "set" to field a ball as a preliminary to a further play, sees the ball, not simply as an approaching object, but as ball-to-be-caught-and-then-thrown-to-first-base. Moreover, the ball, while still on the way, is a ball-that-may-bound-to-the-right-or-to-the-left.   The corresponding movements of the player to the right or left, and the act of throwing, although present only as inhibited or incipient acts, are nevertheless embodied in the visual experience. Similarly my couch looks soft and inviting, because the optical stimulation suggests or prompts, not only the act of lying down, but also the kind of relaxation that is made possible by a comfortable bed. So likewise the tiger's jaws and claws look cruel and horrible, because in that perception are reflected the incipient movements of defense and recoil which are going on in the body of the observer. Perception, like our air-castles, or like dreams in the Freudian theory, presents what is at best but a suggestion or program in the guise of accomplished fact.

This projection, however, of our submerged activities into our perceptions requires a more precise statement. According to the foregoing contention, the appearance, for example, of a razor's edge as sharp is the sensory correlate of an incipient response which, if it were to attain full-blown perfection, would be the reaction to a cut. By hypothesis, however, the response is inhibited, and it is this inhibition which calls forth the perception of the object. If the response encountered no obstruction, adaptation would be complete and perception would not occur. Since there is a blocking of the response, nature resorts to a special device in order to overcome the difficulty, and this device consists in furnishing the organism with a new type of stimulus. The razor as perceived does not actually cut just now, but it bodies forth the quality 'will cut,' i.e., the perceived attribute derives its character from what the object will, or may, do at a future time. That is, a perceived object is a stimulus which controls or directs the organism by results which have not yet occurred, but which will, or may, occur in the future. The uniqueness of such a stimulus lies in the fact that a contingent result somehow becomes operative as a present fact; the future is transferred into the present so as to become effective in the guidance of behavior.

This control by a future that is made present is what constitutes consciousness. A living body may respond to an actual cut by a knife on purely mechanical or reflex principles; but to respond to a cut by anticipation, i.e., to behave with reference to a merely possible or future injury, is manifestly an exhibition of intelligence. Not that there need be any conscious reference to the future as future in the act. Merely to see the object as "sharp" is sufficient to give direction to conduct. But "sharp" is equivalent to "will cut"; the quality of sharpness is a translation of future possibility into terms of present fact, and as thus translated the future possibility becomes a factor in the control of behavior. Perception, therefore, is a point where present and future coincide. What the object *will* do is, in itself, just a contingency, an abstract possibility, but in perception this possibility clothes itself in the garments of present, concrete fact and thus provides the organism with a different environment. The environment provides a new stimulus by undergoing a certain kind of change, i.e., by exercising a peculiar function of control. This control is seeing, and the whole mystery of consciousness is just this rendering of future stimulations or results into terms of present existence. Consciousness, accordingly, is a name for a certain change that takes place in the stimulus; or, more specifically, it is a name for the control of conduct by future results or consequences.

To acquire such a stimulus and to become conscious are one and the same thing. As was indicated previously, the conscious stimulus is correlated with the various inherited and acquired motor tendencies which have been set off and which are struggling for expression, and the uniqueness of the stimulus lies in the fact that the adaptive value of these nascent motor tendencies becomes operative as the determining principle in the organization of the response. The response, for example, to "sharp" or "will cut" is reminiscent of an earlier reaction in which the organism engaged in certain defensive movements as the result of an actual injury. That is, the response to "sharp" is a nascent or incipient form of a response which at the time of its first occurrence was the expression of a maladaptation. The response that is induced when an object is seen as sharp would be biologically bad, if it were completed, and the fact that the object is seen as sharp means that this result is foreshadowed and operates as a stimulus to prevent such maladaptation. Similarly the couch which meets my weary eye becomes a stimulus to repose because the nascent activity which is aroused would be biologically good if completed. In any case the character of the stimulus is determined by the adaptive value which the incipient activity would have if it were carried out. Consciousness, accordingly, is just a future adaptation that has been set to work so as to bring about its own realization. The future thus becomes operative in the present, in much the same way as the prospects for next year's crop may be converted by the farmer into ready money with which to secure the tools for its production.

To justify this conclusion by a detailed and extensive application of this interpretation to every form of quality and relation would carry us beyond the limits of the present undertaking. It is a view, however, which offers possibilities that have not as yet been properly recognized. Certain considerations, besides those already discussed, may be mentioned as giving it an antecedent plausibility. As regards simple sense-qualities, there is abundant reason for believing that Locke's doctrine of "simple ideas" is a violent perversion of the facts. To assume that the last results of analysis are the first things in experience is to give a fatal twist to psychology and to commit us to the fruitless agonies of epistemology. The original "blooming, buzzing confusion" with which experience starts becomes differentiated into specific qualities only to the extent that certain typical and organized forms of response are built up within the body. Sense-qualities, in other words, are functionally not simple but extremely complex; they owe their distinctiveness or individuality to the fact that each of them embodies a specific set of cues or anticipations, with reference to further experiences. The difference between a quality like "sharpness" and a quality like "red" lies in the fact that the former is a translation of a relatively simple possibility, viz., "will cut," whereas the latter embodies a greater variety of anticipations. The perception of red, being the outcome of many comparisons and associations, presupposes a complex physical response which contains multitudinous tendencies to reinstate former responses; and the combined effect of these suppressed tendencies is the perception of a color which offers possibilities of control over behavior in such directions as reminiscences, idle associations, or perhaps scrutiny and investigation. A similar explanation evidently applies to abstract ideas, which neither admit of reduction to "revived sensations" nor compel the adoption of a peculiarly "spiritual" or "psychic" existence in the form of unanalyzable meanings. Here again a complex mode of response must be assumed, having as its correlate an experience describable only in terms of its functioning, which is such as to enable the organism to act intelligently, i.e., with reference to future results, which are sufficiently embodied in the experience to secure appropriate behavior. Again, this point of view offers a satisfactory solution for the time-worn puzzle of relativity. If perception is just the translation of future possible stimulations into present fact, there is assuredly no justification for the notion that perception distorts the facts or that discrepancies among different perceptions prove their "subjectivity." There remains but one test by which the correctness or validity of perception may be judged, viz., whether the perceived object proves to be the kind of stimulus which is reported or anticipated in the present experience.

So far our discussion has emphasized the anticipatory character of the conscious stimulus. Future consequences come into the present as *conditions* for further behavior. These anticipations are based, indeed, upon previous happenings, but they enter into the present situation as conditions that must be taken into account. But to take them into account means that the conscious situation is essentially incomplete and in process of transformation or reconstruction. This peculiar incompleteness or contingency stands out prominently when the situation rises to the level of uncertainty and perplexity. To borrow the classical illustration of the child and the candle, the child is in a state of uncertainty because the neural activity of the moment comprises two incompatible systems of discharge, the one being a grasping and holding, the other a withdrawal and such further movements as may be induced by contact with fire. Hence the candle has the seductiveness of a prize, but at the same time carries the suggestion of burning the fingers. That is, the perceived object has a unique character of uncertainty, which inheres in it as a present positive quality. We are here confronted with genuine contingency, such as is encountered nowhere else. Other modes of behavior may be uncertain in the sense that the incoming stimulation finds no fixed line of discharge laid down for itself within the organism. In seeking to convert itself into response it may either sweep away the obstructions in its path or work itself out along lines of less resistance, in ways that no man can foretell.

There may be moments of equilibrium, moments when it remains to be seen where the dam will break and the current rush through. Such uncertainty, however, is the uncertainty of the bystander who attempts to forecast what will happen next. It is not the uncertainty that figures as an integral part of conscious behavior.

This inherent uncertainty means that conscious behavior, as contrasted with the mechanical character of the reflexes, is essentially experimental. The uncertainty exists precisely because an effort is under way to clear up the uncertainty. The resort to eye or ear or to reflective thinking is suggested by the corresponding nascent responses and is an endeavor to secure something which is still to seek, but which, when found, will meet the requirements of the situation. Translating this process into terms of stimulus and response, we may say that the conscious stimulus of the moment induces the investigation or scrutiny which presently results in the arrival of a stimulus that is adequate to the situation. The stimulus, in other words, provides for its own successor; or we may say that the process as a whole is a self-directing, self-determining activity. Stimulus and response are not successive stages or moments, but rather simultaneous functions or phases of the total process. Within this process the given situation is the stimulus because it is that aspect or function which guides the subsequent course of the activity, while the bodily movements are the response because they already embody the activity that is to follow. The significant circumstance here is that stimulus and response resist the temporal separation that we find in a purely reflex act; stimulus and response are bound together as correlated functions in a unitary, self-directing process, so that these twain are one flesh.

Situations of uncertainty and expectancy, as exemplified by the familiar child-candle incident, are of interest, because they emphasize both the anticipatory character of experience and the peculiar reconstruction of the stimulus. These situations, however, differ merely in degree, not in kind, from other experiences; their merit is that in them the distinctive character of conscious life is writ large. To say that they are conscious situations is to say that they are so constituted that the possibilities of a subsequent moment are embodied in them as a positive quality. In them the present moment embodies a future that is contingent. And similarly the response has neither the predetermined organization of the reflex nor the aimless character of a response that issues in a set of random movements. It is, so to speak, of a generalized character, like the paleontological specimens that foreshadow in their structure the advent of both fish and reptile. This form of organization, however, while exemplified most strikingly in situations of uncertainty, pertains to all conscious behavior. In uttering a sentence, for example, we know in advance what we are going to say, yet the sentence shapes itself into definite form only as we proceed; or perhaps we get "stuck," and by hemming and hawing bear witness that a struggle for a certain kind of organization is going on. The same word in different contexts is a different word in each instance, by virtue of the coloring that it takes on from what is to follow after. And this is equally true of our most casual experiences. The auditory or visual object that we happen to notice and immediately afterwards ignore is apprehended with reference to the possibility of warranting further attention, or else it presents itself as an intruder that is to be excluded in order that we may go on with the concern of the moment. All experience is a kind of intelligence, a control of present behavior with reference to future adjustment. To be in experience at all is to have the future operate in the present.

This reference to the future may be in the nature of an end or goal that controls a series of activities or it may be of a momentary and casual kind. In any case the character of the stimulus changes with the progress of the act. The book on the table must become successively book-to-be-reached-for, book-to-be-picked-up, and book-to-be-opened, unless the process is to drop back to the type of reflex. This development of the stimulus gives genuine continuity, since every moment in the process comes as a fulfilment of its predecessor and as a transition-point to its successor. In a purely mechanical act response follows stimulus like the successive strokes of a clock. It is a touch-and-go affair;

the stimulus presses the button and then subsides, while the neural organization does the rest. In conscious behavior, on the other hand, stimulus and response keep step with each other. A mere succession of stimuli would reduce conscious behavior to a series of explosive jerks, on the principle of the gasoline engine. To be conscious at all is to duplicate in principle the agility of the tight-rope performer, who continuously establishes new co-ordinations according to the exigencies of the moment and with constant reference to the controlling consideration of keeping right side up. The sensory stimulus provides continuously for its own rehabilitation or appropriate transformation, and in a similar way the neural organization is never a finished thing, but is in constant process of readjustment to meet the demands of an adaptation that still lies in the future.

It is this relationship of present response to the response of the next moment that constitutes the distinctive trait of conscious behavior. The relatively unorganized responses of the present moment, in becoming reflected in the experienced object, reveal their outcome or meaning before they have become overt, and thus provide the conditions of intelligent action. In other words, future consequences become transformed into a stimulus for further behavior. We are confronted here with a distinctive mode of operation, which must be properly recognized, if we are to give a consistent and intelligent account of conscious behavior. On the other hand, if we refuse to recognize the advent here of a new category, intelligence becomes an anomaly and mystery deepens into contradiction. Since intelligence or consciousness must be provided for somehow, we are forced back upon either interactionism or else epiphenomenalism, more or less disguised under a euphonious name, such as psycho-physical parallelism or the double-aspect theory. That is, the relation of stimulus and response is either reduced to plain cause and effect or else is rejected altogether and supplanted by a bare concomitance of the physical and mental series. In either case conscious behavior is reduced to the type of reflex action, the only issue between the two doctrines being the question whether or not it is necessary or permissible to interpolate mental links in the causal chain.

According to the doctrine of parallelism, conscious behavior is nothing more than a complicated form of reflex, which goes on without any interference on the part of mind or intelligence. Intelligence adds nothing to the situation except itself; it carries no implications or new significance with regard to conduct. The psychic correlate is permitted to tag along, but the explanations of response remain the same in kind as they were before they reached the level of consciousness. "Mere complexity should not becloud the issue. Every brain process, like every reflex activity, is presumably the result of physico-chemical processes. The assumption of a mysterious intuition or 'psychic force' adds nothing to the mechanistic explanation, even when the latter is most fragmentary. The interactionists go out of their way unnecessarily in assuming a special activity of consciousness to account for the dislocation of reactions from sensations. The nervous organization suffices to explain it. Distant-stimuli and central stimuli co-operate to bring about anticipatory reactions; foresight is but the conscious side of this process. The phenomenon is *both* physical and mental."39

The passage just quoted is fairly typical. Since the mental is an aspect or concomitant of the physical it is clearly entitled to an occasional honorable mention, but the fact remains that the explanation of behavior is to be given wholly in terms of neural organization. The mental is quite literally an "also ran." To say that a physico-chemical process is also mental is of no particular significance as long as it is implied that the end or goal of the process plays no part in shaping the course of events. The mental simply gives dignity to the occasion, like the sedan chair with no bottom, in which the Irishman's admirers, according to James's story, ran him along to the place of banquet and which prompted the hero to remark: "Faith, if it wasn't for the honor of the thing, I might as well have come on foot."

It is this empty show of respect which the interactionists seek to avoid when they make the mental a distinct link in the causal sequence. The physical first causes the mental, and the mental in turn brings about a change in the physical. In this way a certain importance is indeed secured to mental facts, but it appears that, so far as purposive action is concerned, we are no better off than we were before. The mental is simply another kind of cause; it has as little option regarding its physical effect as the physical cause has with regard to its mental effect. Non-mechanical behavior is again ruled out, or else a vain attempt is made to secure a place for it through the introduction of an independent psychic agency.

It is true, indeed, that we are under no antecedent obligation to maintain the existence of an activity that is not entirely reducible to the type of everyday cause and effect. But neither does scientific zeal and incorruptibility require us to do violence to the facts in order to secure this uniformity of type. Not to speak at all of the difficulties inherent in this dualism, it seems undeniable that some facts persistently refuse to conform to the type of mechanism, unless they are previously clubbed into submission. Foresight and the sense of obligation, for example, must learn to regard themselves as nothing more than an interesting indication of the way in which the neural machinery is operating before they will fit into the scheme. And similarly the progress of an argument is no way controlled or directed by the end in view, or by considerations of logical coherence, but by the impact of causation. Ideas lose their power to guide conduct by prevision of the future, and truth and error consequently lose their significance, save perhaps as manifestations of cerebral operations. Since reasoning involves association, it must be reducible to bare association; the sequence of the process is just sequence and nothing more. A description of this kind is on a par with the celebrated opinion that violin music is just a case of scraping horse-hair on catgut. Everything that is distinctive in the facts is left out of account, and we are forced to the conclusion that no conclusion has any logical significance or value.

In the end these difficulties, and in fact most of our philosophic ills, may be traced back to the prejudice that experience or knowing is a process in which the objects concerned do not participate and have no share. This assumption commits us at once to various corollaries and thus breeds a set of abstractions that pass themselves off as entities and add themselves to the world of our experience as demonstrable facts. In philosophy, as in the financial world, there is a constant temptation to do business on a basis of fictitious capitalization. Our abstract physico-chemical processes, with their correlates, such as passive, independent objects, souls, minds, or absolutes, do not represent actual working capital, but watered stock, and their inevitable tendency is to convert the legitimate business of philosophy into a campaign of exploitation, which is none the less exploitation because it is frequently done in the interests of what are supposed to be the spiritual values of man. A careful inventory of our assets brings to light no such entities as those which have been placed to our credit. We do not find body and object *and* consciousness, but only body and object. We do not find objects that remain indifferent to the experiential process, but rather objects that exhibit a flexibility and mobility which defy all description. We do not find a self-sufficient environment or absolute *to* which intelligence must needs adjust itself, but an environment that is at odds with itself and struggling in the throes of a reconstruction. The process of intelligence is something that goes on, not in our minds, but in things; it is not photographic, but creative. From the simplest perception to the most ideal aspiration or the wildest hallucination, our human experience is reality engaged in the guidance or control of behavior. Things undergo a change in becoming experienced, but the change consists in a doing, in the assumption of a certain task or duty. The experiential object hence varies with the response; the situation and the motor activity fit together like the sections of a broken bowl.

The bearing of this standpoint on the interpretation of psychology is readily apparent. If it be granted that consciousness is just a name for behavior that is guided by the results of acts not yet performed but reflected beforehand in the objects of experience, it follows that this behavior is the peculiar subject-matter of psychology. It is only by reference to behavior that a distinctive field can be marked off for psychological enterprise. When we say that the flame is hot, the stone hard, and the ice cold and slippery, we are describing objects and nothing more. These qualities are, indeed, anticipations of future possibilities, but this means simply that the objects are described in terms of their properties or capacities as stimuli of the organism. Such an account leaves out of consideration certain changes which things undergo when they exercise the function of controlling or directing changes in the adjustment of the body. A quality, such as "sharp" or "hot," is not mental or constituted by consciousness, but the function of the quality in giving direction to behavior through certain changes which it undergoes is consciousness. The changes that take place in things as a result of association, attention, or memory, are changes that have no significance, save with regard to their function as stimuli to new adjustments. Psychology, therefore, is properly a study of the conditions which determine the change or development of stimuli; more specifically it is a study of the conditions which govern such processes as those by which problems are solved, lessons are memorized, habits and attitudes are built up, and decisions are reached. To call such study "applied" psychology is to misunderstand the proper scope and purpose of the subject. Psychology frequently has occasion to draw extensively upon physics and physiology, but it has its own problem and its own method of procedure.

That this view of conscious behavior should involve an extensive reinterpretation of familiar facts is altogether natural and inevitable. If consciousness is a form of control, the question, for example, what is "in" consciousness and what is not must be interpreted with reference to this function of control. In a sense we perceive many things to which we are not paying attention, such as the light in the room or the familiar chairs and bookcases. These are perceived "marginally," as we say, in the sense that the presence of these objects affects the total adjustment of the moment in such a way that the experience *would* become a clue to these objects if they were withdrawn. And similarly we may speak of marginal sensations of strain or movement, to indicate possible clues to certain bodily activities which are factors in the process. These marginal perceptions or images are not actual existences, but are symbols and nothing more. The significance of these symbols is that they point to certain conditions by which the experiences in question are determined. Thus the question whether a given experience involves certain "sensations" is just a question whether certain bodily or extra-bodily conditions are involved in the experience. If this reference to conditions is ignored and experience is explained in terms of sensory material that blends and fuses and otherwise disposes itself, the explanation is no longer science but sleight-of-hand. Psychology has no proper concern with such mythical constituents of consciousness; its business is with things as related to conduct, which is to say that psychology is a science of behavior.

II

According to the standpoint set forth in the preceding discussion, the key to a consistent and fruitful interpretation of consciousness and psychology lies in behavior. If we turn now to the psychology of introspection, which has been dominant so many years, we find a standpoint and mode of procedure which, on the surface at least, is of a radically different kind. It behooves us, therefore, to consider this standpoint in some detail in order to justify the attempt to reinterpret and "evaluate" it in the light of our own doctrine.

The point of departure for introspective psychology is to be found, so it seems, not in the facts of behavior, but in the distinction between focal and marginal experience. It is on this distinction that the introspective psychologist bases the attempt to give a psychological analysis and description of the contents of experience. To analyze and describe the facts of consciousness is to bring the marginal constituents of experience into the white light of attention. Analysis and description are possible just because experience is so largely a welter of elements that disguise their identity and character. In some way these unrecognized and unidentified elements are constituents of the total experience. To borrow the language of a writer quoted by James, "However deeply we may suppose the attention to be engaged by any thought, any considerable alteration of the surrounding phenomena would still be perceived; the most abstruse demonstration in this room would not prevent a listener, however absorbed, from noticing the sudden extinction of the lights."40 Or, as James remarks: "It is just like the overtones in music. Different instruments give the 'same note,' namely, various upper harmonics of it which differ from one instrument to another. They are not separately heard by the ear; they blend with the fundamental note and suffuse it, and alter it."41 Let the attention be directed to these overtones, however, and they at once detach themselves from their surroundings and step forth into the light of day. Even so the ticking of the clock may pass unnoticed in the sense that it is an undiscriminated element in the background of our consciousness; but if the ticking comes to a sudden stop, the feeling of a void in our consciousness proclaims the fact that something has gone out from it.

The observation and description of the facts of consciousness, then, is based directly on the fact that experience, as the psychologist deals with it, possesses a focus and margin. Nature as conceived by the physical sciences presents no such distinction. The facts are what they are, and their character as focal or marginal, as clear or obscure, depends altogether upon their relation to an intelligence. Or we may say that if the facts of experience were always focal and never marginal, it would never occur to us to speak of consciousness as we do at present. As long as we confine ourselves to a given color, shape or temperature, as experienced focally, we are not dealing with consciousness, but with objects. An analysis of such facts that does not bring in the marginal is not an analysis of consciousness, but an analysis of physical reality. Even if we consider non-physical objects, such as mathematical or economic concepts, we find that our analysis   is not psychological as long as the marginal is left out. The consideration of the margin, however, brings us into the presence of facts which are of a distinctive kind and which warrant a new science. Let the margin be eliminated and psychology disappears at the same time.

The psychological doctrine of focus and margin, then, is a matter of fundamental importance. On the interpretation of this doctrine depend our systems of psychology and of philosophy. What, then, is meant by focus and margin? If we turn to our psychologies, we seem to be confronted once more with something that everybody knows and nobody can define. But since we have to do with a distinction, the obligation to differentiate cannot be wholly ignored. Consciousness is sometimes likened to a visual field and sometimes to the waves of the sea. Like the visual field it has a foreground and a background, a near and a remote, a center and a margin or periphery. The contents of consciousness are vivid or clear in the center of this field and fade away into vagueness or obscureness in proportion to their approach to the periphery. Or, to take the other comparison, the focus may be represented by the crest of a wave and the margin by what we may call its base. This illustration has the advantage that it indicates the difference between higher and lower degrees of concentration. As concentration increases, the crest of the wave rises higher and its width decreases, while the reverse is true where the concentration of attention is less intense. All consciousness possesses the distinction of focus and margin in some degree; however much we may be absorbed in an object or topic, there is always an indirect mental vision that informs us of other facts, which for the time being are in the background of our consciousness.

For purposes of description a metaphor is at best a clumsy device. It has a tendency to substitute itself for the thing to be described and thus to conceal its limitations and inaccuracies. The present case is no exception. I am forced to think that the visual field in particular is a thoroughly vicious metaphor when employed to body forth the distinction of focus and margin.

Whatever this distinction may in the end turn out to be, it is not such as this comparison would lead one to suppose. Objects seen in indirect vision appear obscure and blurred precisely because they are in the focus of consciousness. We get pretty much the same sort of obscureness or blur on a printed page when we look at it in indirect vision as we do when we look at it from a distance that is just too great to make out the words or characters. What the illustration shows is that things look different according as the circumstances under which we see them are different, but what bearing this has on marginal consciousness is not at all obvious to an unsophisticated intelligence.

When we speak of a focus and margin in consciousness, we are presumably dealing with conscious fact. Now this illustration of the visual field does not represent conscious fact. Ordinary perception carries with it no sense of obscureness at all, and when it does we have exactly the same kind of situation as when an object is too distant or in some other way inaccessible to satisfactory perception. That is, the object perceived is in the 'focus' and not in the margin. The obscureness of objects when seen with the margin of the retina has no more to do with the margin of consciousness than the obscureness caused by an attack of dizziness or by a morning fog.

It will be said, perhaps, that consciousness may be unclear even though there be no sense of unclearness, that there is such a thing as intrinsic clearness, quite apart from obstacles and problems. In other words, the same sensation is capable of realizing various degrees of clearness. It is not at all obvious, however, why the different experiences that are concerned in such a comparison should be called the same sensation. As long as we abstract from objective reference, each sensation is just what it is and there is no opportunity to make comparisons on the basis of clearness. A sensation as such—if we are bound to speak of sensations—can by no possibility be an obscure sensation, for the trait that we call obscureness or vagueness constitutes the intrinsic being of that sensation. If we permit ourselves to speak of clearness at all, we should rather say that it possesses a maximum of clearness, since it has managed to express or present its whole nature with not one trait or feature lacking. What more could be demanded, in the way of clearness, of any conscious fact than that it should body forth every detail that it possesses?

If sensations or states of consciousness possess degrees of clearness, it seems to follow that we may scrutinize them for the purpose of discovering characteristics that were present though scarcely perceived, in much the same way that the polishing of old furniture brings out the grain in the wood. But such a parallel, I submit, is plain nonsense. The supposition that consciousness is something that in due time and with good fortune may attain consciousness is too absurd for discussion, even though it is a supposition that plays a considerable rôle in present-day psychology.

The purpose of the discussion, up to this point, has not been to deny the validity of the distinction between focus and margin, but to insist upon the necessity of reconsidering the meaning of this distinction, if we are to attain to a workable definition of consciousness and a fruitful or even intelligible conception of the problem of psychology. I have endeavored to show, in the first place, that the doctrine of focus and margin involves the *raison d'être* of psychology. Apart from this doctrine we have no task or problem that psychology can claim as its distinctive possession. The analysis of what is in the focus of consciousness is adequately provided for in the other sciences; it is only with the introduction of what is called the margin that an enterprise of a different kind becomes necessary. But, secondly, this distinction of focus and margin cannot be drawn on the basis of the experienced contrast between clearness and obscureness. The very fact that anything is experienced as obscure means that it is an object of attention, or, in other words, that it is in the focus of consciousness and not in the margin. The comparison of focus and margin with direct and indirect vision is misleading, because it suggests that experiences are marginal in proportion as they are felt as obscure. And, thirdly, if we undertake to distinguish between focus and margin on the basis of a difference in clearness or vividness of which no note is taken at the time, we encounter the difficulty that experience or consciousness, taken abstractly, does not admit of such variations in degree, and so this criterion likewise goes by the board.

The situation is indeed peculiar. That there is a realm of psychological fact is universally conceded. As a consequence of this conviction a great body of fact and of doctrine has been built up. It would be folly to deny either the distinctiveness or the significance of this achievement. And yet James's description of psychology as "a string of raw facts; a little gossip and wrangle about opinions; a little classification and generalization on the mere descriptive level; a strong prejudice that we *have* states of mind and that our brain conditions them,"[42] is not wholly untrue even today. It is even possible for a present-day critic to outdo James and maintain that the legitimacy of psychology as a separate inquiry is a matter of faith rather than of sight. The 'raw facts' of which James speaks resolve themselves into physical and physiological material on the one hand and metaphysical dogmas on the other; the gossip and wrangle are largely over fictitious problems; the classifications and generalizations as a rule involve trespassing on other fields; the prejudice that we have states of mind has less standing-ground today than it had twenty years ago. In other words, there is still plausible ground for James's pessimistic comment: "This is no science, it is only the hope of a science." A situation such as this carries with it the insistent suggestion that the trouble lies, not primarily in the nature of the subject-matter, but in our conception of the problem. "The matter of a science," as James says, "is with us." And if the distinction of focus and margin constitutes the starting-point and justification for a science of psychology, a better understanding of this distinction will mean a more adequate appreciation of the problem with which psychology has to deal.

As a starting-point for a reconsideration of focus and margin, we may take those experiences in which the distinction of clearness and obscureness is presented as an experienced fact. Let us then turn once more to the familiar illustration of the visual field. "When we look at a printed page, there is always some one portion of it, perhaps a word, which we see more clearly than we do the rest; and out beyond the margin of the page we are still conscious of objects which we see only in a very imperfect way."[43] That is, we appreciate the distinction between what lies in the center of our visual field and what is more remote, just because in this experiment we are trying to see what lies beyond the center without turning our eyes in that direction. We set ourselves the task of seeing what is on the page, and at the same time we interpose an artificial obstacle. Hence the sense of effort, and the contrast between what is clear and what is obscure. The present experience is obscure, not inherently, but only with reference to a certain problem or question. It is inadequate as an anticipation of further experience. The contrast between clear and obscure is created by our attempt to overcome the difficulty, and is therefore absent from ordinary, unobstructed visual perception.

The situation described in the following familiar quotation from James is an illustration of the same thing: "Suppose we try to recall a forgotten name. The state of our consciousness is peculiar. There is a gap therein; but no mere gap. It is a gap that is intensely active. A sort of wraith of the name is in it, beckoning us in a given direction, making us at moments tingle with the sense of our closeness, and then letting us sink back without the longed-for term."[44]

'I met this man on the train, and later at the reception; but what is his name?' The struggle rends our consciousness in twain. The occasions of our meeting, his appearance, his conversation, are solid fact, yet all suffused with the pervasive, evanscent "wraith" that tantalizes us with glimpses which half reveal and half conceal the name we seek to grasp.

To account for such experiences simply in terms of half-submerged "sensations" and "images" is to do violence to all the requirements for clear thinking. If we rule out explanations of this kind, we are evidently forced to the conclusion that these experiences are obscure, not in themselves or in the abstract, but with reference to the function of putting us in possession of the name to which they are inadequate clues. It is   the subsequent, satisfactory experience of the name which furnishes our standard for clearness; in other words, the implications of obscureness are of a functional, and not of a static or structural, kind. The marginal character of an experience is simply a reference to its function as a clue or cue to some further experience, i.e., a reference to its character as a changing stimulus. Or we may say that the distinction between focus and margin is just another aspect of the distinction between the conditions for further activity and the incompleteness which leads to further adjustment. The transfer of the future into the present gives us a fact, here and now, and in this respect the experience is entirely focal in character, and as such it is subject-matter for the various sciences. Whatever the nature of the experience, it is just what it is, and not something else. With respect to the further experience, however, which it conditions or for which it prepares the way, the present experience is entirely marginal, i.e., in its character as a changing stimulus it is subject-matter for psychology. The distinction of focus and margin, then, is based ultimately upon the function of experience in the control of behavior. The given situation is a present fact and is in functional change; or, in terms of our present discussion, it has both a focus and a margin. As present fact it is a reality which requires recognition in the form of adjustment; as in functional change it provides opportunity for bringing the adjustment to fruition. That is, the experience both sets a task or makes a demand and it points the way. The distinction is a distinction of function, not of static existence, and it is this distinction which is represented by the contrast of focus and margin.

If we compare this interpretation of focus and margin with that of traditional psychology, we find that the latter construes the relation of the present to the future experience wholly in static terms, the functional relation being left out of account. The later experience is read back into its predecessor in the form of dim or marginal images, which need but show themselves more completely to make the two identical. If these sensations were intended only as symbols of a functional relationship, it would perhaps be scarcely worth while to enter a protest against them. But when the functional relationship is quite overlooked, the explanation that is given becomes exceedingly dubious. The ticking of the clock, for example, that is present, though unnoticed, the overtones of the note that suffuse the whole without diverting attention to their individual qualities,—in what precise way are facts of this kind concerned in the description of the experience which they modify? A study of the clock or of the overtones can hardly pass as an analysis of consciousness; it is too obviously an affair of physics. Such a study becomes merely an excuse for repeating the analyses of physics and reading them off in terms of sensations and images. Moreover, the transfer of all this material to consciousness looks suspiciously like a transaction in mental chemistry. Where, then, is psychology to gain a foothold? What is the meaning of these uncanny sensations and images, which nobody experiences, unless it be their character as symbols of adjustment? They have no legitimate status, and psychology, by consequence, has no legitimate problem, except in so far as they represent those possible acts of adaptation which are the sole and proper concern of psychology.

It remains to point out briefly the bearing of these results on what is called "the method of introspection." We are sometimes assured that introspection has discarded the belief in a separate mental stuff or subject-matter, but there is ground for the suspicion that such protestations are made in the same spirit that we affirm our belief in the Ten Commandments or the Golden Rule, with no thought of being taken seriously. At all events, without a literal "looking within" it seems to become exceedingly difficult to differentiate introspection from ordinary observation as practised in the other sciences. The reason for this difficulty is that there is nothing left in introspection by which it can be differentiated. The term introspection properly designates, not a method but a problem; the problem, namely, of interpreting given facts with reference to their function in the control of behavior. If psychology is to justify its claim to the status of a science, it is in duty bound to secure for itself both an objective criterion for the adjudication of disputes which otherwise are of necessity interminable, and a subject-matter that is not simply a heritage of metaphysical prejudice, but a realm of fact that is attested by everyday observation and experience.

III

Within recent years the doctrine that psychology is a science of behavior has acquired a certain prominence. It is presupposed, of course, that the behavior with which psychology is concerned is of a distinctive sort; but the differentia is unfortunately the very thing that the "behaviorist" has hitherto left out of account. In his revolt against introspectionism, which has been accustomed to give to its subject-matter a subjectivistic and "psychic" interpretation, he goes to the other extreme and relies on behavior pure and simple. Being without a serviceable differentia, he is unable to mark off the field of psychology from contiguous territory. The selection of certain problems within the general range of behavior, with no recognition of any distinctive trait to guide and justify the selection, is hardly enough to warrant a new science. Even an arbitrary principle of selection is better than none, and it would, therefore, be quite as reasonable to subdivide the field of botany in the interests of a new science, and group together for separate botanical study those flowers which have enabled poets to give symbolic expression to the beauty of women.

That the principle of selection is, in the end, the ability to modify behavior through the anticipation of possible consequences, appears from the fact that the category of stimulus and response is otherwise found to be unworkable. It is true that in the simpler forms of behavior stimulus and response may be correlated without practical difficulty. But when we deal with what has been called "delayed overt response," the matter becomes more complicated and the theoretical difficulty becomes more prominent. The behaviorist would not seriously undertake to record everything that happens between stimulus and response.

He proceeds selectively, taking the relation of stimulus and response as his clue. He is properly interested in the movements which result from the application of the stimulus only in so far as they constitute response. Otherwise his study is not a study of behavior, but a study of movements. But when does a movement constitute a response? Do we label as stimulus the spoken word which results in overt action a week later, or the visual perception which sets a complicated and long-drawn-out problem, for no other reason than that it appears somewhere as an antecedent in the causal chain of events? If so, there is no obvious reason why the event which occurred just before or immediately after the *soi-disant* stimulus should not be regarded as the true stimulus. Unless a satisfactory reason is forthcoming, it would seem better to substitute cause and effect for stimulus and response and to drop the term behavior from our vocabulary. Psychology then becomes a study of certain causal relationships, but is still without a principle for the selection of those causal events which are supposed to constitute its peculiar subject-matter.

Even if we manage to become reconciled to this situation, however, our troubles are not yet at an end. There still remains the difficulty in certain cases of showing that the event which is selected as stimulus or cause bears any significant relationship to the event which figures in our scheme as the response. The stimulus is supposed to have a causal connection with the response, but how are we to know that this is the fact? How are we to know that the engineer who solves a problem for me at my request might not have done so anyway? No behaviorist can possibly show that the air waves set in motion by my vocalization were an indispensable stimulus. We doubtless believe that the spoken word was in fact the spark which lit the fuse and finally exploded the mine, but this belief involves a complication of causes which it is wholly beyond our power to control or to verify.

It is true, of course, that we are able, as a matter of fact, to correlate stimulus and response. I know that it was the spoken word which caused the commission to be executed, for the expert reminds me of the fact and presents a bill. But neither of us makes any pretense that his belief is derived from a scrutiny of the causal sequence. Memory furnishes us with a shortcut to the result. While our present acts are doubtless connected with the past through causation, we do not regard them as simply the effects of antecedent causes. They are rather responses to present stimuli. The expert presents his bill, being moved thereto by a stimulus which may be indicated by saying that it is the spoken-word-constituting-a-commission-now-completed-and-entitling-me-to-compensation. That is, the stimulus cannot be pushed back and anchored at a fixed point in the past, but is a present factor at the moment of response and is operative by virtue of its anticipation of future events.

If, then, psychology is to be regarded as a study of behavior, it is plainly necessary to reinterpret the category of behavior. For example, a purely mechanical response to a light-stimulus may properly be viewed as response to the ether-vibration or wave-length upon which it follows in temporal sequence. But if this stimulation results in what is commonly called consciousness, a different kind of response ensues. The light-stimulus becomes a cause or occasion for the act of looking. But why look, unless it be to secure a new stimulus for further response? We stop to look, precisely because the first stimulus does not run smoothly off the reel. The response will not go forward, but is halted and expends itself in the effort to secure a further stimulus. This is the moment of attention, in which the stimulus undergoes a process of transformation, concomitantly with the process of reorganization in the motor responses, and in the direction of ends or results that are foreshadowed in it. This change in the stimulus takes place under certain specifiable conditions, and the study of these conditions is a study of such processes as perceiving, attending, remembering, and deliberating, which are distinctively psychological in their nature. Processes of this kind, if taken as changes in stimuli, find an objective criterion in the adaptive behavior for the sake of which they occur, and they provide psychology with a distinctive task and subject-matter.

As against the introspectionist, then, the behaviorist is justified in his contention that psychological procedure must be objective and experimental in character. The danger to which he has exposed himself is the failure to differentiate his problem from that of physiology and physics. It is only by a proper recognition of both the objective and the distinctive character of conscious behavior that psychology can free itself of the reproach which is heaped upon it by members of its own household and take the place that rightfully belongs to it in the community of the sciences.

IV

According to the preceding exposition, the current psychological doctrine of focus and margin is an attempt to reduce the changes in the stimulus to terms of static entities denominated sensations and images. By abstracting from change we convert the new stimulus that is already on the way into inert sensory material, which lends itself to purely analytic treatment. In this way the suggested hardness of the rock becomes a "centrally aroused sensation" of a stubbed toe, the heat of the candle becomes an image of a burn, etc. As was said before, the sensations are not existences, but representatives or symbols of our nascent activities; they are the static equivalents of this foreshadowing or reference to the future. The explanation of experience that we find in James and Bergson approximates this view so closely in one respect and departs from it so widely in another as to warrant a brief discussion.

A prominent characteristic of the doctrine advocated by James and Bergson is the emphasis given to the foreshadowings or anticipations of the future. Experiences of conflict, such as the struggle to recall a name, take on their peculiar coloring, so these writers contend, from their relationship to a beyond, to something which is yet to be. If we are to understand experience as it really is, we must guard against the besetting temptation to translate everything into spatial equivalents. This forward reference is usually read off as a distinction and contrast between simultaneously existing components. Some constituent is first set apart as the nucleus or focus and is then enveloped with an elusive, intangible wraith of meaning, which is called the margin. We have been taught to think of the focus as made up of sensory material of some sort and silhouetted against a background lit up by the fitful, inconsequential heat-lightning of meaning. But this is a perversion of the facts. When we are engaged in a problem it is precisely these unformed meanings that are of interest and importance. They are in the focus of consciousness, in so far as we can speak of a focus at all. They absorb our attention and direct our energies. They inform us of a margin, not by refusing to compete for our attention with more important or more interesting facts, but by bodying forth the *unfinished* character of the situation. Hence this beckoning, this tingling with the sense of closeness, this sinking back when our efforts meet with defeat. Focus and margin, in short, have to do with movement, with transition, and not with a static field. These situations are felt as inherently unstable and in process of reconstruction. There is a peculiar sense of activity, of "something doing," of a future knocking on the door of the present. What is thus on its way to the present we can designate only in terms of the object as it is after it has arrived. To call it marginal is to immerse the object in this temporal flux, which embodies perfectly the characteristics of Bergsonian duration.

But this is only a first step. If we turn now to those experiences from which this inner diremption of fact and meaning is absent, we find a process that is essentially the same in kind. They likewise constitute a temporal flow, even though there be no sense of duration or of change as such. The different moments of these experiences are not mechanically juxtaposed, but blend together in much the same way as when the process is experienced as a process. In principle we have the same transition, the same becoming, the same growth from less to more, the same activity of continuous reconstruction. Conscious life, we find, is a continuous adjustment; each of its moments is a "transitive state." The more evenly flowing experiences are likewise endowed with a focus and margin, not in the form of static elements, but as a dynamic relationship of what is with what is to be.

Such an interpretation of experience, moreover, opens the way for a proper valuation of the psychologist's procedure. The concept of sensation is methodology pure and simple. Granted that focus and margin are such as was indicated a moment ago, how are they to be described, unless we resort to some *Hilfsbegriff* such as sensations? James's description of the effort to recall a forgotten name is not description at all in a scientific sense, since the "wraith of the name" that we are trying to recover is of too unearthly a fabric to be weighed and measured by accepted scientific standards. It makes us "tingle," it lets us "sink back," but such portrayal is literature rather than science. Our first step must be to resolve our material into components. These components we identify with genuine elements if we can, with pious fictions if we must; but until this is done there can be no exact description. There can be no precision in our statement of the facts and no formulation of the laws that govern their changes.

This view undeniably has a certain plausibility. As long as the results are attained which the psychologist sets out to reach, we need not be hypersensitive on the score of methods. In the field of natural science, at all events, this Jesuitical principle is not incompatible with respectability. If it be true, however, that sensation is but a tool or artifact, a means to an end, what is the end that is to be attained by this device? It is at this point that we come to the parting of the ways. According to the view previously elaborated, the anticipations of the future have to do with the results of our possible acts, and sensations are simply symbols for the various elements in our complex motor responses. In the case of Bergson and James, however, the clue that is furnished by response is discarded. The reference to the future, being dissociated from behavior, is taken as evidence of an abstract or metaphysical duration, so that experience is somehow other than it seems; and sensation is regarded as the translation of duration into the language of space. Associationism is justified in its belief that reality is different from its appearance in our experience, but is criticized for attempting to interpret the real in terms of space rather than time. In both cases the lead of the subject-matter is abandoned in favor of an explanation that is derived from a fourth-dimensional plane of existence.

The suspicion that these two positions have a deep-seated affinity is strengthened if we call to mind that the concept of sensation was originated, not in the interests of methodology, but as the expression of a historic preconception that mistook fiction for fact. The fundamental error back of it was the preposterous notion that consciousness consists of subconscious or unconscious constituents, which by their mechanical or chemical combinations make our experience what it is. The question which it raises and which has afflicted us even to the present day is not primarily the question of fact, but the question of intelligibility, as the controversy over mindstuff abundantly attests. Whether we regard experience as made up of sensory material, however, or as constituted in a Bergsonian fashion, is a matter of detail; the primary question is whether a distinction between consciousness as it appears and as it "really" is has any meaning. In so far as this distinction is maintained, we are beating the thin air of mythology, despite our reinterpretations and justifications. True conversion does not consist in a renaming of old gods, but demands a humble and a contrite heart. To call sensation an artifact, a methodological device, without a surrender of the metaphysical assumption that lies back of Associationism is not to correct the evil, but is more likely to be treated as an indulgence for sins that are yet to be committed.

This fundamental identity is presumably the reason for certain other similarities, which would perhaps not be readily anticipated. Both doctrines undertake to tell us what is going on behind the scenes, what consciousness or experience "really" is. The descriptions present an astonishing difference of vocabulary, but if we take care not to be misled by superficial differences, we find an equally astonishing agreement as to content. From the one side consciousness is explained as a juxtaposition of elements;

from the other as an interpenetration of elements so complete that the parts can be neither isolated nor distinguished from the whole. On the one hand we find a multiplicity without unity, on the other a unity without multiplicity. In the one account the temporal unit is a sensation devoid of internal temporal diversity; in the other duration as such is a unity in which past, present, and future blend into an undifferentiated whole. The one position gathers its facts by a mystifying process called introspection; the other obtains its results from a mystical faculty of intuition. The difference in language remains, but both accounts lead us away into a twilight region where words substitute themselves for facts.

As was suggested a moment ago, the contrast between ordinary experience and something else of which it is the appearance is the result of the failure to give proper recognition to the facts of behavior. If we connect the forward reference of experience with the operations of our nascent activities, we have no need of a pure duration or of bridging the gulf between reality and its appearances. In the same way, if we construe sensations as just symbols of our responses, we rid ourselves of problems that are insoluble because they are unintelligible. Such problems constitute metaphysics in the bad sense of the word, whether they show themselves in the domain of science or of philosophy. To describe experience by reference to such a real is to explain what we know in terms of what we do not know. The question what is real is absolutely sterile. Our descriptions and explanations must remain on the same plane as the experiences with which they deal, and not seek after a real of a different order. If we are to have an explanation of consciousness at all, the explanation must not take us back to hypothetical sensations that are almost but not quite experienced, nor to a duration in which all distinctions are swallowed up, but must be rendered in terms of other facts that dwell in the light of common day.

By way of conclusion I venture to urge once more that a proper consideration of the facts of behavior will furnish us with a key that will unlock many a door. The conception of stimulus and response gives us a differentia for experience and also enables us to distinguish within experience between consciousness and object. If, however, we disregard behavior, we are bound to lose our way. The distinction between the experienced and the unexperienced is either wiped out or else is permitted to convert itself into a distinction between appearance and reality that leads nowhere and explains nothing. The significance of truth as the successful guidance of behavior, in accordance with the program laid down in the organization of stimulus and response, is lost to sight and recourse is had to a fourth-dimensional truth or reality for the miracle of breathing life into the dead bones of our philosophic abstractions. The study of behavior constitutes a mode of approach that holds out the hope of deliverance from questions that should never have been asked. We are on a different and, let us hope, a higher level when we cease to ask how consciousness can lay hold of passive objects, or how knowledge *überhaupt* is possible, and concern ourselves rather with the wondrous activity whereby this plastic dance of circumstance that we call the universe transcends the domain of mechanism and embodies itself in the values of conscious life.

THE PHASES OF THE ECONOMIC INTEREST

HENRY WALDGRAVE STUART

§ I. In the logic of Instrumentalism, truth has been identified with usefulness and the good with the satisfactory. Classifying critics have seen in this the damaging mark of Utilitarianism, certain of them deeming "Amerikanismus" an even shrewder and more specific diagnosis. The association of these terms together and the aptness of either to express what the critics have in mind are matters of small interest. It is of more importance to discover, behind the reproach implied, the assumptions which may have made the reproach seem pertinent. One cannot, of course, suppose it to express a sheer general aversion to the useful or an ascetic abhorrence of all satisfaction on principle. Puritanism, æstheticism, and pedantry should be last resorts in any search for an interpretative clue.

The distrust of Utilitarianism need be ascribed to none of these. It comes instead from a conception of the true Utilitarian as a dull and dogmatic being with no interests beyond the range of his own uninquiring vision, no aspiration beyond the complacent survey of his own perfections and no standards beyond the inventory of his own *bourgeois* tastes and prejudices. The type is indeed not yet extinct in our day: but is it plausible to charge a "new" philosophy with conspiring to perpetuate it? Is Instrumentalism only philistinism called by a more descriptive name? It professes at least to be a logic of hypothesis and experiment, whereas for the perfect philistine there are no ultimate problems and hence no logic but the logic of self-evidence. When Instrumentalism speaks of needs and interests in its analysis of truth and goodness does it then mean the needs and interests that define the individual in what is sometimes invidiously termed a "biological" sense—interests that control him before his conduct becomes in any way a problem for himself? Quite as a matter of course, just this has been the assumption. The satisfactoriness of prompt and cogent classification has had a hand in the vindication of truth's supremacy over satisfaction. In the view of instrumentalism this ready interpretation of its meaning is nothing less than the thinking of the unthinkable and the bodying-forth of what is not. The man who has solved a problem simply *is* not the man he was before—if his problem was a genuine one and it was he who solved it. He cannot measure and judge the outcome by his earlier demands for the very good reason·that the outcome of real deliberation empties these earlier demands of their interest and authority for him.

Can the conception thus suggested of personal growth through exercise of creative or constructive intelligence be in any measure verified by a general survey of the economic side of life? Has it any important bearings upon any parts of economic theory? These are the questions to which this essay is addressed.

I

§ 2. How have the real or fancied needs of the average person of today come to be what they are? For all sorts and conditions of men, the ways and means of living have, during the past century or two—even during the past decade or two—undergone revolutionary changes. It is true that many of these changes have been relatively superficial, touching only certain externalities and entering in no important way into life's underlying and dominant motives. Others, no doubt, may fairly be held to confuse and disperse the energies of men, instead of making for wholeness, sanity and development of human interest and power. And critics of industrial and social progress who have felt the need for reservations of this sort fall easily into a certain mood of historic homesickness for the supposed "simplicity" of an earlier age. But our interest, in this discussion, is in the genesis, the actual process of becoming, of our present "standards of living," not their value as rated by any critical (or uncritical) standard. And accordingly we shall take it for a fact that on the whole the average person of today is reasonably, perhaps unreasonably, well satisfied with his telephone, his typewriter, and his motor-car; with his swift and easy journeyings over land and sea; with his increasingly scientific medical attendance and public sanitation; with his virtually free supplies of literature and information, new and old, and with his electric light or his midnight oil (triple distilled) to aid in the perusal. More than this, he is so well satisfied with all these modern inventions that, historical or æsthetical or other "holidays" apart, he would never for a moment dispense with any one of them as a matter of free choice. Grossly material and humbly instrumental though they are, these things and their like constitute the framework sustaining the whole system of spiritual functions that make up the life we live today, as a society and as individuals. And our present problem simply is the way in which they were first received by those who were to use them, and passed into their present common acceptance. To put the matter in general terms, how is it that novel means of action or enjoyment, despite their novelty, are able to command fair scrutiny and hearing and can contrive to make their way, often very speedily, into a position of importance for industry and life?

There is an easy and not unnatural way of thinking of this process as we see it going on about us that may keep us long unmindful of even the possibility of such a question. In every field of action, we habitually look back upon accomplished changes from some present well-secured vantage-point, and as we trace the steps by which they have come to pass it is almost inevitable that we should first see the sequence as an approach, direct or devious but always sure, to the stage on which we happen to have taken our stand. It seems clear to us that what we have attained is better than aught that has gone before—if it were not distinctly satisfactory on its own merits we should not now be taking it as the standpoint for a survey. But once it is so taken, our recognition of its appreciable and satisfying superiority passes over insensibly into metaphysics. What we now find good we find ourselves perceiving to have been all the while predestined in the eternal scheme of things! We pause in retrospect like the wayfarer who has reached the turning of a mountain road or the man of middle age who for the first time feels that his professional position is assured. This, we say, justifies the effort it has cost, *this* at last is really living! And the next step in retrospective reconstruction follows easily; this was my true goal from the first, the dim and inexpressible hope of which would not let me pause and kept me until now dissatisfied. The end was present in the beginning, provoking the first groping efforts and affording progressively the test and measure by which their results were found ever wanting.

This retrospective logic may explain the presence and perennial charm of those panoramic pages in our encyclopædias purporting to show forth the gradual perfecting of great instrumentalities upon which our modern life depends. We survey the "evolution" of printing, for example, from the wooden blocks of the Chinese or of Laurens Coster down to the Hoe press, the stereotype plate, and the linotype machine. Or we see the forms of written record from pictured papyrus, cuneiform brick, and manuscript scroll down to the printed book and the typewritten page; the means of carriage by land from the ox-cart of the patriarchs to the stage-coach, the Cannonball Limited, the motor-truck, and the twelve-cylinder touring-car. And as one contemplates these cheerfully colored exhibits there is in each case an almost irresistible suggestion of a constant and compelling need of "universal man" seeking in more and more marvellously ingenious ways an adequate expression and satisfaction. This need seems never to have lapsed or changed its nature. All along both driving power and direction, it has been the one fixed factor in a long process in which all else has been fluctuating, contingent, and imperfect—all else except the nature of the materials and the principles of mechanics, which, too, are seen in the end to have been mutely conspiring toward the result. Essential human nature, it seems clear, does not and happily cannot change. Spiritual progress, in this ultimate optimism, means simply clearer vision, completer knowledge, and a less petulant and self-assertive habit of insistence upon the details of particular purposes as individual "impulse" and "idiosyncrasy" define them. We fortunate beings of today have available, in the various departments of our life, certain instrumentalities, and to these our interests attach. These interests of ours in their proportional strength (so the argument runs) express our native and generic constitution in so far as this constitution has been able as yet to achieve outward expression and embodiment. And accordingly, in interpreting the long history of technological evolution, we take what we conceive ourselves now to be as normative and essential. We project back into the lives of primitive man, of our own racial ancestors, or of our grandfathers, the habits and requirements which we acknowledge in ourselves today and we conceive the men of the past to have been driven forward on the ways of progress by the identical discontent that would presumably beset ourselves if we were to be suddenly carried back to their scale and manner of existence.

§ 3. Whatever else may be thought of it, there is at least this to be said for the cult of historic homesickness to which reference has just been made: it happens to be at one with modern ethnology and history in suggesting that earlier cultures were on the whole not less content and self-satisfied in their condition than our own. It is primitive man, not the modern, who is slow to move and is satisfied, as a matter of course, with the manner of life in which he fancies his people to have lived from time immemorial. Change in early social groups is tragic when it is not insensible. It comes through conquest and enslavement by outsiders or through stress of the dread of these, or by gradual adaptation of custom to failing environmental resources or to increasing wealth. Assent to change is in general grudging or tacit at best and is commonly veiled by some more or less transparent fiction.

And our suspicion of fallacy lurking somewhere in the type of retrospective Idealism we have been considering is strengthened when we come to look a little closely to details. To take a commonplace example—can it be held that the difference between using a typewriter and "writing by hand" is purely and simply a matter of degree—that the machine serves the same purpose and accomplishes the same *kind* of result as the pen, but simply does the work more easily, rapidly, and neatly? Undoubtedly some such impression may easily be gathered from an external survey of the ways that men have used at different times for putting their ideas on record. But it ignores important aspects of the case. For one thing, the modern invention effects a saving of the writer's time which can be used in further investigation or in more careful revision or in some way wholly unrelated to literary work, and if the machine makes any part of the writer's task less irksome, or the task as a whole less engrossing, the whole matter of literary effort becomes less forbidding and its place and influence as a social or a personal function may for better or for worse be altered. The difference brought to pass transcends mere technical facility—it ramifies into a manifold of differences affecting the entire qualitative character and meaning of the literary function. And only by an arbitrary sophistication of the facts can this complexity of new outcome be thought of as implicit and dynamic in the earlier stage.

In the same way precisely, the motor-car, as every one knows, has "vanquished distance" and has "revolutionized suburban life." In England it is said to have made acute the issue of plural voting. In America it is hailed by the optimistic as the solution of the vexed problem of urban concentration and the decline of agriculture. Even as a means of recreation it is said by the initiated to transform the whole meaning of one's physical environment, exploiting new values in sky and air and the green earth, which pass the utmost possibilities of family "carry-all" or coach and four. Or consider the ocean steamship and its influence: today we travel freely over the world, for all manner of reasons, sufficient or otherwise. A hundred years ago distant journeyings by sea or land were arduous and full of peril, undertaken only by the most adventurous or the most curious or for urgent need. Now commodities of every sort can be transported to virtually every quarter of the globe—rails and locomotives, cement and structural steel, machinery of all kinds from the motor and the dynamo to the printing press and the cinematograph, in a word whatever is necessary to recreate the waste places of the earth and to make life in these regions humanly liveable. The sheer scale and magnitude of such operations lifts them above the level of the international trade of five hundred or even a hundred years ago. And their far-reaching results of every sort in the lives of nations and of individuals the world over can in no intelligible sense be understood as mere homogeneous multiples of what trade meant before our age of steam, iron, and electricity. Finally, we may think of modern developments in printing as compared, for example, with the state of the craft in the days when the New England Primer served to induct juvenile America into the pleasant paths of "art and literature." And it is clear that the mechanical art that makes books and reading both widely inviting and easily possible of enjoyment today is not merely a more perfect substitute for the quill and ink-horn of the mediæval scribe or even for the printing press of Caxton or of Benjamin Franklin. The enormously and variously heightened "efficiency" of the mechanical instrumentalities nowadays available has for good and for evil carried forward the whole function of printing and publication into relations and effects which are qualitatively new and beyond the possible conception of the earlier inventors and readers.

§ 4. The real evolution in such cases of the coming of a new commodity or a new instrument into common and established use is an evolution of a more radical, more distinctly epigenetic type than the pictured stories of the encyclopædia-maker serve to suggest. At each forward step the novelty makes possible not merely satisfactions more adequate as measured by existing requirements or more economical in terms of cost, but new satisfactions also for which no demand or desire before existed or could possibly exist—satisfactions which, once become habitual, make the contentment of former times in the lack of them hard to understand or credit. And indeed the story is perhaps never quite one-sided; the gain we reckon is perhaps never absolutely unmixed. There may be, perhaps must in principle be, not only gain but loss. The books we read have lost something of the charm of the illuminated manuscript; our compositors and linotypers, it may be, have forgotten something of the piety and devotion of the mediæval scribe and copyist. So everywhere in industry the machine depreciates and pushes out the skilled artisan and craftsman, summoning into his place the hired operative whose business is to feed and serve instead of to conceive and execute. For cheapness and abundance, for convenience of repair and replacement we everywhere sacrifice something of artistic quality in the instrumentalities of life and action and something of freedom and self-expression in the processes of manufacture. Thus again, to change the venue, there are those who miss in democratic government or in an ethical type of religion the poignant and exalting spiritual quality of devotion to a personal sovereign or a personal God. Whatever one's judgment may be in particular cases, there can be no reason for disputing that in epigenetic or creative evolution there is, in a sense, loss as well as gain. There is no more reason for supposing that all that was wholesome or ennobling or beautiful in an earlier function *must* somehow have its specific compensation in kind infallibly present in the new than for supposing that all that is desirable in the new must surely have been present discernibly or indiscernibly in the old.

If we are on the whole satisfied with the new on its intrinsic merits as a present complex fact, we have therein sufficient ground for saying that it marks a stage in progress. This, in fact, is what such a proposition means. And the old then appears more or less widely discontinuous with the new—not merely that it shows, in units of measure, less of the acceptable quality or qualities which the *new* fact or situation is found to possess, but that it belongs for us to a qualitatively different level and order of existence. How, we wonder, could our ancestors have found life tolerable in their undrained and imperfectly heated dwellings, without the telephone, the morning's news of the world by cable, and the phonograph? How, again, could feudal homage and fealty have ever been the foundation of social order in countries where today every elector is wont to think and to act in his public relations no longer as a subject but as a citizen. And how, in still a different sphere, could the father or the mother of a happy family of children ever have found the freedom and irresponsibility of bachelorhood endurable? Shall we say that in changes like these we have to do simply with the quantitative increase of some quality, present in small measure in the earlier stages and in larger measure in the later? Or shall we evade the issue with the general admission that *of course*, as every schoolboy knows, there are in this world many differences of degree that somehow "amount to differences of kind"? As a matter of fact what has happened in every case like these is an actual change of standard, a new construction in the growing system of one's norms of value and behavior. Provisionally, though hopefully, a step has been taken— a real event in personal and in social history has been given place and date. From some source beyond the scope and nature of the earlier function a suggestion or an impulse has come by which the agent has endeavored to move forward. The change wrought is a transcendence of the earlier level of experience and valuation, not a widening and clarification of vision on that level. And the standards which govern on the new level serve not so much to condemn the old as to seal its consignment to disuse and oblivion. Least of all can a judgment or appraisal of the old from the standpoint of the new be taken for a transcript of the motives which led to the transition.

We must confine ourselves more closely, however, to the sphere of material goods and their uses. And in this sphere objection to the view proposed will run in some such terms as the following: Take our ancestors, for example, and their household arrangements to which invidious reference has been made: why should we suppose that their seeming contentment was anything more (or less) than a dignified composure in which we might well imitate them—an attitude in no way precluding a definite sense of specific discomforts and embarrassments and a distinct determination to be rid of them as soon as might be? And, in fact, if they were satisfied with what they had why did they receive the new when it was offered? If, on the other hand, they were not satisfied, how is the fact intelligible except upon the assumption that they had distinct and definite wants not yet supplied, and were wishing (but patiently) for conveniences and comforts of a sort not yet existent. And this latter hypothesis, it will be urged, is precisely what the foregoing argument has sought to discredit as an account of the moving springs in the evolution of consumption.

§ 5. Any adequate discussion of the central issue thus presented would fall into two parts. In the first place, before a consumption good can come into general acceptance and currency it must have been in some way discovered, suggested or invented, and the psychology of invention is undoubtedly a matter of very great complexity and difficulty. But for the purposes of the present inquiry all this may be passed over. The other branch of a full discussion of our problem has to do with the reception of the newly invented commodity or process into wider and wider use—and this again is a social phenomenon not less complex than the other. It is this phenomenon of increasing extension and vogue, of widening propagation from person to person, that is directly of present concern for us—and in particular the individual person's attitude toward the new thing and the nature of the interest he takes in it.

It has recently been argued by a learned and acute investigator of economic origins that "invention is the mother of necessity," and not the child.45 Such a complete reversal of all our ordinary thought about the matter seems at first sheer paradox. What, one may ask, can ever suggest an invention and what can give it welcome and currency but an existing need— which, if it happens to be for the time being latent and unconscious, needs only the presentation of its appropriate means of satisfaction to "arouse" and "awaken" it fully into action? But this paradox as to invention is at all events not more paradoxical than the view as to the reception of new commodities and the rise of new desires that has been above suggested. What it appears to imply is in principle identical with what has seemed, from our consideration of the other aspect of the general situation, to be the simple empirical fact; neither the existence of the new commodity nor our interest in it when it is presented admits of explanation as an effect on each particular occasion of a preëxisting unsatisfied desire for it. What both sides of the problem bring to view is a certain original bent or constitutive character of human nature—a predisposition, an *élan vital* perhaps, which we must recognize as nothing less than perfectly general and comprehensive—finding expression in inventive effort and likewise in the readiness with which the individual meets a new commodity halfway and gives it opportunity to become for him, if it can, a new necessity and the source of a new type of satisfaction.

From the point of view of "logic," as William James might have said, such a version of psychological fact may seem essentially self-contradictory. Unless, it may be argued, a novelty when presented excites some manner of desire for itself in the beholder, the beholder will make no effort towards it and thus take no step away from his existing system of life to a new system in which a new desire and a new commodity shall have a place. So much would seem clear enough but the question immediately follows: How can a thing that is new arouse desire? In so far as it is new it must *ex vi termini* be unknown and wanting definition in terms of remembered past experiences; and how can a thing unknown make that connection with the present character of the individual which must be deemed necessary to the arousal of desire in him? A new thing would seem, then, from this point of view, to be able to arouse desire only in so far as it is able to conceal or subordinate its aspects of novelty and appear as known and well-accredited—either this or there must be in the individual some definite instinctive mechanism ready to be set in action by the thing's presentment. And on neither of these suppositions can having to do with the new thing effect any fundamental or radical difference in the individual—it can serve at most only to "bring out" what was already "there" in him in a "latent" or "implicit" status. Whatever new developments of power or desire may be attained and organized into the individual's character through his commerce with the novelty must be new in only a superficial sense—they will be new only as occurrences, only as the striking of the hour by the clock and the resulting abrasion of the bell and hammer are new events. But the clock was made to strike; it is the nature of metal to wear away and likewise these changes in the individual are in deeper truth not new at all but only a disclosure of the agent's character, a further fulfilment along preëstablished and unalterable lines which all along was making headway in the agent's earlier quests and efforts and attainments.

There is a sense, no doubt, in which some such version of the facts as this is unanswerable, but controversial advantage is paid for, here as elsewhere in the logic of absolute idealism, at the cost of tangible meaning and practical importance. Just what does the contention come to? Let us say, for example, that one has learned to use a typewriter. What has happened is like an illiterate person's learning to read and write. Correspondence with one's friends begins to take on new meaning and to acquire new value; one begins to find a new pleasure and stimulation taking the place of the ineffectual drivings of an uneasy conscience. All this, let us say, has come from the moderate outlay for a superior mechanical instrument. And now let it be granted that it would not have come if the fortunate individual had not been "what he was." If it has come it is because the individual and the rest of the world were "of such a sort" that the revival and new growth of interest *could* take its rise with the provision of the new instrumentality. But what, precisely, does such a statement mean? What sort of verification does it admit of? What fruitful insight into the concrete facts of the case does it convey? Of *what* sort, prior to the event, does it show the individual to have been?

The truth is, of course, that he was of *no* sort, then and there and with reference to the purchase—he was of no sort decisively. He was neither purchaser nor rejector. He was neither a convinced "typist" nor piously confirmed in his predilection for writing "by hand." He was neither wholly weary of his correspondence nor fully cognizant of the importance of intercourse with his friends for his soul's good. He may have been dissatisfied and rebellious or he may have been comfortably persuaded that letter-writing, though an irksome labor, was even at that sufficiently worth while. The most that can be said is simply that he must have been willing and desirous to try the experiment for the sake of any good, imaginable or beyond present imagination, that might come of it. But being of "such a sort" as this could not prejudge the issue—although, undoubtedly, in willingness to raise an issue there lies always the possibility of change. All the plausibility of the dogma we are here considering comes from its hasty inclusion of this general attitude of constructively experimental inquiry and effort, this essential character of creative intelligence, as *one among* the concrete interests which constitute and define our particular problems in their inception. To say *ex post facto* that the individual must have been "of such a sort" as to do what he has in fact done is a purely verbal comment which, whatever may be its uses, can assuredly be of no use whatever in suggesting either solution or method for the next situation to arise. It may be comfortably reassuring afterwards, but it is an empty oracle beforehand.

§ 6. If then "logic" is unable to express the nature of our forward looking interest in the unexperienced and unpredictable, perhaps the empirical fact will speak for itself. We call things new; we recognize their novelty and their novelty excites our interest. But just as we are sometimes told that we can only *know* the new in terms of its resemblances to what we have known before, so it may be held that in the end we can *desire* it only on the like condition. Are we, then, to conclude that the seeming novelty of things new is an illusion, or shall we hold, on the contrary, that novelty need not be explained away and that a spontaneous constructive interest stands more or less constantly ready in us to go out to meet it and possess it?

Unquestionably, let us say the latter. Any new commodity will, of course, resemble in part or in a general way some old one.

It is said that bath-tubs are sometimes used in "model tenements" as coal-bins. Old uses persist unchanged in the presence of new possibilities. But in general new possibilities invite interest and effort because our experimental and constructive bent contrives on the whole to make head against habituation and routine. We recognize the new as new. And if it be contended that novelty in its own right cannot be a ground of interest, that novelty must first get restatement as the old with certain "accidents" externally adhering, the answer is that the "accidents" interest us nevertheless. They may prove their right to stand as the very essence of some new "kind" that one may wish to let take form and character for him. Instead of the chips and shavings, they are in fact the raw material of the logical process. For if we can know the new *as new*, if we can know the "accident" *as accidental* in a commodity before us, the fact betrays an incipient interest in the quality or aspect that its novelty or contingency at least does not thwart. And is this quite all? Will it be disputed that a *relation* of a quality or feature to ourselves which we can know, name, and recognize—like "novelty"—must be known, as anything else is known, through an interest of which it is the appropriate terminus?46

And there is no difficulty in pointing to instances in which the character of novelty seems fundamental. Consider, for example, the interest one feels in spending a day with a friend or in making a new acquaintance or, say, in entering on the cares of parenthood. Or again, take the impulse toward research, artistic creation, or artistic study and appreciation. Or again, take the interest in topography and exploration. That there is in such phenomena as these a certain essentially and irreducibly forward look, a certain residual freedom of our interest and effort from dependence on the detail of prior experience down to date, probably few persons without ulterior philosophical prepossessions will dispute. If we call these phenomena instinctive we are using the term in a far more loose and general sense than it seems to have in the best usage of animal psychology. If we call them attitudes or dispositions, such a term has at least the negative merit of setting them apart from the class of instinctive acts, but it may carry with it a connotation of fixity and unconsciousness that after all surrenders the essential distinction. It will suffice to look at a single one of these instances.

In friendship, for example, there is undoubtedly strongly operative a desire for the mere recurrence, in our further friendly intercourse, of certain values that have become habitual and familiar. We may have long known and become attached to a friend's tones of voice, peculiarities of manner and external appearance, turns of speech and thought and the like, which we miss in absence and which give us pleasure when we meet the friend again. But if the friendship is not one of "pleasure" or "utility" simply, but of "virtue"47 as well, there is also present on both sides a constructive or progressive or creative interest. And this interest, stated on its self-regarding and introspective side, is more than a desire for the mere grateful recurrence of the old looks and words "recoined at the old mint." It is an interest looking into the "undone vast," an interest in an indefinite prolongation, an infinite series, of joint experiences the end of which cannot and need not be foreseen and the nature of which neither can nor need be forecasted. And there is the same characteristic in all the other instances mentioned in this connection. It is not a desire for recurrent satisfactions of a determinate type, but an interest in the active development of unexperienced and indeterminate possibilities. If finally the question be pressed, how there can be an interest of this seemingly self-contradictory type in human nature, the answer can only be that we must take the facts as we find them. Is such a conception inherently more difficult than the view that all ramifications and developments of human interest are concretely predetermined and implicit *a priori*? To ignore or deny palpable fact because it eludes the reach of a current type of conceptual analysis is to part company with both science and philosophy. We are in fact here dealing with the essential mark and trait of what is called self-conscious process. If there are ultimates and indefinables in this world of ours, self-consciousness may as fairly claim the dignity or avow the discredit as any other of the list.

§ 7. Does our interest in economic goods on occasion exhibit the trait of which we are here speaking? Precisely this is our present contention. And yet it seems not too much to say that virtually all economic theory, whether the classical or the present dominant type that has drawn its terminology and working concepts from the ostensible psychology of the Austrian School, is founded upon the contradictory assumption. The economic interest, our desire and esteem for solid and matter-of-fact things like market commodities and standardized market services, has been conceived as nothing visionary and speculative, as no peering into the infinite or outreaching of an inexpressible discontent, but an intelligent, clear-eyed grasping and holding of known satisfactions for measured and acknowledged desires. Art and religion, friendship and love, sport and adventure, morality and legislation, these all may be fields for the free play and constructive experimentation of human faculty, but in our economic efforts and relations we are supposed to tread the solid ground of fact. Business is business. Waste not, want not. First a living, then (perhaps) a "good life."[48] And we are assured one need not recoil from the hard logic of such maxims, for they do not dispute the existence of spacious (and well-shaded) suburban regions fringing the busy areas of industry and commerce.

Such is the assumption. We have said that it precludes the admission of speculation as an economic factor. Speculation for economic theory is a purely commercial phenomenon, a hazarding of capital on the supposition that desires will be found ready and waiting for the commodity produced—with a sufficient offering of purchasing power to afford a profit. And the "creation of demand," where this is part of the program of speculative enterprise, means the arousal of a "dormant" or implicit desire, in the sense above discussed—there is nothing, at all events, in other parts of current theory to indicate a different conception. The economist will probably contend that what the process of the creation of demand may *be* is not his but the psychologist's affair;

that his professional concern is only whether or not the economic demand, as an objective market fact, be actually forthcoming. But what we here contend for as a fact of economic experience is a speculation that is in the nature of personal adventure and not simply an "adventuring of stock."

§ 8. For what is the nature of the economic "experience" or situation, considered as a certain type of juncture in the life of an individual? It may be shortly described as the process of determining how much of one's time, strength, or external resources of any sort shall be expended for whatever one is thinking of doing or acquiring. Two general motives enter here to govern the estimate and each may show the routine or the innovative phase. In any work there is possible, first, more or less of the workman's interest—an interest not merely in a conventional standard of excellence in the finished result but also in betterment of the standard and in a corresponding heightened excellence of technique and spirit in the execution.49 These interests, without reference to the useful result and "for their own sake" (i.e., for the workman's sake, in ways not specifiable in advance), may command a share of one's available time, strength, and resources. In the second place, any work or effort or offer to give in exchange has a nameable result of some kind in view—a crop of wheat, a coat, a musical rendition, or the education of a child. Why are such things "produced" or sought for? Verbally and platitudinously one may answer: For the sake of the "satisfactions" they are expected to afford. But such an answer ignores the contrast of attitudes that both workmanship and productive or acquisitive effort in the ordinary sense display. As the workman may conform to his standard or may be ambitious to surpass it, so the intending consumer may be counting on known satisfactions or hoping for satisfactions of a kind that he has never known before. Both sorts of effort may be of either the routine or the innovative type. In neither workmanship nor acquisition can one fix upon routine as the "normal" type, hoping to derive or to explain away the inevitable residue of "outstanding cases." For as a matter of fact the outstanding cases prove to be our only clue to a knowledge of how routine is made.<u>50</u>

The above formula will apply, with the appropriate changes of emphasis, to buyers and sellers in an organized market, as well as to the parties to a simple transaction of barter. Two main empirical characteristics of the economic situation are suggested in putting the statement in just these terms. In the first place, the primary problem in such a situation is that of "exchange valuation," the fixation of a "subjective" (or better, a "personal") price ratio between what the agent wishes to acquire and whatever it is that he offers in exchange. The agent thus is engaged in determining what shall be the relative importance for himself of *two* commodities or exchangeable goods. And in the second place these goods get their values determined together and in relation to each other,   never singly and with a view to *subsequent* comparison. These values when they have been determined will be measured in terms of marginal utility in accordance with familiar principles, but the marginal utilities that are to express the attained and accepted ratio at which exchange eventually takes place are not known quantities at all in the inception of the process of comparison. If these dogmatic statements seem to issue in hopeless paradox or worse, then let us not fear to face the paradox and fix its lines with all possible distinctness. Can a man decide to offer so much of one commodity for so much of another unless he *first* has settled what each is worth to him in some intelligible terms or other? And is not this latter in point of fact the real decision—at all events clearly more than half the battle? Does not the exchange ratio to which one can agree "leap to the eyes," in fact, as soon as the absolute values in the case have been once isolated and given numerical expression?

In a single word we here join issue. For the comparison in such a case is *constructive comparison*, not a mechanical measuring of fixed magnitudes, as the above objection tacitly assumes. And constructive comparison is essentially a transitive or inductive operation whereby the agent moves from one level to another, altering his standard of living in some more or less important way, embarking upon a new interest, entering upon the formation of a new habit or upon a new accession of power or effectiveness—making or seeking to make, in short, some transformation in his environment and in himself that shall give his life as an entire system a changed tenor and perspective. The term "constructive comparison" is thus intended, among other things, to suggest that the process is in the nature of adventure, not calculation, and, on the other hand, that though adventurous it is not sheer hazard uncontrolled. And the motive dominant throughout the process—the economic motive in its constructive phase—is neither more nor less than a supposition, on the agent's part, that there may be forthcoming for him in the given case in hand just such an "epigenetic" development of new significance and value as we have found actual history to disclose as a normal result of economic innovation. It is the gist of hedonism, in economic theory as in its other expressions, that inevitably the agent's interests and motives are restricted in every case to the precise range and scope of his existing tendencies and desires; he can be provoked to act only by the hope of just those particular future pleasures or means of pleasure which the present constitution of his nature enables him to enjoy. Idealism assumes that the emergent new interest of the present was wrapped up or "implied," in some sense, in the interests of the remote and immediate past—interests of which the agent at the time could of course be but "imperfectly" aware. Such differences as one can discern between the two interpretations seem small indeed—like many others to which idealism has been wont to point in disparagement of the hedonistic world view. For in both philosophies the agent is without initiative and effect; he is in principle but the convergence of impersonal motive powers which it is, in the one view, absurdly futile, in the other misguidedly presumptuous, to try to alter or control.

§ 9. A commodity sought or encountered may then be of interest to us for reasons of the following three general sorts. In the first place it may simply be the normal and appropriate object of some established desire of ours. We may be seeking the commodity because this desire has first become active, or encountering the commodity in the market may have suddenly awakened the desire. Illustration seems superfluous; tobacco for the habitual smoker, clothing of most sorts for the ordinary person, regular supplies of the household staples—these will suffice. This is the province within which a hedonistic account of the economic motive holds good with a cogency that anti-hedonistic criticism has not been able to dissolve. Our outlays for such things as these may as a rule be held in their due and proper relation to each other—at all events in their established or "normal" relation—simply by recalling at critical times our relative marginal likes and dislikes for them. That these likes and dislikes are not self-explanatory, that they are concrete expectations and not abstract affective elements, does not seem greatly to matter where the issue lies between maintaining or renouncing an existing schedule of consumption. And in this same classification belong also industrial and commercial expenditures of a similarly routine sort. Even where the scale of operations is being enlarged, expenditures for machines, fuel, raw materials, and labor may have been so carefully planned in advance with reference to the desired increase of output or pecuniary profit that no special problem of motivation attaches directly to them. And these outlays are so important in industry and commerce that the impression comes easily to prevail that all business undertaking, and then all consumption of finished goods, fall under the simple hedonistic type.

But if we keep to the plane of final consumption, there appears a second sort of situation. Our interest in the commodity before us may be due to a suggestion of some sort that prompts us to take a step beyond the limits that our present formed desires mark out. The suggestion may be given by adroit advertising, by fashion, by the habits of another class to which one may aspire or by a person to whom one may look as guide, philosopher, and friend. An authority of one sort or another invites or constrains us to take the merits of the article on trust. Actual trial and use may show, not so much that it can minister to a latent desire as that we have been able through its use to form a habit that constitutes a settled need.

And, finally, in the third place, there is a more spontaneous and intrinsically personal type of interest which is very largely independent of suggestion or authority. A thing of beauty, a new author, a new acquaintance, a new sport or game, a new convenience or mechanical device may challenge one's curiosity and powers of appreciation, may seem to offer a new facility in action or some unimagined release from labor or restriction. The adventure of marriage and parenthood, the intimate attraction of great music, the mystery of an unknown language or a forbidden country, the disdainful aloofness of a mountain peak dominating a landscape are conspicuous instances inviting a more spontaneous type of constructive interest that finds abundant expression also in the more commonplace situations and emergencies of everyday life. It is sheer play upon words to speak in such cases of a pleasure of adventurousness, a pleasure of discovery, a pleasure of conquest and mastery, assigning this as the motive in order to bring these interests to the type that fits addiction to one's particular old coat or easy-chair. The specific "pleasure" alleged could not exist were the tendency not active beforehand. While the same is true in a sense for habitual concrete pleasures in relation to their corresponding habits, the irreducible difference in constructive interest as a type lies in the *transition* which this type of interest purposes and effects from one level of concrete or substantive desire and pleasure to another. Here one consciously looks to a result that he cannot foresee or foretell; in the other type his interest as interest goes straight to its mark, sustained by a confident forecast.51

§ 10. But constructive interests, whether provoked by suggestion or of the more freely imaginative type, may, as has been said, be held to lie outside the scope of economic theory. How a desire for a certain thing has come to get expression may seem quite immaterial—economically speaking. Economics has no concern with human folly as such or human imitativeness, or human aspiration high or low or any other of the multitude of motives that have to do with secular changes in the "standard of living" and in the ideals of life at large. It has no concern with anything that lies behind the fact that I am in the market with my mind made up to buy or sell a thing at a certain price. And the answer to this contention must be that it first reverses and then distorts the true perspective of our economic experience. Let it be admitted freely—indeed, let it be insisted on—that the definition of a science must be determined by the pragmatic test. If an economist elects to concern himself with the problems of what has been called the "loose mechanics of trade" there can be no question of his right to do so or of the importance of the services he may render thereby, both to theory and to practice. But on the other hand economic theory cannot be therefore, once and for all, made a matter of accounting—to the effacement of all problems and aspects of problems of which the accountant has no professional cognizance. Just this, apparently, is what it means to level down all types of interest to the hedonistic, leaving aside as "extra-economic" those that too palpably resist the operation. It is acknowledged that freshly suggested modes of consumption and ends of effort require expenditure and sacrifice no less than the habitual, that the exploration of Tibet or of the Polar Seas affects the market for supplies not less certainly than the scheduled voyages of oceanic liners. Moreover, behind these scheduled voyages there are all the varied motives that induce people to travel and the desires that lead to the shipment of goods. Shall it be said that all of these motives and desires must be traceable back to settled habits of behavior and consumption? And if this cannot be maintained is it not hazardous to assume that such general problems of economic theory as the determination of market values or of the shares in distribution require no recognition of the other empirical types of interest? These types, if they are genuine, are surely important; they may well prove to be, in many ways, fundamentally important. For a commodity that has become habitual must once have been new and untried.

§ II. The economic demands which make up the budget of a particular person at a particular time are clearly interdependent. A man's income or the greater part of it is usually distributed among various channels of expenditure in a certain fairly constant way. In proportion to the definiteness of this distribution and the resoluteness with which it is maintained does the impression gain strength that the man is carrying out a consistent plan of some sort. Such a regular plan of expenditure may be drawn out into a schedule, setting forth the amounts required at a certain price for the unit of each kind. And such a schedule is an expression in detail, in terms of ways and means, of the type of life one has elected to lead. For virtually any income above the level of bare physical subsistence, there will be an indefinite number of alternative budgets possible. A little less may be spent for household conveniences and adornments and a little more for food. Some recreations may be sacrificed for an occasional book or magazine. One may build a house or purchase a motor-car instead of going abroad. And whichever choice is made, related expenditures must be made in consequence for which, on the assumption of a definite amount of income, compensation must be made by curtailment of outlay at other points. What seems clear in general is that one's total budget is relative to the general plan and manner of life one deems for him the best possible and that this plan, more or less definitely formulated, more or less steadily operative, is what really determines how far expenditure shall go in this direction and in that. The budget as a whole will define for the individual an equilibrium among his various recognized wants; if the work of calculating it has been carefully done there will be for the time being no tendency to change in any item.

If, then, we choose to say in such a case that the individual carries his expenditure along each line to the precise point at which the last or marginal utility enjoyed is precisely equal to the marginal utility on every other line, it seems not difficult to grasp what such a statement means. Quite harmlessly, all that it can mean is that the individual has planned precisely what he has planned and is not sorry for it, and for the time being does not think he can improve upon it. As there is one earth drawing toward its center each billiard ball of the dozen in equilibrium in a bowl, so there is behind the budget of the individual one complex personal conception of a way of life that fixes more or less certainly and clearly the kinds and intensities of his wants and assigns to each its share of purchasing power. That the units or elements in equilibrium hold their positions with reference to each other for reasons capable of separate statement for each unit seems a supposition no less impossible in the one case than in the other. To think of each kind of want in the individual's nature as holding separately in fee simple and clamoring for full and separate "satisfaction" in its separate kind, is the characteristic illusion of a purely formal type of analysis. The permanence of a budget and its carrying out no doubt require the due and precise realization of each plotted marginal utility—to go further than this along any one line would inevitably mean getting not so far along certain others, and thus a distorted and disappointing total attainment in the end. But to say that one actually plans and controls his expenditures along various lines by the ultimate aim of attaining equivalent terminal utilities on each is quite another story. It is much like saying that the square inches of canvas assigned in a picture to sky and sea and crannied wall are arranged upon the principle of identical and equal effects for artist or beholder from the last inches painted of each kind. The formula of the equality of marginal effects is no constructive principle; it is only a concise if indeed somewhat grotesque way of phrasing the essential fact that no change of the qualitative whole is going to be made, because no imperfection in it as a whole is felt.52

§ 12. We come, then, to the problem of the individual's encounter with a new commodity. In general, a purchase in such a case must amount to more or less of a departure from the scheme of life in force and a transition over to a different one. And a new commodity (in the sense in which the term has been used above) is apt to be initially more tempting than an addition along some line of expenditure already represented in the budget. The latter, supposing there has been no change of price and no increase of income, is usually a mere irregularity, an insurgent departure from some one specification of a total plan without preliminary compensating adjustment or appropriate change at other points. The erratic outlay, if considerable, will result in sheer disorder and extravagance—indefensible and self-condemned on the principles of the individual's own economy. But with a new commodity the case stands differently. It is more interesting to consider a really new proposal than to reopen a case once closed when no evidence distinctly new is offered. A sheer "temptation" or an isolated impulse toward new outlay along a line already measured in one's scheme has the force of habit and a presumption of un-wisdom to overcome. If the case is one not of temptation but of "being urged" one is apt to answer, "No, I can make no use of any more of *that*." But a new commodity has the charm of its novelty, a charm consisting in the promise, in positive fashion, of new qualitative values about which a new entire schedule will have to be organized. Partly its strength of appeal lies in its radicalism; it gains ready attention not only by its promise but by its boldness. "Preparedness" gains a more ready acclaim than better schools or the extirpation of disease. The automobile and the "moving picture" probably have a vogue today far surpassing any use of earlier "equivalents" that a mere general augmentation of incomes could have brought about. Indeed, the economic danger of the middle classes in present-day society lies not in mere occasional excess at certain points but in heedless commitment to a showy and thinned-out scheme of life in which the elements are ill-chosen and ill-proportioned and from which, as a whole, abiding satisfaction cannot be drawn. It is where real and thoroughgoing change in the manner of life is hopeless that irregular intemperance of various sorts appears to bulk relatively largest as an economic evil.

Shall we not say, however, that the superior attraction of the new in competition with established lines of expenditure only indicates the greater "satiation" of the wants the latter represent and the comparative freshness of the wants the novelty will satisfy? On the contrary the latter wants are in the full sense not yet existent, the new satisfactions are untried and unmeasured; the older wants have the advantage of position, and if satiated today, will reassert themselves with a predictable strength tomorrow. The new wants, it is true, if they are acquired, will be part of a new system, but the present fact remains that their full meaning cannot be known in advance of trial and the further outlines of the new scheme of uses and values cannot be drawn up until this meaning has been learned. If, then, the new commodity is taken, it is not because the promised satisfaction and the sum of known utilities to be sacrificed are found equal, nor again because the new commodity will fit neatly into a place in the existing schedule that can be vacated for it. This latter is the case of substitution. Such an interpretation of the facts is retrospective only; it is a formal declaration that the exchange has been deemed on the whole worth while, but the reasons for this outcome such a formula is powerless to suggest.

In general the new commodity and the habits it engenders could not remain without effect upon a system into which they might be mechanically introduced. Certain items in the schedule, associated in use with those dispensed with for the new, must be rendered obsolete by the change. The new interests called into play will draw to themselves and to their further development attention which may be in large measure diverted from the interests of older standing. And in the new system all interests remaining over from the old will accordingly stand in a new light and their objects will be valued, will be held important, for reasons that will need fresh statement.53

In similar fashion it might be argued that the commodities or uses which one sacrifices for the sake of a new venture are inevitably more than a simple deduction that curtails one's schedule in a certain kind and amount. Such a deduction or excision must leave the remaining lines of the original complex hanging at loose ends. The catching-up of these and their coördination with the new interest must in any event amount, as has been contended, to a thoroughgoing reorganization. What must really happen then, in the event of action, is in principle nothing less than the disappearance of the whole from which the sacrificed uses are dissevered. These latter, therefore, stand in the process of decision as a symbol for the existing personal economy as a whole. The old order and the new confront each other as an accepted view of fact and a plausible hypothesis everywhere confront each other and the issue for the individual is the practical issue of making the transition to a new working level. To declare that the salient elements of the confronting complexes are quantitatively equivalent is only to announce in symbolic terms that the transition has been effected, the die cast.54

§ 13. The statement thus given has been purposely made, for many transactions of the sort referred to, something of an over-statement. If I contemplate purchasing a typewriter or a book on an unfamiliar but inviting subject it may well seem somewhat extravagant to describe the situation as an opposition between two schemes of life. Is the issue so momentous; is the act so revolutionary? But the purpose of our over-statement was simply to make clear the type of situation without regard to the magnitudes involved. No novelty that carries one in any respect beyond the range of existing habits can be wholly without its collateral effects nor can its proximate and proper significance be measured in advance. This is in principle as true of a relatively slight innovation as of a considerable one. And our present conscious exaggeration departs less widely from the truth than the alternative usual preoccupation of economic theory with the logic of routine desire and demand. For the phenomena of routine and habit are thereby made a standard by which all others, if indeed recognized as real at all, must be judged "exceptional." And, as we shall see, to do this introduces difficulty into certain parts of substantive economic theory.

Again, objection may attach to the view that equivalence of the "salient members" of the opposing systems is only another name for the comprehensive fact of the novelty's acceptance. For if we hesitate in such a case, is this not because we judge the price too high? What can this signify but that the service or satisfaction we expect from the novelty falls short of sufficing to convince us? And unless we are dealing with measured quantities, how can we come to this conclusion? Moreover, if the novel commodity is divided into units we may take a smaller quantity when the price demanded is "high" than if the price were lower. And does this not suggest predetermined value-magnitudes as data? But if one takes thus a smaller amount, as the argument contends, it is because there is a presumption of being able to make some important total use of it and there is no general reason apparent for supposing that this will be merely a fractional part of a larger but like significance that might be hoped for from a larger quantity. And on the other hand, the prospect simply may not tempt at all; the smaller quantity may be deemed an improbable support for a really promising total program and the present program will hold its ground, not seriously shaken. The total demand of a market for a given commodity is no doubt in some sort a mathematical function of the price. The lower the price the greater in some ratio will be the number of persons who will buy and in general the greater the number of units taken by those who are already buyers. But that such a proposition admits of statistical proof from the observation of a series of price changes in a market affords no presumption concerning the nature of the reasons that move any individual person to his action. The theoretical temptation is strong, here as elsewhere, in passing from the study of markets to the personal economy of the individual forthwith to find this also a trafficking in unit-quantities and marginal satisfactions to which the concepts and notation of market analysis will readily apply.

It remains to consider certain implications of this view of economic desire and demand.

II

§ 14. It is evident that the issue finally at stake in any economic problem of constructive comparison, is an ethical issue. Two immediate alternatives are before one—to expend a sum of money in some new and interesting way, or to keep it devoted to the uses of one's established plan. Upon the choice, one recognizes, hinge consequences of larger and more comprehensive importance than the mere present enjoyment or non-enjoyment of the new commodity.55 And these "more important" consequences *are* important because there appears to lie in them the possibility of a type of personal character divergent from the present type and from any present point of view incommensurable with it.56 The ethical urgency of such a problem will impress one in the measure in which one can see that such an issue really does depend upon his present action and irretrievably depends. And we are able now to see what that economic quality is that attaches to ethical problems at a certain stage of their development and calls for a supplementary type of treatment.

Let us first consider certain types of juncture in conduct that will be recognized at once as ethical and in which any economic aspect is relatively inconspicuous. Temperance or intemperance, truth or falsehood, idleness or industry, honesty or fraud, social justice or class-interest—these will serve. What makes such problems as these ethical is their demand for creative intelligence. In each, alternative types of character or manners of life stand initially opposed. If the concrete issue is really problematical, if there is no rule that one can follow in the case with full assurance, constructive comparison, whether covertly or openly, must come into play. How long, then, will a problem of temperance or intemperance, idleness or industry, preserve its obviously ethical character without admixture? Just so long, apparently, as the modes of conduct that come into view as possible solutions are considered and valued with regard to their *directly physiological and psychological* consequences alone. Any given sort of conduct, that is to say, makes inevitably for the formation of certain habits of mind or muscle, weakening, or precluding the formation of, certain others. Attention is engrossed that is thereby not available elsewhere, time and strength are expended, discriminations are dulled and sharpened, sympathies and sensitivities are narrowed and broadened, every trait and bent of character is directly or indirectly affected in some way by every resolve concluded and every action embarked upon. If one moves a certain way along a certain line he can never return to the starting-point and set out unchanged along any other. If one does one thing one cannot do another. And when the sufficient reasons for this mutual exclusion lie in the structure and organization of the human mind and body our deliberation as between the two alternatives, our constructive comparison of them remains upon the ethical plane.

If one does one thing one cannot do another. If we substitute the well-worn saying "one cannot eat his cake and have it" we indicate the economic plane of constructive comparison with all needful clearness.

This is in fact the situation that has been already under discussion at such length above and the economic quality of which we are just now in quest arises from neither more nor less than the fact of our dependence in the working out of our personal problems upon limited external resources. The eventual solution sought under these circumstances remains ethical as before. But to reach it, it is necessary to bring into consideration not only such other interests and ends as the psycho-physical structure of human nature and the laws of character-development show to be involved, but a still wider range of interests less intimately or "internally" related to the focal interest of the occasion but imperatively requiring to be heard. If my acquisition of a phonograph turns upon the direct psychological bearing of the new interest upon my other interests, its probable effects whether good or bad upon my musical tastes and the diplomatic complications with my neighbors in which the possession of the instrument may involve me, the problem of its purchase remains clearly in the ethical phase. But when I count the cost in terms of sacrifices which the purchase price makes necessary, from literature down to food and fuel, and must draw this whole range of fact also into the adjustment if I can, the economic phase is reached. In principle two entire and very concrete schemes of life now stand opposed. Just *what* concrete sacrifices I shall make I do not know—this, in fact, is one way of stating my problem. Nor, conversely, do I know just what I shall be able to make the phonograph worth to me. It is my task to come to a conclusion in the case that shall be explicit and clear enough to enable me to judge in *the event* whether my expectation has been realized and I have acted wisely or unwisely. Thus a problem is economic when the fact of the limitation of my external resources must be eventually and frankly faced. The characteristic quality of a problem grown economic is a certain vexatiousness and seeming irrationality in the ill-assorted array of nevertheless indisputable interests, prosaic and ideal, that have to be reduced to order.

It is perhaps this characteristic emotional quality of economic problems that has insensibly inclined economists to favor a simpler and more clear-cut analysis. As for ethical problems—they have been left to "conscience" or to the jurisdiction of a "greatest happiness" principle in which the ordinary individual or legislator has somehow come to take an interest. That they arise and become urgent in us of course does human nature unimpeachable credit and economics must by all means wait respectfully upon their settlement. So much is conceded. But economics is economics, when all is said and done. What we mean by the economic interest is an interest in the direct and several satisfactions that a man can get from the several things he shrewdly finds it worth his while to pay for. And shrewdness means nicety of calculation, accuracy of measurement in the determination of tangible loss and gain. Here, then, is no field for ethics but a field of fact. Thus ethics on her side must also wait until the case is fully ready for her praise or blame. Such is the *modus vivendi*. But its simplicity is oversimple and unreal. It pictures the "economic man" as bound in the chains of a perfunctory deference that he would throw off if he could. For the theory of constructive comparison or creative intelligence, on the other hand, instead of a seeker and recipient of "psychic income" and a calculator of gain and loss, he is a personal agent maintaining continuity of action in a life of discontinuously changing levels of interest and experience. His measure of attainment lies not in an accelerating rate of "psychic income," but in an increasing sense of personal effectiveness and an increasing readiness and confidence before new junctures.

The possession and use of commodities are, then, not in themselves and directly economic facts at all. As material things commodities serve certain purposes and effect certain results. They are means to ends and their serving so is a matter of technology. But do I seriously want their services? This is a matter of my ethical point of view. Do I want them at the price demanded or at what price and how many? This is the economic question and it obviously is a question wholly ethical in import— more broadly and inclusively ethical, in fact, than the ethical question in its earlier and more humanly inviting form. And what we have now to see is the fact that no consideration that has a bearing upon the problem in its ethical phase can lose its importance and relevance in the subsequent phase.

There can be no restriction of the economic interest, for example, to egoism. If on general principles I would really rather use goods produced in safe and cleanly factories or produced by "union labor," there is no possible reason why this should not incline me to pay the higher prices that such goods may cost and make the needful readjustment in my budget. Is there reason why my valuation of these goods should *not* thus be the decisive act that takes me out of one relation to industrial workers and sets me in another—can anything else, indeed, quite so distinctly do this? For economic valuation is only the fixation of a purchase price, or an exchange relation in terms of price and quantity, upon which two schemes of life, two differing perspectives of social contact and relationship converge—the scheme of life from which I am departing and the one upon which I have resolved to make my hazard. It is this election, this transition, that the purchase price expresses—drawing all the strands of interest and action into a knot so that a single grasp may seize them. The only essential egoism in the case lies in the "subjectivism" of the fact that inevitably the emergency and the act are mine and not another's. This is the "egocentric predicament" in its ethical aspect. And the egocentric predicament proves Hobbes and La Rochefoucauld as little as it proves Berkeley or Karl Pearson. No social interest, no objective interest of any sort, is shown ungenuine by my remembering in season that if I cannot fill my coal-bin I shall freeze.<u>57</u>

§ 15. This logical and psychological continuity of the ethical and economic problems suggests certain general considerations of some practical interest. In the first place as to "egoism." I am, let us say, an employer. If I am interested in procuring just "labor," in the sense of foot-pounds of energy, then undoubtedly labor performed under safe and healthful conditions is worth no more to me than other labor (provided it does not prove more efficient). But is this attitude of interest in just foot-pounds of energy the attitude *par excellence* or solely entitled to be called economic? And just this may be asserted for the reason that an exclusive interest in just *labor* is the only interest in the case that men of business, or at least many of them, can entertain without going speedily to the wall. If, then, I do *in fact* pay more than I must in wages or if I expend more than a bare minimum for conveniences and safety-guards this is not because of the valuation I put upon *labor*, but only because I take pleasure in the contentment and well-being of others. And this is not "business" but "uplift"—or else a subtle form of emotional self-indulgence. Suppose, however, that by legislation similar working conditions have been made mandatory for the entire industry and suppose that the community approves the law, even to the extent of cheerfully paying so much of the additional cost thereby imposed as may be shifted upon them.

Shall we say that this is an ethical intrusion into the sphere of economics or shall we say that the former economic demand for labor "as such" has given place to an economic demand for labor better circumstanced or better paid? The community at all events is paying the increase of price or a part of the increase. It seems arbitrary to insist that the old price is still the *economic* price of the commodity and the increase only the price of a quiet conscience. The notion of a strictly economic demand for labor pure and simple seems in fact a concept of accounting. To meet the community's demand for the commodity a number of producers were required. The least capable of these could make both ends meet at the prevailing price only by ignoring all but the severely impersonal aspects of the process. Taking these costs as a base, other more capable or more fortunate producers may have been able to make additional expenditures of the sort in question, charging these perhaps to "welfare" account. The law then intervenes, making labor in effect more expensive for all by requiring the superior conveniences or by compelling employers' insurance against accidents to workmen or by enforcing outright a higher minimum wage. The old basic labor cost becomes thus obsolete. And without prejudging as to the expediency of such legislation in particular industrial or business situations may we not protest against *a priori* and wholesale condemnation of such legislation as merely irresponsibly "ethical" and "unscientific"? Is it not, rather, economically experimental and constructive, amounting in substance to a simple insistence that henceforth the hiring and paying of labor shall express a wider range of social interests—shall signalize a more clearly self-validating level of comprehension, on the part of employers and consumers, of the social significance of industry than the old? And may we not protest also, as a matter of sheer logic, against carrying over a *producer's* distinction of accounting between "labor" cost and "welfare" cost into the *consumer's* valuation of the article? How and to what end shall a distinction be drawn between *his* "esteem" for the trimmed and isolated article and *his* esteem for the men who made it—which, taken together, dispose him to pay a certain undivided price for it?

For the egoism of men is no fixed and unalterable fact. Taking it as a postulate, a mathematical theory of market phenomena may be erected upon it, but such a postulate is purely formal, taking no note of the reasons which at any given time lie behind the individuals' "demand" or "supply schedules." It amounts simply to an assumption that these schedules will not change during the lapse of time contemplated in the problem in hand. And it therefore cannot serve as the basis for a social science. As an actual social phenomenon egoism is merely a disclosure of a certain present narrowness and inertness in the nature of the individual which may or may not be definitive for him. It is precisely on a par with anemia, dyspepsia or fatigue, or any other like unhappy fact of personal biography.

§ 16. There is another suggestion of ethical and economic continuity that may be briefly indicated. If our view of this relation is correct, a problem, by becoming economic, may lose something in dramatic interest and grandiosity but gains in precision and complexity. In the economic phase an issue becomes sensibly crucial. It is in this phase that are chiefly developed those qualities of clear-headedness, temperateness of thought and action, and well-founded self-reliance that are the foundation of all genuine personal morality and social effectiveness. And one may question therefore the ethical consequences of such measures as old age, sickness, and industrial accident insurance or insurance against unemployment. In proportion as these measures are effective they amount to a constant virtual addition to the individual's income from year to year without corresponding effort and forethought on his part. They may accordingly be condemned as systematic pauperization—the "endowment of the unfit." There is evidently a fundamental problem here at issue, apart from all administrative difficulties. Clearly this type of criticism assumes a permanent incapacity in "human nature" or in most actual beings therewith endowed, to recognize as seriously important other interests than those upon which hinge physical life and death. The ordinary man, it is believed, is held back from moral Quixotism as from material extravagance by the fear of starvation alone; and it is assumed that there are no other interests in the "normal" man that can or ever will be so wholesomely effective to these ends. And two remarks in answer appear not without a measure of pertinence. First, if what is alleged be true (and there is evidence in Malthus' *Essay* and elsewhere to support it) it seems less a proof of original sin and "inperfectibility" than a reproach to a social order whose collective tenor and institutions leave the mass untouched and unawakened above the level of animal reproduction and whose inequalities of opportunity prevent awakened life from growing strong. And second, the democratic society of the future, if it exempts the individual in part or wholly from the dread of premature physical extinction must leave him on higher levels of interest similarly dependent for success or failure upon his ultimate personal discretion. And is it inconceivable that on higher levels there should ever genuinely be such a persisting type of issue for the multitude of men?58

§ 17. We have held constructive comparison in its economic phase to be a reciprocal evaluating of the "salient members" of two budgets. The respective budgets in such a case express in the outcome (I) the plane of life to which one is to move and (2) the plane one is forsaking. It was the salient member of the former that presented the problem at the outset. In the course of the process its associates were *gathered about* it in their due proportions and perspective. The salient member of the latter (i.e., whatever the purchase is to oblige one to do without), it was the business of constructive comparison to *single out* from among its associates and designate for sacrifice. In any case at all departing from the type of substitution pure and simple, the commodities sacrificed will come to have a certain "value in exchange" that clearly is a new fact, a new judgment, in experience. This value in exchange, this "subjective" or "personal" exchange value, may fittingly be termed a "value for transition." The transition once made, the exchange once concluded, I shall deem the motor-car, for example, that I have *not* bought to replace one used-up, to be worth less than the piano I *have* bought instead. This indeed (in no disparaging sense) is a tautology. But does this lesser relative value equal or exceed or fall short of the value the car would have had if no question of a piano had been raised at all and I had bought it in replacement of the old one as a matter of course? How can one say? The question seems unmeaning, for the levels of value referred to are different and discontinuous and the magnitudes belong to different orders.

In a word, because a "value for transition" marks a resolve and succinctly describes an act, it cannot be broken in two and expressed as an equating of two magnitudes independently definable apart from the relation. The motor-car *had* its value as a member of the old system—the piano *has* its value as a member of the new. "The piano is worth more than the car"; "the car is worth less than the piano"—these are the prospective and retrospective views across a gulf that separates two "specious presents," not judgments of static inequality in terms of a common measure.

Is value, then, absolute or relative? Is value or price the prior notion? Was the classical English economics superficial in its predilection for the relative conception of value? Or is the reigning Austrian economics profound in its reliance upon marginal utility? By way of answer let us ask—What in our world can be more absolute a fact than a man's transition from one level of experience and action to another? Can the flight of time be stayed or turned backward? And if not can the acts by whose intrinsic uniqueness and successiveness time becomes filled for me and by which I feel time's sensible passage as swift or slow, lose their individuality? But it is not by a mere empiric temporalism alone that the sufficient absoluteness of the present act is attested. My transition from phase to phase of "finitude" is a thing so absolute that Idealism itself has deemed an Absolute indispensable to assure its safe and sane achievement. And with all Idealism's distrust of immediate experience for every evidential use, the Idealist does not scruple to cite the "higher obviousness" of personal effort, attainment, and fruition as the best of evidence for his most momentous truth of all.[59] And accordingly (in sharp descent) we need not hesitate to regard value in exchange as a primary fact in its own right, standing in no need of resolution into marginal pseudo-absolutes. A price agreed to and paid marks a real transition to another level. There are both marginal valuation and *Werthaltung* on this level, but they are subordinate incidents to this level's mapping and the conservation of its resources. On this level every marginal utility is relative, as we have seen, to every other through their common relation to the complex plan of organization as a whole.60

§ 18. In conclusion one more question closely related to the foregoing may be briefly touched upon. We have held that the individual's attitude toward a commodity is in the first instance one of putting a price-estimate upon it and only secondarily that of holding it in a provisionally settled marginal esteem. If this principle of the priority of price-estimation or exchange value is true, it seems evident that there can be no line of demarcation drawn (except for doubtfully expedient pedagogical purposes) between (1) "Subjective valuations" with which individuals are conceived to come to a market and (2) a mechanical equilibration of demand and supply which it is the distinctive and sole function of market concourse to effect. In such a view the market process in strict logic must be timeless as it is spaceless; a superposition of the two curves is effected and they are seen to cross in a common point which their shapes geometrically predetermine. Discussion, in any proper sense, can be no inherent part of a market process thus conceived. Once in the market, buyers and sellers can only declare their "subjective exchange valuations" of the commodity and await the outcome with a dispassionate certainty that whoever may gain by exchanging at the price to be determined, those who cannot exchange will at all events not lose. But considered as a typical likeness of men who have seen a thing they want and are seeking to possess it, this picture of mingled hope and resignation is not convincing. Most actual offering of goods for sale that one observes suggests less the dispassionate manner of the physiologist or psychologist taking the measure of his subject's reactions, sensibilities, and preferences than the more masterful procedure of the physician or the hypnotist who seeks to uproot or modify or reconstruct them. This is the process known in economic writing since Adam Smith as "the higgling and bargaining of the market."

In fact, the individual's ante-market valuation, when there temporarily is one, is an exchange valuation of the constructive or experimental and therefore (in any significant sense of the word) perfectly objective type, and the market process into which this enters is only a perfectly homogeneous temporal continuation of it that carries the individual forward to decisive action. There is no more reason for a separation here than for sundering the ante-experimental sketching out of an hypothesis in any branch of research from the work of putting the hypothesis to experimental test. The results of experiment may serve in a marked way in both sorts of process to elucidate or reconstruct the hypothesis.

The "higgling and bargaining of the market" has been accorded but scant attention by economists. It has apparently been regarded as a kind of irrelevance—a comedy part, at best, in the serious drama of industry and trade, never for a moment hindering the significant movement and outcome of the major action. As if to excuse the incompetence of this treatment (or as another phase of it) theory has tended to lay stress upon, and mildly to deplore, certain of the less amiable and engaging aspects of the process. The very term indeed as used by Adam Smith, imported a certain æsthetic disesteem, albeit tempered with indulgent approbation on other grounds. In Böhm-Bawerk's more modern account this approbation has given place to a neutral tolerance. A certain buyer, he says (in his discussion of simple "isolated" exchange), will give as much as thirty pounds for a horse; the horse's owner will take as little as ten pounds—these are predetermined and fixed valuations brought to the exchange negotiations and nothing that happens in the game of wits is conceived to modify them. The price will then be fixed somewhere between these limits. But how? "Here ..." we read, "is room for any amount of 'higgling.' According as in the conduct of the transaction the buyer or the seller shows the greater dexterity, cunning, obstinacy, power-of-persuasion, or such like, will the price be forced either to its lower or to its upper limit."61 But the higgling cannot touch the underlying attitudes. Even "power of persuasion" is only one part of "skill in bargaining," with all the rest and like all the rest; if it were more than this there would be for Böhm-Bawerk no theoretically grounded price limits to define the range of accidental settlement and the whole explanation, as a theory of price, would reduce to nullity.62

With this, then, appears to fall away all ground for a one-sided, or even a sharply two-sided, conception of the process of fixation of market-values. A "marginal utility" theory and a "cost of production" theory of market price alike assume that the factor chosen as the ultimate determinant is a fixed fact defined by conditions which the actual spatial and temporal meeting-together of buyers and sellers in the market cannot affect. In this logical sense, the chosen determinant is in each case an ante-market or extra-market fact and the same is true of the blades of Marshall's famous pair of scissors.

The price of a certain article let us say is $5. According to the current type of analysis this is the price because, intending buyers' and sellers' valuations of the article being just what they are, it is at this figure that the largest number of exchanges can occur. Were the price higher there would be more persons willing to sell than to buy; were it lower there would be more persons willing to buy than to sell. At $5 no buyer or seller who means what he says about his valuation when he enters the market goes away disappointed or dissatisfied. With this price established all sellers whose costs of production prevent their conforming to it must drop out of the market; so must all buyers whose desire for the article does not warrant their paying so much. More fundamentally then, Why is $5 the price? Is it because intending buyers and the marginal buyer in particular do not desire the article more strongly? Or is it because conditions of production, all things considered, do not permit a lower marginal unit cost? The argument might seem hopeless. But the advantage is claimed for the principle of demand. Without demand arising out of desires expressive of wants there would simply *be* no value, no production, and no price. Demand evokes production and sanctions cost. But cost expended can give no value to a product that no one wants.

Does it follow, however, that the cost of a commodity in which on its general merits I have come to take a hypothetical interest can in no wise affect my actual price-offer for it? Can it contribute nothing to the preciser definition of my interest which is eventually to be expressed in a price offer? If the answer is "No, for how can this external fact affect the strength of your desire for the object?"—then the reason given begs the question at issue. *Is* my interest in the object an interest in the object alone? And *is* the cost of the object a fact for me external and indifferent? It is, at all events, not uncommon to be assured that an article "cannot be produced for less," that one or another of its elements of cost is higher than would be natural to suppose. Not always scientifically accurate, such assurances express an evident confidence that they will not be without effect upon a hesitant but fair-minded purchaser. And in other ways as well, the position of sellers in the market is not so defenseless as a strict utility theory of price conceives—apart from the standpoint of an abstract "normality" that can never contrive to get itself realized in empirical fact.63 It is true that, in general, one tends to purchase an article of a given familiar kind where its price, all things considered, is lowest. In consequence the less "capable" producers or sellers must go to the wall. But the fact seems mainly "regulative" and of subordinate importance. Is it equally certain that as between branches of expenditure, such as clothing, food, and shelter, children, books, and "social" intercourse, the shares of income we expend upon them or the marginal prices we are content to pay express the original strength of separate and unmodified extra-market interests? On the contrary we have paid in the past what we have had to pay, what we have deemed just and reasonable, what we have been willing experimentally to hazard upon the possibility of the outlay's proving to have been worth while. In these twilight-zones of indetermination, cost as well as other factors of supply have had their opportunity. Shall we nevertheless insist that our "demands" are *ideally* fixed, even though in fallible human fact they are more or less indistinct, yielding and modifiable? On the contrary they are "in principle and for the most part" indeterminate and expectant of suggested experimental shaping from the supply side of the market. It is less in theory than in fact that they have a salutary tendency (none too dependable) toward rigidity.

CONCLUSION

§ 19. The argument may now be summarily reviewed.

I. How are we to understand the acquisition, by an individual, of what are called new economic needs and interests? Except by a fairly obvious fallacy of retrospection we cannot regard this phenomenon as a mere arousal of so-called latent or implicit desires. New products and new means of production afford "satisfactions" and bring about objective results which are unimaginable and therefore unpredictable, in any descriptive fashion, in advance. In a realistic or empirical view of the matter, these constitute genuinely new developments of personality and of social function, not mere unfoldings of a preformed logical or vital system. "Human nature" is modifiable and economic choice and action are factors in this indivisible process (§§ 2-4). Now "logically" it would seem clear that unless a new commodity is an object of desire it will not be made or paid for. On the other hand, with equal "logic," a *new* commodity, it would seem, *cannot* be an object of desire because all desire must be for what we already know. We seem confronted with a complete *impasse* (§ 5). But the *impasse* is conceptual only. We have simply to acknowledge the patent fact of our recognition of the new as novel and our interest in the new in its outstanding character of novelty. We need only express and interpret this fact, instead of fancying ourselves bound to explain it away. It is an interest not less genuine and significant in economic experience than elsewhere (§§ 6, 7). Its importance lies in the fact that it obliges us to regard what is called economic choice not as a balancing of utilities, marginal or otherwise, but as a process of "constructive comparison." The new commodity and its purchase price are in reality symbols for alternatively possible systems of life and action. Can the old be relinquished for the new? Before this question is answered each system may be criticized and interpreted from the standpoint of the other, each may be supplemented by suggestion, by dictate of tradition and by impulsive prompting, by inference, and by conjecture. Finally in experimental fashion an election must be made. The system as accepted may or may not be, in terms, identical with one of the initial alternatives; it can never be identical in full meaning and perspective with either one. And in the end we have not chosen the new because its value, as seen beforehand, measured more than the value of the old, but we now declare the old, seen in retrospect, to have been worth less (§§ 8-12). There are apparently no valid objections to this view to be drawn from the current logical type of marginal-utility analysis (§ 13).

II. Because so-called economic "choice" is in reality "constructive comparison" it must be regarded as essentially ethical in import. Ethics and economic theory, instead of dealing with separate problems of conduct, deal with distinguishable but inseparable stages belonging to the complete analysis of most, if not all, problems (§ 14). This view suggests, (*a*) that no reasons in experience or in logic exist for identifying the economic interest with an attitude of exclusive or particularistic egoism (§ 15), and (*b*) that social reformers are justified in their assumption of a certain "perfectibility" in human nature—a constructive responsiveness instead of an insensate and stubborn inertia (§ 16). Again, in the process of constructive comparison in its economic phase, Price or Exchange Value is, in apparent accord with the English classical tradition, the fundamental working conception. Value as "absolute" is essentially a subordinate and "conservative" conception, belonging to a status of system and routine, and is "absolute" in a purely functional sense (§ 17). And finally constructive comparison, with price or exchange value as its dominant conception, is clearly nothing if not a market process. In the nature of the case, then, there can be no such ante-market definiteness and rigidity of demand schedules as a strictly marginal-utility theory of market prices logically must require (§ 18).

§ 20. In at least two respects the argument falls short of what might be desired. No account is given of the actual procedure of constructive comparison and nothing like a complete survey of the leading ideas and problems of economic theory is undertaken by way of verification. But to have supplied the former in any satisfactory way would have required an unduly extended discussion of the more general, or ethical, phases of constructive comparison. The other deficiency is less regrettable, since the task in question is one that could only be hopefully undertaken and convincingly carried through by a professional economist.

For the present purpose, it is perhaps enough to have found in our economic experience and behavior the same interest in novelty that is so manifest in other departments of life, and the same attainment of new self-validating levels of power and interest, through the acquisition and exploitation of the novel. In our economic experience, no more than elsewhere, is satisfaction an ultimate and self-explanatory term. Satisfaction carries with it always a reference to the level of power and interest that makes it possible and on which it must be measured. To seek satisfaction for its own sake or to hinge one's interest in science or art upon their ability to serve the palpable needs of the present moment— these, together, make up the meaning of what is called Utilitarianism. And Utilitarianism in this sense (which is far less what Mill meant by the term than a tradition he could never, with all his striving, quite get free of), this type of Utilitarianism spells routine. It is the surrender of initiative and control, in the quest for ends in life, for a philistine pleased acceptance of the ends that Nature, assisted by the advertisement-writers, sets before us. But this type of Utilitarianism is less frequent in actual occurrence than its vogue in popular literature and elsewhere may appear to indicate. As a matter of fact, we more often look to satisfaction, not as an end of effort or a condition to be preserved, but as the evidence that an experimental venture has been justified in its event. And this is a widely different matter, for in this there is no inherent implication of a habit-bound or egoistic narrowness of interest in the conceiving or the launching of the venture.

The economic interest, as a function of intelligence, finds its proper expression in a valuation set upon one thing in terms of another—a valuation that is either a step in a settled plan of spending and consumption or marks the passing of an old plan and our embarkation on a new. From such a view it must follow that the economic betterment of an individual or a society can consist neither in the accumulation of material wealth alone nor in a more diversified technical knowledge and skill. For the individual or for a collectivist state there must be added to these things alertness and imagination in the personal quest and discovery of values and a broad and critical intelligence in making the actual trial of them. Without a commensurate gain in these qualities it will avail little to make technical training and industrial opportunity more free or even to make the rewards of effort more equitable and secure. But it has been one of the purposes of this discussion to suggest that just this growth in outlook and intelligence may in the long run be counted on—not indeed as a direct and simple consequence of increasing material abundance but as an expression of an inherent creativeness in man that responds to discipline and education and will not fail to recognize the opportunity it seeks.

Real economic progress is ethical in aim and outcome. We cannot think of the economic interest as restricted in its exercise to a certain sphere or level of effort—such as "the ordinary business of life" or the gaining of a "livelihood" or the satisfaction of our so-called "material" wants, or the pursuit of an enlightened, or an unenlightened, self-regard. Economics has no special relation to "material" or even to commonplace ends. Its materialism lies not in its aim and tendency but in its problem and method. It has no bias toward a lower order of mundane values. It only takes note of the ways and degrees of dependence upon mundane resources and conditions that values of every order must acknowledge. It reminds us that morality and culture, if they are genuine, must know not only what they intend but what they cost. They must understand not only the direct but the indirect and accidental bearing of their purposes upon all of our interests, private and social, that they are likely to affect. The detachment of the economic interest from any particular level or class of values is only the obverse aspect of the special kind of concern it has with values of every sort. The very generality of the economic interest, and the abstractness of the ideas by which it maintains routine or safeguards change in our experience, are what make it unmistakably ethical. Without specific ends of its own, it affords no ground for dogmatism or apologetics. And this indicates as the appropriate task of economic theory not the arrest and thwarting but the steadying and shaping of social change.

THE MORAL LIFE AND THE CONSTRUCTION OF VALUES AND STANDARDS[64]

JAMES HAYDEN TUFTS

Writing about ethics has tended to take one of two directions. On the one hand we have description of conduct in terms of psychology, or anthropology. On the other a study of the concepts right and wrong, good and bad, duty and freedom. If we follow the first line we may attempt to explain conduct psychologically by showing the simple ideas or feelings and the causal connections or laws of habit and association out of which actions arise. Or anthropologically we may show the successive stages of custom and taboo, or the family, religious, political, legal, and social institutions from which morality has emerged. But we meet at once a difficulty if we ask what is the bearing of this description and analysis. Will it aid me in the practical judgment "What shall I do?" In physics there is no corresponding difficulty. To analyze gravity enables us to compute an orbit, or aim a gun; to analyze electric action is to have the basis for lighting streets and carrying messages. It assumes the uniformity of nature and takes no responsibility as to whether we shall aim guns or whether our messages shall be of war or of peace. Whereas in ethics it is claimed that the elements are so changed by their combination—that the *process* is so essential a factor—that no prediction is certain. And it is also claimed that the ends themselves are perhaps to be changed as well as the means. Stated otherwise, suppose that mankind has passed through various stages, can mere observation of these tell me what next? Perhaps I don't care to repeat the past; how can I plan for a better future? Or grant that I may discover instinct and emotion, habit and association in my thinking and willing, how will this guide me to direct my thinking and willing to right ends?

The second method has tended to examine concepts. Good is an eternal, changeless pattern; it is to be discovered by a vision; or right and good are but other terms for nature's or reason's universal laws which are timeless and wholly unaffected by human desires or passions; moral nature is soul, and soul is created not built up of elements,—such were some of the older absolutisms. Right and good are unique concepts not to be resolved or explained in terms of anything else,—this is a more modern thesis which on the face of it may appear to discourage analysis. The ethical world is a world of "eternal values." Philosophy "by taking part in empirical questions sinks both itself and them." These doctrines bring high claims, but are they more valuable for human guidance than the empirical method?65

"The knowledge that is superhuman only is ridiculous in man." No man can ever find his way home with the pure circle unless he has also the art of the impure. It is the conviction of this paper that in ethics, as in knowledge, thoughts without contents are empty; percepts without concepts are blind. Description of what has been—empiricism—is futile in itself to project and criticize. Intuitions and deductions a priori are empty. The "thoughts" of ethics are of course the terms right, good, ought, worth, and their kin. The "percepts" are the instincts and emotions, the desires and aspirations, the conditions of time and place, of nature, and institutions.

Yet it is misleading to say that in studying the history of morals we are merely empiricists, and can hope to find no criterion. This would be the case if we were studying non-moral beings. But moral beings have to some degree guided life by judgments and not merely followed impulse or habit. Early judgments as to taboos, customs, and conduct may be crude and in need of correction; they are none the less judgments. Over and over we find them reshaped to meet change from hunting to agriculture, from want to plenty, from war to peace, from small to large groupings. Much more clearly when we consider civilized peoples, the interaction between reflection and impulse becomes patent. To study this interaction can be regarded as futile for the future only if we discredit all past moral achievement.

Those writers who have based their ethics upon concepts have frequently expressed the conviction that the security of morality depends upon the question whether good and right are absolute and eternal essences independent of human opinion or volition. A different source of standards which to some offers more promise for the future is the fact of the moral life *as* a constant process of forming and reshaping ideals and of bringing these to bear upon conditions of existence. To construct a right and good is at least a process tending to responsibility, if this construction is to be for the real world in which we must live and not merely for a world of fancy or caprice. It is not the aim of this paper to give a comprehensive outline of ethical method. Four factors in the moral life will be pointed out and this analysis will be used to emphasize especially certain social and constructive aspects of our concepts of right and good.

I

The four factors which it is proposed to emphasize are these:

(1) Life as a biological process involving relation to nature, with all that this signifies in the equipment of instincts, emotions, and selective activity by which life maintains itself.

(2) Interrelation with other human beings, including on the one hand associating, grouping, mating, communicating, coöperating, commanding, obeying, worshiping, adjudicating, and on the psychological side the various instincts, emotions, susceptibilities to personal stimulation and appropriate responses in language and behavior which underlie or are evoked by the life in common.

(3) Intelligence and reason, through which experience is interrelated, viewed as a whole, enlarged in imagination.

(4) The process of judgment and choice, in which different elements are brought together, considered in one conscious universe, evaluated or measured, thereby giving rise reciprocally to

a self on the one hand and to approved or chosen objects on the other.

(I) Life. Life is at least the raw material of all values, even if it is not in itself entitled to be called good without qualification. For in the process of nourishing and protecting itself, the plant or animal selects and in the case of higher animals, manipulates; it adapts itself to nature and adapts nature to itself; it shows reciprocal relation of means to end, of whole to part. It foreshadows the conscious processes in so many ways that men have always been trying to read back some degree of consciousness. And life in the animal, at least, is regarded as having experiences of pleasure and pain, and emotions of fear, anger, shame, and sex, which are an inseparable aspect of values. If it is not the supreme or only good, if men freely sacrifice it for other ends, it is none the less an inevitable factor. Pessimistic theories indeed have contended that life is evil and have sought to place good in a will-less Nirvana. Yet such theories make limited appeal. Their protest is ultimately not against life as life but against life as painful. And their refutation is rather to be intrusted to the constructive possibilities of freer life than to an analysis of concepts.

Another class of theories which omit life from the good is that which holds to abstractly ontological concepts of good as an eternal essence or form. It must be remembered, however, that the idea of good was not merely a fixed essence. It was also for Plato the self-moving and the cause of all motion. And further, Plato evidently believed that life, the very nature of the soul, was itself in the class of supreme values along with God and the good. The prize of immortality was καλόν and the hope great. And with Aristotle and his followers the good of contemplation no less truly than the good of action had elements of value derived from the vital process. Such a mystic as Spinoza, who finds good in the understanding values this because in it man is "active," and would unite himself with the All because in God is Power and Freedom. The Hebrew prophet found a word capable of evoking great ethical values when he urged his countrymen to "choose life," and

Christian teaching found in the conception of "eternal life" an ideal of profound appeal. It is not surprising that with his biological interests Spencer should have set up life of greatest length and breadth as a goal.

The struggle of the present war emphasizes tremendously two aspects of this factor of life. National life is an ideal which gets its emotional backing largely from the imagery of our physical life. For any one of the small nations involved to give up its national life—whatever the possibilities of better organized industry or more comfortable material conditions—seems to it a desperate alternative. Self-defense is regarded by the various powers at war as a complete justification not merely for armed resistance or attack but for ruthless acts. And if we are tempted to say that the war involves a prodigal waste of individual life on a scale never known before, we are at the same time compelled to recognize that never before has the bare destruction of life aroused such horror.

For never before has peace set its forces so determinedly to protect life. The span of human life has been lengthened: the wastefulness of accident and disease has been magnified. The dumb acquiescence with which former generations accepted the death of infants and children and those in the prime of life has given way to active and increasingly successful efforts to preserve. The enormous increase in scientific study of biology, including eugenics, reflects not only an advance of science but a trend in morality. It is scarcely conceivable that it should grow less in absolute importance, whatever crises may temporarily cause its depreciation relatively to other values.

One exception to the growing appreciation calls for notice—the interest in immortality appears to be less rather than greater. The strong belief in life beyond the grave which since the days of ancient Egypt has prevailed in the main stream of Western culture seems not only to be affected by the scientific temper of the day, but also to be subject to a shift in interest. This may be in part a reaction from other-worldliness. In part it may be due to loss of fervor for a theological picture of a future heaven of a rather monotonous sort and may signify not so much loss of interest in life as desire for a more vital kind of continuance. It is not true that all that a man hath will he give for his life, yet it is true that no valuing process is intelligible that leaves out life with its impulses, emotions, and desires as the first factor to be reckoned with.

(2) The second factor is the life in common, with its system of relations, and its corresponding instincts, emotions, and desires.

So much has been written in recent years on the social nature of man that it seems unnecessary to elaborate the obvious. Protest has even been raised against the exaggeration of the social. But I believe that in certain points at least we have not yet penetrated to the heart of the social factor, and its significance for morals.

So far as the moral aspect is concerned I know nothing more significant than the attitude of the Common Law as set forth by Professor Pound.66 This has sought to base its system of duties on relations. The relation which was prominent in the Middle Ages was that of landlord and tenant; other relations are those of principal and agent, of trustee, etc. An older relation was that of kinship. The kin was held for the wergeld; the goël must avenge his next of kin; the father must provide for prospective parents-in-law; the child must serve the parents. Duty was the legal term for the relation. In all this there is no romanticism, no exaggeration of the social; there is a fair statement of the facts which men have recognized and acted upon the world over and in all times. Individualistic times or peoples have modified certain phases. The Roman law sought to ground many of its duties in the contract, the will of the parties. But covenants by no means exhaust duties. And according to Professor Pound the whole course of English and American law today is belying the generalization of Sir Henry Maine, that the evolution of law is a progress from status to contract. We are shaping law of insurance, of public service companies, not by contract but by the relation of insurer and insured, of public utility and patron.

Psychologically, the correlate of the system of relations is the set of instincts and emotions, of capacity for stimulation and response, which presuppose society for their exercise and in turn make society possible. There can be no question as to the reality and strength of these in both animals and men. The bear will fight for her young more savagely than for her life. The human mother's thoughts center far more intensely upon her offspring than upon her own person. The man who is cut dead by all his acquaintance suffers more than he would from hunger or physical fear. The passion of sex frequently overmasters every instinct of individual prudence. The majority of men face poverty and live in want; relatively few prefer physical comfort to family ties. Aristotle's φιλία is the oftenest quoted recognition of the emotional basis of common life, but a statement of Kant's earlier years is particularly happy. "The point to which the lines of direction of our impulses converge is thus not only in ourselves, but there are besides powers moving us in the will of others outside of ourselves. Hence arise the moral impulses which often carry us away to the discomfiture of selfishness, the strong law of duty, and the weaker of benevolence. Both of these wring from us many a sacrifice, and although selfish inclinations now and then preponderate over both, these still never fail to assert their reality in human nature. Thus we recognize that in our most secret motives, we are dependent upon the rule of the general will."[67]

The "law of duty," and I believe we may add, the conception of right, do arise objectively in the social relations as the common law assumes and subjectively in the social instincts, emotions, and the more intimate social consciousness which had not been worked out in the time of Kant as it has been by recent authors. This point will receive further treatment later, but I desire to point out in anticipation that if right and duty have their origin in this social factor there is at least a presumption against their being subordinate ethically to the conception of good as we find them in certain writers. If they have independent origin and are the outgrowth of a special aspect of life it is at least probable that they are not to be subordinated to the good unless the very notion of good is itself reciprocally modified by right in a way that is not usually recognized in teleological systems.

(3) Intelligence and reason imply (*a*) considering the proposed act or the actually performed act as a whole and in its relations. Especially they mean considering consequences. In order to foresee consequences there is required not only empirical observation of past experience, not only deduction from already formulated concepts—as when we say that injustice will cause hard feelings and revolt—but that rarer quality which in the presence of a situation discerns a meaning not obvious, suggests an idea, "injustice," to interpret the situation. Situations are neither already labeled "unjust," nor are they obviously unjust to the ordinary mind. Analysis into elements and rearrangement of the elements into a new synthesis are required. This is eminently a synthetic or "creative" activity. Further it is evident that the activity of intelligence in considering consequences implies not only what we call reasoning in the narrower sense but imagination and feeling. For the consequences of an act which are of importance ethically are consequences which are not merely to be described but are to be imagined so vividly as to be felt, whether they are consequences that affect ourselves or affect others.

(*b*) But it would be a very narrow intelligence that should attempt to consider only consequences of a single proposed act without considering also other possible acts and their consequences. The second important characteristic of intelligence is that it considers either other means of reaching a given end, or other ends, and by working out the consequences of these also has the basis for deliberation and choice. The method of "multiple working hypotheses," urged as highly important in scientific investigation, is no less essential in the moral field. To bring several ends into the field of consideration is the characteristic of the intelligent, or as we often say, the open-minded man. Such consideration as this widens the capacity of the agent and marks him off from the creature of habit, of prejudice, or of instinct.

(*c*) Intelligence implies considering in two senses all persons involved, that is, it means taking into account not only how an act will affect others but also how others look at it. It is scarcely necessary to say that this activity of intelligence cannot be cut off from its roots in social intercourse. It is by the processes of give and take, of stimulus and response, in a social medium that this possibility of looking at things from a different angle is secured. And once more this different angle is not gained by what in the strict sense could be called a purely intellectual operation, although it has come to be so well recognized as the necessary equipment for dealing successfully with conditions that we commonly characterize the person as stupid who does not take account of what others think and feel and how they will react to a projected line of conduct. This social element in intelligence is to a considerable degree implied in the term "reasonable," which signifies not merely that a man is logical in his processes but also that he is ready to listen to what others say and to look at things from their point of view whether he finally accepts it or not.

The broad grounds on which it is better to use the word intelligence than the word reason in the analysis with which we are concerned are two. (I) It is not a question-begging term which tends to commit us at the outset to a specific doctrine as to the source of our judgments. (2) The activity of intelligence which is now most significant for ethical progress is not suggested by the term reason, for unless we arbitrarily smuggle in under the term practical reason the whole activity of the moral consciousness without inquiry as to the propriety of the name we shall be likely to omit the constructive and creative efforts to promote morality by positive supplying of enlarged education, new sources of interest, and more open fields for development, by replacing haunting fears of misery with positive hopes, and by suggesting new imagery, new ambitions in the place of sodden indifference or sensuality. The term reason as used by the Stoics and by Kant meant control of the passions by some "law"—some authority cosmic or logical. It prepared for the inevitable; it forbade the private point of view. But as thus presenting a negative aspect the law was long ago characterized by a profound moral genius as "weak." It has its value as a schoolmaster, but it is not in itself capable of supplying the new life which dissolves the old sentiment, breaks up the settled evil habit, and supplies both larger ends and effective motives.

If we state human progress in objective fashion we may say that although men today are still as in earlier times engaged in getting a living, in mating, in rearing of offspring, in fighting and adventure, in play, and in art, they are also engaged in science and invention, interested in the news of other human activities all over the world; they are adjusting differences by judicial processes, coöperating to promote general welfare, enjoying refined and more permanent friendships and affections, and viewing life in its tragedy and comedy with enhanced emotion a roader sympathy. Leaving out of consideration the work of the religious or artistic genius as not in question here, the great objective agencies in bringing about these changes have been on the one hand the growth of invention, scientific method, and education, and on the other the increase in human intercourse and communication. Reason plays its part in both of these in freeing the mind from wasteful superstitious methods and in analyzing situations and testing hypotheses, but the term is inadequate to do justice to that creative element in the formation of hypotheses which finds the new, and it tends to leave out of account the social point of view involved in the widening of the area of human intercourse. More will be said upon this point in connection with the discussion of rationalism.

(4) The process of judgment and choice. The elements are not the sum. The moral consciousness is not just the urge of life, plus the social relations, plus intelligence. The *process* of moral deliberation, evaluation, judgment, and choice is itself essential. In this process are born the concepts and standards good and right, and likewise the moral self which utters the judgment. It is in this twofold respect synthetic, creative. It is as an interpretation of this process that the concept of freedom arises. Four aspects of the process may be noted.

(*a*) The process involves holding possibilities of action, or objects for valuation, or ends for choice, in consciousness and measuring them one against another in a simultaneous field—or in a field of alternating objects, any of which can be continually recalled. One possibility after another may be tried out in anticipation and its relations successively considered, but the comparison is essential to the complete moral consciousness.

(*b*) The process yields a universe of valued *objects* as distinguished from a subjective consciousness of desires and feelings. We say, "This is right," "That is good." Every "is" in such judgments may be denied by an "is not" and we hold one alternative to be true, the other false. As the market or the stock exchange or board of trade fixes values by a meeting of buyers and sellers and settles the price of wheat accurately enough to enable farmers to decide how much land to seed for the next season, so the world of men and women who must live together and coöperate, or fight and perish, forces upon consciousness the necessity of adjustment. The preliminary approaches are usually hesitant and subjective—like the offers or bids in the market—e.g., "I should like to go to college; I believe that is a good thing"; "My parents need my help; it does not seem right to leave them." The judgments finally emerge. "A college education is good;" "It is wrong to leave my parents"—both seemingly objective yet conflicting, and unless I can secure both I must seemingly forego actual objective good, or commit actual wrong.

(*c*) The process may be described also as one of "universalizing" the judging consciousness. For it is a counterpart of the objective implication of a judgment that it is not an affirmation as to any individual's opinion. This negative characterization of the judgment is commonly converted into the positive doctrine that any one who is unprejudiced and equally well informed would make the same judgment. Strictly speaking the judgment itself represents in its completed form the elimination of the private attitude rather than the express inclusion of other judges. But in the making of the judgment it is probable that this elimination of the private is reached by a mental reference to other persons and their attitudes, if not by an actual conversation with another. It is dubious whether an individual that had never communicated with another would get the distinction between a private subjective attitude and the "general" or objective.

Moreover, one form of the moral judgment: "This is right," speaks the language of law—of the collective judgment, or of the judge who hears both sides but is neither. This generalizing or universalizing is frequently supposed to be the characteristic activity of "reason." I believe that a comparison with the kindred value judgments in economics supports the doctrine that in judgments as to the good as well as in those as to right, there is no product of any simple faculty, but rather a synthetic process in which the social factor is prominent. A compelling motive toward an objective and universal judgment is found in the practical conditions of moral judgments. Unless men agree on such fundamental things as killing, stealing, and sex relations they cannot get on together. Not that when I say, "Killing is wrong," I mean to affirm "I agree with you in objecting to it"; but that the necessity (a) of acting as if I either do or do not approve it, and (b) of either making my attitude agree with yours, or yours agree with mine, or of fighting it out with you or with the whole force of organized society, compels me to put my attitude into objective terms, to meet you and society on a common platform. This is a *synthesis*, an achievement. To attribute the synthesis to any faculty of "practical reason," adds nothing to our information, but tends rather to obscure the facts.

(*d*) The process is thus a reciprocal process of valuing objects and of constructing and reconstructing a self. The object as first imaged or anticipated undergoes enlargement and change as it is put into relations to other objects and as the consequences of adoption or rejection are tried in anticipation. The self by reflecting and by enlarging its scope is similarly enlarged. It is the *resulting* self which is the final valuer. The values of most objects are at first fixed for us by instinct or they are suggested by the ethos and mores of our groups—family, society, national religions, and "reign under the appearance of habitual self-suggested tendencies." The self is constituted accordingly.

Collisions with other selves, conflicts between group valuations and standards and individual impulses or desires, failure of old standards as applied to new situations, bring about a more conscious definition of purposes. The agent identifies himself with these purposes, and values objects with reference to them. In this process of revaluing and defining, of comparing and anticipation, freedom is found if anywhere. For if the process is a real one the elements do not remain unaffected by their relation to each other and to the whole. The act is not determined by any single antecedent or by the sum of antecedents. It is determined by the process. The self is not made wholly by heredity, or environment. *It is itself creating for each of its elements a new environment*, viz., the process of reflection and choice. And if man can change the heredity of pigeons and race horses by suitable selection, if every scientific experiment is a varying of conditions, it is at least plausible that man can guide his own acts by intelligence, and revise his values by criticism.

The self is itself creating for each of its elements a new environment—this is a fact which if kept in mind will enable us to see the abstractness and fallacies not merely of libertarianism and determinism, but of subjectivism and objectivism. Subjective or "inward" theories have sought standards in the self; but in regarding the self as an entity independent of such a process as we have described they have exposed themselves to the criticism of providing only private, variable, accidental, unauthoritative sources of standards—instincts, or emotions, or intuitions. The self of the full moral consciousness, however,—the only one which can claim acceptance or authority—is born only in the process of considering real conditions, of weighing and choosing between alternatives of action in a real world of nature and persons. Its judgments are more than subjective. Objectivism in its absolutist and abstract forms assumes a standard—nature, essence, law—independent of process. Such a standard is easily shown to be free from anything individual, private, or changing. It is universal, consistent, and eternal, in fact it has many good mathematical characteristics, but unfortunately it is not moral. As mathematical, logical, biological, or what not, it offers no standard that appeals to the moral nature as authoritative or that can help us to find our way home.

II

If we are dissatisfied with custom and habit and seek to take philosophy for the guide of life we have two possibilities: (1) we may look for the good, and treat right and duty as subordinate concepts which indicate the way to the good, that is, consider them as good as a means, or (2) we may seek first to do right irrespective of consequences, in the belief that in willing to do right we are already in possession of the highest good. In either case we may consider our standards and values either as in some sense fixed or as in the making.68 We may suppose that good is objective and absolute, that right is discovered by a rational faculty, or we may consider that in regarding good as objective we have not made it independent of the valuing process and that in treating right as a standard we have not thereby made it a fixed concept to be discovered by the pure intellect. The position of this paper will be (1) that good while objective is yet objective as a value and not as an essence or physical fact; (2) that a social factor in value throws light upon the relation between moral and other values; (3) that right is not merely a means to the good but has an independent place in the moral consciousness; (4) that right while signifying order does not necessarily involve a timeless, eternal order since it refers to an order of personal relations; (5) that the conception of right instead of being a matter for pure reason or even the "cognitive faculty" shows an intimate blending of the emotional and intellectual and that this appears particularly in the conception of the reasonable.

(1) We begin with the question of the synthetic and objective character of the good. With G. E. Moore as with the utilitarians the good is the ultimate concept. Right and duty are means to the good. Moore and Rashdall also follow Sidgwick in regarding good as unique, that is, as "synthetic." Sidgwick emphasized in this especially the point that moral value cannot be

decided by physical existence or the course of evolution, nor can the good be regarded as meaning the pleasant. Moore and Russell reinforce this. However true it may be that pleasure is one among other good things or that life is one among other good things, good does not mean either pleasure or survival. Good means just "good."

A similar thought underlies Croce's division of the Practical into the two spheres of the Economic and the Ethical. "The economic activity is that which wills and effects only what corresponds to the conditions of fact in which a man finds himself; the ethical activity is that which, although it correspond to these conditions, also refers to something that transcends them. To the first correspond what are called individual ends, to the second universal ends; the one gives rise to the judgment concerning the greater or less coherence of the action taken in itself, the other to that concerning its greater or less coherence in respect to the universal end, which transcends the individual.[69] Utilitarianism is according to Croce an attempt to reduce the Ethical to the Economic form, although the utilitarians as men attempt in various ways to make a place for that distinction which as philosophers they would suppress. "Man is not a consumer of pleasures. He is a creator of life." With this claim of the distinctive, synthetic, character of the moral consciousness and of the impossibility of testing the worth of ideals by cosmic laws, or by gratification of particular wants as measured by pleasure, I have no issue. The analysis of the moral judgment made above points out just how it is that good is synthetic. It is synthetic in that it represents a measuring and valuing of ends—instinctive and imagined, individual and social—against each other and as part of a whole to which a growing self corresponds. It is synthetic in that it represents not merely a process of evaluating ends which match actually defined desires, but also a process in which the growing self, dissatisfied with any ends already in view, gropes for some new definition of ends that shall better respond to its living, creative capacity, its active synthetic character. Good is the concept for just this valuing process as carried on by a conscious being that is not content to take its desire as ready made by its present construction, but is reaching out for ends that shall respond to a growing, expanding, inclusive, social, self. It expresses value *as* value.

Value *as value!* not as being; nor as independent essence; nor as anything static and fixed. For a synthetic self, a living personality, could find no supreme value in the complete absence of valuing, in the cessation of life, in the negation of that very activity of projection, adventure, construction, and synthesis in which it has struck out the concept good. A theory of ethics which upholds the synthetic character of the good may be criticized as being not synthetic enough if it fails to see that on the basis of the mutual determination of percepts and concepts, of self and objects, the synthetic character of the process must be reflected in the ultimate meaning of the category which symbolizes and incorporates the process.

(2) We may find some light upon the question how moral value gets its distinctive and unique character, and how it comes to be more "objective" than economic value if we consider some of the social factors in the moral judgment. For although the concept good is rooted in the life process with its selective activity and attending emotions it involves a subtle social element, as well as the more commonly recognized factors of intelligence.

Within the fundamental selective process two types of behavior tend to differentiate in response to two general sorts of stimulation. One sort is simpler, more monotonous, more easily analyzable. Response to such stimulation, or treatment of objects which may be described under these terms of simple, analyzable, etc., is easily organized into a habit. It calls for no great shifts in attention, no sudden readjustments. There is nothing mysterious about it. As satisfying various wants it has a certain kind of value. It, however, evokes no consciousness of self. Toward the more variable, complex sort of stimuli, greater attention, constant adjustment and readjustment, are necessary.

Objects of the first sort are treated as things, in the sense that they do not call out any respect from us or have any intrinsic value. We understand them through and through, manipulate them, consume them, throw them away. We regard them as valuable only with reference to our wants. On the other hand, objects of the second sort take their place in a bi-focal situation. Our attention shifts alternately to their behavior and to our response, or, conversely, from our act to their response. This back and forth movement of attention in the case of certain of these objects is reinforced by the fact that certain stimuli from them or from the organism, find peculiar responses already prepared in social instincts; gesture and language play their part. Such a bi-focal situation as this, when completely developed, involves persons. In its earlier stages it is the quasi-personal attitude which is found in certain savage religious attitudes, in certain æsthetic attitudes, and in the emotional attitudes which we all have toward many of the objects of daily life.

Economic values arise in connection with attitudes toward things. We buy things, we sell them. They have value just in that they gratify our wants, but they do not compel any revision or change in wants or in the self which wants. They represent a partial interest—or if they become the total interest we regard them as now in the moral sphere. Values of personal affection arise as we find a constant rapport in thought, feeling, purpose, between the two members of our social consciousness. The attitude is that of going along with another and thereby extending and enriching our experiences. We enter into his ideas, range with his imagination, kindle at his enthusiasms, sympathize with his joys or sorrows. We may disagree with our friend's opinions, but we do not maintain a critical attitude toward *him*, that is, toward his fundamental convictions and attitudes. If "home is the place where, when you have to go there, they have to take you in," as Frost puts it, a friend is one who, when you go to him, has to accept you.

Moral values also arise in a social or personal relation—not in relation to things. This is on the surface in the form of judgment; "He is a good man," "That is a good act." If it is less obvious in the practical judgment, "This is the better course of action," i.e., the course which leads to the greater good, or to the good, this is because we fail to discern that the good in these cases is a something with which I can identify myself, not a something which I merely possess and keep separate from my personality. It is something I shall be rather than have. Or if I speak of a share or participation it is a sharing in the sense of entering into a kindred life. It is an ideal, and an ideal for a conscious personal being can hardly be other than conscious. It may be objected that however personal the ideal it is not on this account necessarily social. It embodies what I would be, but does not necessarily imply response to any other personality. This, however, would be to overlook the analyses which recent psychology has made of the personal. The ideal does not develop in a vacuum. It implies for one thing individuality which is conceivable only as other individuals are distinguished. It implies the definition of purposes, and such definition is scarcely if ever attempted except as a possible world of purposes is envisaged.

Æsthetic valuation is in certain respects intermediate between the valuation of things on the one hand and the moral evaluation of acts of persons or conscious states on the other. Æsthetic objects are in many cases seemingly things and yet even as things they are quasi-personal; they are viewed with a certain sympathy quite different from that which we feel for a purely economic object. If it is a work of art the artist has embodied his thought and feeling and the observer finds it there. The experience is that of *Einfühlung*. Yet we do not expect the kind of response which we look for in friendship, nor do we take the object as merely a factor for the guidance or control of our own action as in the practical judgment of morality. The æsthetic becomes the object of contemplation, not of response; of embodied meaning, not of individuality. It is so far personal that no one of æsthetic sensibility likes to see a thing of beauty destroyed or mistreated. The situation in which we recognize in an object meaning and embodied feeling, or at least find sources of stimulation which appeal to our emotions, develops an æsthetic enhancement of conscious experience. The æsthetic value predicate is the outcome of this peculiar enhancement.

It seems that the social nature of the judgment plays a part also in the varying objectivity of values. It is undoubtedly true that some values are treated as belonging to objects. If we cannot explain this fully we may get some light upon the situation by noticing the degree to which this is true in the cases of the kinds of values already described.

Economic values are dubiously objective. We use both forms of expression. We say on the one hand, "I want wheat," "There is a demand for wheat," or, on the other, "Wheat is worth one dollar a bushel." Conversely, "There is no demand for the old-fashioned high-framed bicycle" or "It is worthless." The Middle Ages regarded economic value as completely objective. A thing had a *real value*. The retailer could not add to it. The mediæval economist believed in the externality of relations; he prosecuted for the offenses of forestalling and regrating the man who would make a profit by merely changing things in place. He condemned usury. We have definitely abandoned this theory. We recognize that it is the want which makes the value. To make exchange possible and socialize to some degree the scale of prices we depend upon a public market or a stock exchange.

In values of personal affection we may begin with a purely individual attitude, "I love or esteem my friend." If I put it more objectively I may say, "He is an honored and valued friend." Perhaps still more objectively, we—especially if we are feminine—may say "Is not X dear?" We may then go on to seek a social standard. We perhaps look for reinforcement in a small group of like-minded. We are a little perplexed and, it may be, aggrieved if other members of the circle do not love the one whom we love. In such a group judgment of a common friend there is doubtless greater objectivity than in the economic judgment. The value of a friend does not depend upon his adjustment to our wants. As Aristotle pointed out, true friendship is for its own sake. Its value is "disinterested." If a man does not care for an economic good it does not reflect upon him. He may be careless of futures, neglectful of corn, indifferent to steel. It lessens the demand, lowers the values of these goods, an infinitesimal, but does not write him down an inferior person. To fail to prize a possible friend is a reflection upon us. However the fact that in the very nature of the case one can scarcely be a personal friend to a large, not to say a universal group, operates to limit the objectivity.

In the æsthetic and moral attitudes we incorporate value in the object decisively. We do not like to think that beauty can be changed with shifting fashions or to affirm that the firmament was ever anything but sublime. It seems to belong to the very essence of right that it is something to which the self can commit itself in absolute loyalty and finality. And, as for good, we may say with Moore in judgments of intrinsic value, at least, "we judge concerning a particular state of things that it would be worth while—would be a good thing—that that state of things should exist, even if nothing else were to exist besides."

With regard to this problem of objectivity it is significant in the first place that the kind of situation out of which this object value is affirmed in æsthetic and moral judgments is a social situation. It contrasts in this respect with the economic situation. The economic is indeed social in so far as it sets exchange values, but the object valued is not a social object. The æsthetic and moral object is such an object. Not only is there no contradiction in giving to the symbolic form or the moral act intrinsic value: there is entire plausibility in doing so. For in so far as the situation is really personal, *either member is fundamentally equal to the other and may be treated as embodying all the value of the situation.* The value which rises to consciousness in the situation is made more complete by eliminating from consideration the originating factors, the plural agents of admiration or approval, and incorporating the whole product abstractly in the object. In thus calling attention to the social or personal character of the æsthetic or moral object it is not intended to minimize that factor in the judgment which we properly speak of as the universalizing activity of thought, much less to overlook the importance of the judgmental process itself. The intention is to point out some of the reasons why in one case the thinking process does universalize while in the other it does not, why in one case the judgment is completely objective while in the other it is not. In both æsthetic and moral judgments social art, social action, social judgments, through collective decisions prepare the way for the general non-personal, objective form. It is probable that man would not say, "This is right," using the word as an adjective, if he had not first said, as member of a judicially acting group, "This is right," using the word as a noun. And finally whatever we may claim as to the "cognitive" nature of the æsthetic and moral judgment, the only test for the beauty of an object is that persons of taste discover it. The only test for the rightness of an act is that persons of good character approve it. The only test for goodness is that good persons on reflection approve and choose it—just as the test for good persons is that they choose and do the good.

(3) Right is not merely a means to good but has a place of its own in the moral consciousness. Many of our moral choices or judgments do not take the form of choice between right and wrong, or between duty and its opposite; they appear to be choices between goods. That is, we do not always consider our value as crystallized into a present standard or feel a tension between a resisting and an authoritative self. But when they do emerge they signify a distinct factor. What Moore says of good may be said also of right. Right means just "right," nothing else. That is, we mean that acts so characterized correspond exactly to a self in a peculiar attitude, viz., one of adequate standardizing and adjustment, of equilibrium, in view of all relations. The concept signifies that in finding our way into a moral world into which we are born in the process of valuing and judging, we take along the imagery of social judgment in which through language and behavior the individual is constantly adjusting himself, not only to the social institutions, and group organization but far more subtly and unconsciously to the social consciousness and attitudes.

This conception of an order to which the act must refer has usually been regarded as peculiarly a "rational" factor. It is, however, rather an order of social elements, of a nature of persons, than of a "nature of things." In savage life the position of father, wife, child, guest, or other members of the household, is one of the most prominent facts of the situation. The relationship of various totem groups and inter-marrying groups is the very focus of moral consciousness. Even in the case of such a cosmic conception of order as Dike and Themis, Rita and Tao, the "Way" is not impersonal cosmos. It is at least quasi-personal. And if we say such primitive myth has no bearing on what the "nature" of right or the "true" meaning of right is, it is pertinent to repeat that concepts without percepts are empty; that the term means nothing except the conceptual interpretation of a unique synthetic process in which an act placed in relation to a standard is thereby given new meaning. So long as custom or law forms the only or the dominant factor in the process, we have little development of the ideal concept right as distinct from a factual standard. But when reason and intelligence enter, particularly when that creative activity of intelligence enters which attempts a new construction of ends, a new ordering of possible experience, then the standardizing process is set free; a new self with new possibilities of relation seeks expression. The concept "right" reflects the standardizing, valuing process of a synthetic order and a synthetic self. Duty born similarly in the world of social relations and reflecting especially the tension between the individual and the larger whole is likewise given full moral significance when it becomes a tension within the synthetic self. And as thus reflecting the immediate attitudes of the self to an ideal social order both right and duty are not to be treated merely as means to any value which does not include as integrant factors just what these signify.

This view is contrary to that of Moore, for whom "right does and can mean nothing but 'cause of a good result,' and is thus identical with useful."[70] The right act is that which has the best consequences.[71] Similarly duty is that action which will cause more good to exist in the Universe than any possible alternative. It is evident that this makes it impossible for any finite mind to assert confidently that any act is right or a duty. "Accordingly it follows that we never have any reason to suppose that an action is our duty: we can never be sure that any action will produce the greatest value possible.72

Whatever the convenience of such a definition of right and duty for a simplified ethics it can hardly be claimed to accord with the moral consciousness, for men have notoriously supposed certain acts to be duty. To say that a parent has no reason to suppose that it is his duty to care for his child is more than paradox. And a still greater contradiction to the morality of common sense inheres in the doctrine that the right act is that which has the best consequences. Considering all the good to literature and free inquiry which has resulted from the condemnation of Socrates it is highly probable—or at least it is arguable—that the condemnation had better results than an acquittal would have yielded. But it would be contrary to our ordinary use of language to maintain that this made the act right. Or to take a more recent case: the present war may conceivably lead to a more permanent peace. The "severities," practised by one party, may stir the other to greater indignation and lead ultimately to triumph of the latter. Will the acts in question be termed right by the second party if they actually have this effect? On this hypothesis the more outrageous an act and the greater the reaction against it, the better the consequences are likely to be and hence the more reason to call the act right and a duty. The paradox results from omitting from right the elements of the immediate situation and considering only consequences. The very meaning of the concept right, implies focussing attention upon the present rather than upon the future. It suggests a cross-section of life in its relations. If the time process were to be arrested immediately after our act I think we might still speak of it as right or wrong. In trying to judge a proposed act we doubtless try to discover what it will mean, that is, we look at consequences. But these consequences are looked upon as giving us the meaning of the present act and we do not on this account subordinate the present act to these consequences. Especially we do not mean to eliminate the significance of this very process of judgment. It is significant that in considering what are the intrinsic goods Moore enumerates personal affection and the appreciation of beauty, and with less positiveness, true belief, but does not include any mention of the valuing or choosing or creative consciousness.

(4) If we regard right as the concept which reflects the judgment of standardizing our acts by some ideal order, questions arise as to the objectivity of this order and the fixed or moving character of the implied standard. Rashdall lays great stress upon the importance of objectivity: "Assuredly there is no scientific problem upon which so much depends as upon the answer we give to the question whether the distinction which we are accustomed to draw between right and wrong belongs to the region of objective truth like the laws of mathematics and of physical science, or whether it is based upon an actual emotional constitution of individual human beings."[73] The appraisement of the various desires and impulses by myself and other men is "a piece of insight into the true nature of things."[74] While these statements are primarily intended to oppose the moral sense view of the judgment, they also bear upon the question whether right is something fixed. The phrase "insight into the true nature of things" suggests at once the view that the nature of things is quite independent of any attitude of human beings toward it. It is something which the seeker for moral truth may discover but nothing which he can in any way modify. It is urged that if we are to have any science of ethics at all what was once right must be . conceived as always right in the same circumstances.[75]

I hold no brief for the position—if any one holds the position—that in saying "this is right" I am making an assertion about my own feelings or those of any one else. As already stated the function of the judging process is to determine objects, with reference to which we say "is" or "is not." The emotional theory of the moral consciousness does not give adequate recognition to this. But just as little as the process of the moral consciousness is satisfied by an emotional theory of the judgment does it sanction any conception of objectivity which requires that values are here or there once for all; that they are fixed entities or "a nature of things" upon which the moral consciousness may look for its information but upon which it exercises no influence. The process of attempting to give—or discover—moral values is a process of mutual determination of object and agent. We have to do in morals not with a nature of things but with natures of persons. The very characteristic of a person as we have understood it is that he is synthetic, is actually creating something new by organizing experiences and purposes, by judging and choosing. Objectivity does not necessarily imply changelessness.

Whether right is a term of fixed and changeless character depends upon whether the agents are fixed units, either in fact or in ideal. If, as we maintain, right is the correlate of a self confronting a world of other persons conceived as all related in an order, the vital question is whether this order is a fixed or a moving order. "Straight" is a term of fixed content just because we conceive space in timeless terms; it is by its very meaning a cross-section of a static order. But a world of living intelligent agents in social relations is in its very presuppositions a world of activity, of mutual understanding and adjustment. Rationalistic theory, led astray by geometrical conceptions, conceived that a universal criterion must be like a straight line, a fixed and timeless—or eternal—entity. But in such an order of fixed units there could be no selection, no adjustment to other changing agents, no adventure upon the new untested possibility which marks the advance of every great moral idea, in a word, no morality of the positive and constructive sort. And if it be objected that the predicate of a judgment must be timeless whatever the subject, that the word "is" as Plato insists cannot be used if all flows, we reply that if right=the correlate of a moving order, of living social intelligent beings, it is quite possible to affirm "This is according to that law." If our logic provides no form of judgment for the analysis of such a situation it is inadequate for the facts which it would interpret. But in truth mankind's moral judgments have never committed themselves to any such implication. We recognize the futility of attempting to answer simply any such questions as whether the Israelites did right to conquer Canaan or Hamlet to avenge his father.

(5) The category of right has usually been closely connected, if not identified, with reason or "cognitive" activity as contrasted with emotion. Professor Dewey on the contrary has pointed out clearly76 the impossibility of separating emotion and thought. "To put ourselves in the place of another ... is the surest way to attain universality and objectivity of moral knowledge." "The only truly general, the reasonable as distinct from the merely shrewd or clever thought, is the *generous* thought." But in the case of certain judgments such as those approving fairness and the general good Sidgwick finds a rational intuition. "The principle of impartiality is obtained by considering the similarity of the individuals that make up a Logical Whole or Genus."77 Rashdall challenges any but a rationalistic ethics to explain fairness as contrasted with partiality of affection.

There is without question a properly rational or intellectual element in the judgment of impartiality, namely, analysis of the situation and comparison of the units. But what we shall set up as our units—whether we shall treat the gentile or the barbarian or negro as a person, as end and not merely means, or not, depends on something quite other than reason. And this other factor is not covered by the term "practical reason." In fact no ethical principle shows better the subtle blending of the emotional and social factors with the rational. For the student of the history of justice is aware that only an extraordinarily ingenious exegesis could regard justice as having ever been governed by a mathematical logic. The logic of justice has been the logic of a we-group gradually expanding its area. Or it has been the logic of a Magna Charta—a document of special privileges wrested from a superior by a strong group, and gradually widening its benefits with the admission of others into the favored class. Or it has been the logic of class, in which those of the same level are treated alike but those of different levels of birth or wealth are treated proportionately. Yet it would seem far-fetched to maintain that the countrymen of Euclid and Aristotle were deficient in the ability to perform so simple a reasoning process as the judgment one equals one, or that men who developed the Roman Law, or built the cathedrals of the Middle Ages, were similarly lacking in elementary analysis. Inequality rather than equality has been the rule in the world's justice. It has not only been the practice but the approved principle. It still is in regard to great areas of life. In the United States there is no general disapproval of the great inequalities in opportunity for children, to say nothing of inequalities in distribution of wealth. In England higher education is for the classes rather than for the masses. In Prussia the inequality in voting strength of different groups and the practical immunity of the military class from the constraints of civil law seem to an American unfair. The western states of the Union think it unfair to restrict the suffrage to males and give women no voice in the determination of matters of such vital interest to them as the law of divorce, the guardianship of children, the regulation of women's labor, the sale of alcoholic liquors, the protection of milk and food supply. Are all these differences of practice and conviction due to the fact that some people use reason while others do not? Of course in every case excellent reasons can be given for the inequality. The gentile should not be treated as a Jew because he is not a Jew. The slave should not be treated as a free citizen because he is not a free citizen. The churl should not have the same wergeld as the thane because he is lowborn. The more able should possess more goods. The woman should not vote because she is not a man. The reasoning is clear and unimpeachable if you accept the premises, but what gives the premises? In every case cited the premise is determined largely if not exclusively by social or emotional factors. If reason can then prescribe equally well that the slave should be given rights because he is a man of similar traits or denied rights because he has different traits from his master, if the Jew may either be given his place of equality because he hath eyes, hands, organs, dimensions, senses, affections, passions, or denied equality because he differs in descent, if a woman is equal as regards taxpaying but unequal as regards voting, it is at least evident that reason is no unambiguous source of morality. The devil can quote Scripture and it is a very poor reasoner who cannot find a reason for anything that he wishes to do. A partiality that is more or less consistently partial to certain sets or classes is perhaps as near impartiality as man has yet come, whether by a rational faculty or any other.

Is it, then, the intent of this argument merely to reiterate that reason is and ought to be the slave of the passions? On the contrary, the intent is to substitute for such blanket words as reason and passions a more adequate analysis. And what difference will this make? As regards the particular point in controversy it will make this difference: the rationalist having smuggled in under the cover of reason the whole moral consciousness then proceeds to assume that because two and two are always four, or the relations of a straight line are timeless, therefore ethics is similarly a matter of fixed standards and timeless goods. A legal friend told me that he once spent a year trying to decide whether a corporation was or was not a person and then concluded that the question was immaterial. But when the supreme court decided that a corporation was a person in the meaning of the Fourteenth Amendment it thereby made the corporation heir to the rights established primarily for the negro. Can the moral consciousness by taking the name "reason" become heir to all the privileges of the absolute idea and to the timelessness of space and number?

Suppose I am to divide an apple between my two children— two children, two pieces—this is an analysis of the situation which is obvious and may well be called the analytic activity of reason. But shall I give to each an equal share on the ground that both are equally my children or shall I reason that as John is older or larger or hungrier or mentally keener or more generous or is a male, he shall have a larger piece than Jane? To settle this it may be said that we ought to see whether there is any connection between the size of the piece and the particular quality of John which is considered, or that by a somewhat different use of reason we should look at the whole situation and see how we shall best promote family harmony and mutual affection. To settle the first of these problems, that of the connection between the size of the piece and the size of the hunger or the sex of the child, is seemingly again a question of analysis, of finding identical units, but a moment's thought shows that the case is not so simple; that the larger child should have the larger piece is by no means self-evident. This is in principle doubtless the logic, to him that hath shall be given. It is the logic of the survival of the strong, but over against that the moral consciousness has always set another logic which says that the smaller child should have the larger piece if thereby intelligent sympathy can contribute toward evening up the lot of the smaller. Now it is precisely this attitude of the moral consciousness which is not suggested by the term reason, for it is quite different from the analytic and identifying activity. This analytical and identifying activity may very well rule out of court the hypothesis that I should give John the larger piece because he has already eaten too much or because he has just found a penny or because he has red hair; it has undoubtedly helped in abolishing such practices as that of testing innocence by the ordeal. But before the crucial question of justice which divides modern society, namely, whether we shall lay emphasis upon adjustment of rewards to previous abilities, habits, possessions, character, or shall lay stress upon needs, and the possibility of bringing about a greater measure of equality, the doctrine which would find its standard in an *a priori* reason is helpless.

If we look at the second test suggested, namely, that of considering the situation as a whole with a view to the harmony of the children and the mutual affection within the family, there can be even less question that this is no mere logical problem of the individuals in a logical genus. It is the social problem of individuals who have feelings and emotions as well as thought and will. The problem of distributing the apple fairly is then a complex in which at least the following processes enter. (I) Analysis of the situation to show all the relevant factors with the full bearing of each; (2) putting yourself in the place of each one to be considered and experiencing to the full the claims, the difficulties and the purposes of each person involved; (3) considering all of these *as* members of the situation so that no individual is given rights or allowed claims except in so far as he represents a point of view which is comprehensive and sympathetic. This I take it is the force of President Wilson's utterance which has commanded such wide acceptance: "America asks nothing for herself except what she has a right to ask in the name of humanity." Kant aimed to express a high and democratic ideal of justice in his doctrine that we should treat every rational being as end. The defect in his statement is that the rational process as such has never treated and so far as can be foreseen never will treat *human* beings as ends. To treat a human being as an end it is necessary to put oneself into his place in his whole nature and not simply in his universalizing, and legislative aspects: Kant's principle is profound and noble, but his label for it is misleading and leaves a door open for appalling disregard of other people's feelings, sympathies, and moral sentiments, as Professor Dewey has indicated in his recent lectures on "German Philosophy and Politics."

The term "reasonable," which is frequently used in law and common life as a criterion of right, seems to imply that reason is a standard. As already stated, common life understands by the reasonable man one who not only uses his own thinking powers but is willing to listen to reason as presented by some one else. He makes allowance for frailties in human nature. To be reasonable means, very nearly, taking into account all factors of the case not only as I see them but as men of varying capacities and interests regard them. The type of the "unreasonable" employer is the man who refuses to talk over things with the laborers; to put himself in their place; or to look at matters from the point of view of society as a whole.

Just as little does the term reasonable as used in law permit a purely intellectualistic view of the process or an *a priori* standard. The question as to what is reasonable care or a reasonable price is often declared to be a matter not for the court but for the jury to decide, i.e., it is not to be deduced from any settled principle but is a question of what the average thoughtful man, who considers other people as well as himself, would do under the circumstances. A glance at some of the judicial definitions of such phrases as "reasonable care," "reasonable doubt," "reasonable law," as brought together in *Words and Phrases Judicially Defined*, illustrates this view. We get a picture not of any definite standard but of such a process as we have described in our analysis, namely, a process into which the existing social tradition, the mutual adjustments of a changing society and the intelligent consideration of all facts, enter. The courts have variously defined the reasonable (1) as the customary, or ordinary, or legal, or (2) as according with the existing state of knowledge in some special field, or (3) as proceeding on due consideration of all the facts, or (4) as offering sufficient basis for action. For example, (1) reasonable care means "according to the usages, habits, and ordinary risks of the business," (2) "surgeons should keep up with the latest advances in medical science," (3) a reasonable price "is such a price as the jury would under all the circumstances decide to be reasonable." "If, after an impartial comparison and consideration the jury can say candidly they are not satisfied with the defendant's guilt they have a reasonable doubt." Under (4) falls one of various definitions of "beyond reasonable doubt." "The evidence must be such as to produce in the minds of prudent men such certainty that they would act without hesitation in their own most important affairs." There is evidently ground for the statement of one judge that "reasonable" (he was speaking the phrase "reasonable care," but his words would seem to apply to other cases) "cannot be measured by any fixed or inflexible standard." Professor Freund characterizes "reasonable" as "the negation of precision." In the development of judicial interpretation as applied to the Sherman Law the tendency is to hold that the "rule of reason" will regard as forbidden by the statute (*a*) such combinations as have historically been prohibited and (*b*) such as seem to work some definite injury.

III

The above view of the function of intelligence, and of the synthetic character of the conscious process may be further defined in certain aspects by comparison with the view of Professor Fite, who likewise develops the significance of consciousness and particularly of intelligence for our ethical concepts and social program.

Professor Fite insists that in contrast with the "functional psychology" which would make consciousness merely a means to the preservation of the organic individual in mechanical working order, the whole value of life from the standpoint of the conscious agent consists in its being conscious. Creative moments in which there is complete conscious control of materials and technique represent high and unique individuality. Extension of range of consciousness makes the agent "a larger and more inclusive being," for he is living in the future and past as well as in the present. Consciousness means that a new and original force is inserted into the economy of the social and the physical world."[78] On the basis of the importance of consciousness Professor Fite would ground his justification of rights, his conception of justice, and his social program. The individual derives his rights simply from the fact that he knows what he is doing, hence as individuals differ in intelligence they differ in rights. The problem of justice is that of according to each a degree of recognition proportioned to his intelligence, that is, treat others as ends so far as they are intelligent; so far as they are ignorant treat them as means.[79] "The conscious individual when dealing with other conscious individuals will take account of their aims, as of other factors in his situation. This will involve 'adjustment,' but not abandonment of ends, i.e., self-sacrifice. Obligation to consider these ends of others is based on 'the same logic that binds me to get out of the way of an approaching train.'"[80]

The point in which the conception of rights and justice and the implied social program advocated in this paper differs as I view it from that of Professor Fite is briefly this. I regard both the individual and his rights as essentially synthetic and in constant process of reconstruction. Therefore what is due to any individual at a moment is not measured by his present stage of consciousness. It is measured rather by his possibilities than his actualities. This does not mean that the actual is to be ignored, but it does mean that if we take our stand upon the actual we are committed to a program with little place for imagination, with an emphasis all on the side of giving people what they deserve rather than of making them capable of deserving more. Professor Fite's position I regard as conceiving consciousness itself too largely in the category of the identical and the static rather than in the more "conscious" categories of constant reconstruction. When by virtue of consciousness you conceive new ends in addition to your former particular ideas of present good the problem is, he says, "to secure perfect fulfilment of each of them." The "usefulness" or "advantage" or "profitableness" of entering into social relations is the central category for measuring their value and their obligation.

Now the conception of securing perfect fulfilment of all one's aims by means of society rather than of putting one's own aims into the process for reciprocal modification and adjustment with the aims of others and of the new social whole involves a view of these ends as fixed, an essentially mechanical view. The same is the implication in considering society from the point of view of use and profit. As previously suggested these economic terms apply appropriately to things rather than to intrinsic values. To consider the uses of a fellow-being is to measure him in terms of some other end than his own intrinsic personal worth. To consider family life or society as profitable implies in ordinary language that such life is a means for securing ends already established rather than that it *proves* a good to the man who invests in it and thereby becomes himself a new individual with a new standard of values. Any object to be chosen must of course have value to the chooser. But it is one thing to be valued because it appeals to the actual chooser as already constituted; it is another thing to be valued because it appeals to a moving self which adventures upon this new unproved objective. This second is the distinction of taking an interest instead of being interested.

The second point of divergence is that Professor Fite lays greater stress upon the intellectual side of intelligence, whereas I should deny that the intellectual activity in itself is adequate to give either a basis for obligation or a method of dealing with the social problem. The primary fact, as Professor Fite well states it, is "that men are conscious beings and therefore know themselves and one another." It involves "a mutual recognition of personal ends." "That very knowledge which shows the individual himself shows him also that he is living in a world with other persons and other things whose mode of behavior and whose interests determine for him the conditions through which his own interests are to be realized."

What kind of "knowledge" is it "which shows the individual himself"? Professor Fite has two quite different ways of referring to this. He uses one set of terms when he would contrast his view with the sentimental, or the "Oriental," or justify exploitation by those who know better what they are about than the exploited. He uses another set of terms to characterize it when he wishes to commend his view as human, and fraternal, and as affording the only firm basis for social reform. In the first case he speaks of "mere knowing"; of intelligence as "clear," and "far-sighted," of higher degrees of consciousness as simply "more in one." "Our test of intelligence would be breadth of vision (in a coherent view), fineness and keenness of insight."81

In the second case it is "generous," it will show an "intelligent sympathy"; it seeks "fellowship," and would not "elect to live in a social environment in which the distinction of 'inferiors' were an essential part of the idea."82 The type of intelligence is found not in the man seeking wealth or power, nor in the legal acumen which forecasts all discoverable consequences and devises means to carry out purposes, but in literature and art.83

The terms which cover both these meanings are the words "consider" and "considerate." "Breadth of consideration" gives the basis for rights. The selfish man is the "inconsiderate."[84] This term plays the part of the *amor intellectualis* in the system of Spinoza, which enables him at once to discard all emotion and yet to keep it. For "consideration" is used in common life, and defined in the dictionaries, as meaning both "examination," "careful thought," and "appreciative or sympathetic regard." The ambiguity in the term may well have served to disguise from the author himself the double rôle which intelligence is made to play. The broader use is the only one that does justice to the moral consciousness, but we cannot include sympathy and still maintain that "mere knowing" covers the whole. The insistence at times upon the "mere knowing" is a mechanical element which needs to be removed before the ethical implications can be accepted.

Once more, how does one know himself and others? Is it the same process precisely as knowing a mechanical object? Thoughts without percepts are empty, and what are the "percepts" in the two cases? In the first case, that of knowing things, the percepts are colors, sounds, resistances; in the case of persons the percepts are impulses, feelings, desires, passions, as well as images, purposes, and the reflective process itself. In the former case we construct objects dehumanized; in the latter we keep them more or less concrete. But now, just as primitive man did not so thoroughly de-personalize nature, but left in it an element of personal aim, so science may view human beings as objects whose purposes and even feelings may be predicted, and hence may, as Professor Fite well puts it, view them mechanically. What he fails to note is that just this mechanical point of view is the view of "mere knowing"—if "mere" has any significance at all, it is meant to shut out "sentiment." And this mechanical view is entirely equal to the adjectives of "clear," "far-sighted," and even "broad" so far as this means "more in one." For it is not essential to a mechanical point of view that we consider men in masses or study them by statistics. I may calculate the purposes and actions, yes, and the emotions and values of one, or of a thousand, and be increasingly clear, and far-sighted, and broad, but if it is "mere" knowing—scientific information—it is still "mechanical," i.e., external. On the other hand, if it is to be a knowledge that has the qualities of humaneness, or "intelligent sympathy," it must have some of the stuff of feeling, even as in the realm of things an artist's forest will differ from that of the most "far-sighted," "clear," and "broad" statistician, by being rich with color and moving line.

And this leads to a statement of the way in which my fellow-beings will find place in "my" self. I grant that if they are there I shall take some account of them. But they may be there in all sorts of ways. They may be there as "population" if I am a statistician, or as "consumers," or as rivals, or as enemies, or as fellows, or as friends. They will have a "value" in each case, but it will sometimes be a positive value, and sometimes a negative value. Which it will be, and how great it will be, depends not on the mere fact of these objects being "in consciousness" but on the capacity in which they are there. And this capacity depends on the dominant interest and not on mere knowing. The trouble with the selfish man, says Professor Fite, is that he "fails to consider," "he fails to take account of me."85 Well, then, *why* does he fail? *Why* does he not take account of me? He probably does "consider" me in several of the ways that are possible and in the ways that it suits him to consider me. I call him selfish because he does not consider me in the one particular way in which I wish to be considered. And what will get me into his consideration from this point of view? In some cases it may be that I can speak: "Sir, you are standing on my toe," and as the message encounters no obstacle in any fixed purpose or temperamental bent the idea has no difficulty in penetrating his mind. In other cases it may interfere with his desire to raise himself as high as possible, but I may convince him by the same logic as that of an "approaching railway train"—that he must regard me. In still other cases—and it is these that always test Individualism—I am not myself aware of the injury, or I am too faint to protest. How shall those who have no voice to speak get "consideration"? Only by "intelligent sympathy," and by just those emotions rooted in instinctive social tendencies which an intellectualistic Individualism excludes or distrusts.

IV

What practical conclusion, if any, follows from this interpretation of the moral consciousness and its categories? Moral progress involves both the formation of better ideals and the adoption of such ideals as actual standards and guides of life. If our view is correct we can construct better ideals neither by logical deduction nor solely by insight into the nature of things— if by this we mean things as they are. We must rather take as our starting-point the conviction that moral life is a process involving physical life, social intercourse, measuring and constructive intelligence. We shall endeavor to further each of these factors with the conviction that thus we are most likely to reconstruct our standards and find a fuller good.86

Physical life, which has often been depreciated from the moral point of view, is not indeed by itself supreme, but it is certain that much evil charged to a bad will is due to morbid or defective conditions of the physical organism. One would be ashamed to write such a truism were it not that our juvenile courts and our prison investigations show how far we are from having sensed it in the past. And our present labor conditions show how far our organization of industry is from any decent provision for a healthy, sound, vigorous life of all the people. This war is shocking in its destruction, but it is doubtful if it can do the harm to Great Britain that her factory system has done. And if life is in one respect less than ideals, in another respect it is greater; for it provides the possibility not only of carrying out existing ideals but of the birth of new and higher ideals.

Social interaction likewise has been much discussed but is still very inadequately realized. The great possibilities of coöperation have long been utilized in war. With the factory and commercial organization of the past century we have hints of their economic power. Our schools, books, newspapers, are removing some of the barriers. But how far different social classes are from any knowledge, not to say appreciation, of each other! How far different races are apart! How easy to inculcate national hatred and distrust! The fourth great problem which baffles Wells's hero in the *Research Magnificent* is yet far from solution. The great danger to morality in America lies not in any theory as to the subjectivity of the moral judgment, but in the conflict of classes and races.

Intelligence and reason are in certain respects advancing. The social sciences are finding tools and methods. We are learning to think of much of our moral inertia, our waste of life, our narrowness, our muddling and blundering in social arrangements, as stupid—we do not like to be called stupid even if we scorn the imputation of claiming to be "good." But we do not organize peace as effectively as war. We shrink before the thought of expending for scientific investigation sums comparable with those used for military purposes. And is scholarship entitled to shift the blame entirely upon other interests? Perhaps if it conceived its tasks in greater terms and addressed itself to them more energetically it would find greater support.

And finally the process of judgment and appraisal, of examination and revaluation. To judge for the sake of judging, to analyze and evaluate for the sake of the process hardly seems worth while. But if we supply the process with the new factors of increased life, physical, social, intelligent, we shall be compelled to new valuations. Such has been the course of moral development; we may expect this to be repeated. The great war and the changes that emerge ought to set new tasks for ethical students. As medievalism, the century of enlightenment, and the century of industrial revolution, each had its ethics, so the century that follows ought to have its ethics, roused by the problem of dealing fundamentally with economic, social, racial, and national relations, and using the resources of better scientific method than belonged to the ethical systems which served well their time.

Only wilful misinterpretation will suppose that the method here set forth is that of taking every want or desire as itself a final justification, or of making morality a matter of arbitrary caprice. But some may in all sincerity raise the question: "Is morality then after all simply the shifting mores of groups stumbling forward— or backward, or sidewise—with no fixed standards of right and good? If this is so how can we have any confidence in our present judgments, to say nothing of calling others to an account or of reasoning with them?" What we have aimed to present as a moral method is essentially this: to take into our reckoning all the factors in the situation, to take into account the other persons involved, to put ourselves into their places by sympathy as well as conceptually, to face collisions and difficulties not merely in terms of fixed concepts of what is good or fair, and what the right of each party concerned may be, but with the conviction that we need new definitions of the ideal life, and of the social order, and thus reciprocally of personality. Thus harmonized, free, and responsible, life may well find new meaning also in the older intrinsic goods of friendship, æsthetic appreciation and true belief. And it is not likely to omit the satisfaction in actively constructing new ideals and working for their fulfilment.

Frankly, if we do not accept this method what remains? Can any one by pure reason discover a single forward step in the treatment of the social situation or a single new value in the moral ideal? Can any analysis of the pure concept of right and good teach us anything? In the last analysis the moral judgment is not analytic but synthetic. The moral life is not natural but spiritual. And spirit is creative.

VALUE AND EXISTENCE IN PHILOSOPHY, ART, AND RELIGION

HORACE M. KALLEN

He who assiduously compares the profound and the commonplace will find their difference to turn merely on the manner of their expression; a profundity is a commonplace formulated in strange or otherwise obscure and unintelligible terms. This must be my excuse for beginning with the trite remark that the world we live in is not one which was made for us, but one in which we happened and grew. I am much aware that there exists a large and influential class of persons who do not think so; and I offer this remark with all deference to devotees of idealism, and to other such pietists who persist in arguing that the trouble which we do encounter in this vale of tears springs from the inwardness of our own natures and not from that of the world. I wish, indeed, that I could agree with them, but unhappily their very arguments prevent me, since, if the world were actually as they think it, they could not think it as they do. In fact, they could not think. Thinking—worse luck!—came into being as response to discomfort, to pain, to uncertainty, to problems, such as could not exist in a world truly made for us; while from time immemorial *pure* as distinct from human consciousness has been identified with absolute certainty, with self-absorption and self-sufficiency; as a god, a goal to attain, not a fact to rest in. It is notable that those who believe the world actually to have been made for us devote most of their thinking to explaining away the experiences which have made all men feel that the world was actually not made for us. Their chief business, after proving the world to be all good, is solving "the problem of evil." Yet, had there really been no evil, this evil consequence could not have ensued: existence would have emerged as beatitude and not as adjustment; thinking might in truth have been self-absorbed contemplation, blissful intuition, not painful learning by the method of trial and error.

Alas that what "might have been" cannot come into being by force of discursive demonstration! If it could, goodness alone would have existed and been real, and evil would have been non-existence, unreality, and appearance—all by the force of the Word. As it is, the appearance of evil is in so far forth no less an evil than its reality; in truth, it is reality and its best witnesses are the historic attempts to explain it away. For even as "appearance" it has a definite and inexpugnable character of its own which cannot be destroyed by subsumption under the "standpoint of the whole," "the absolute good," the "over-individual values." Nor, since only sticks and stones break bones and names never hurt, can it be abolished by the epithet "appearance." To deny reality to evil is to multiply the evil. It is to make two "problems" grow where only one grew before, to add to the "problem of evil" the "problem of appearance" without serving any end toward the solution of the real problem how evil can be effectively abolished.

I may then, in view of these reflections, hold myself safe in assuming that the world we live in was not made for us; that, humanly speaking, it is open to improvement in a great many directions. It will be comparatively innocuous to assume also, as a corollary, that in so far as the world was made for mind, it has been made so by man, that civilization is the adaptation of nature to human nature. And as a second corollary it may be safely assumed that the world does not stay made; civilization has brought its own problems and peculiar evils.

I realize that, in the light of my title, much of what I have written above must seem irrelevant, since the "problem of evil" has not, within the philosophic tradition, been considered part of a "problem of values" as such. If I dwell on it, I do so to indicate that the "problem of evil" can perhaps be best understood in the light of another problem: the problem, namely, of why men have created the "problem of evil." For obviously, evil can be problematic only in an absolutely good world, and the idea that the world is absolutely good is not a generalization *upon* experience, but a contradiction *of* experience. If there exists a metaphysical "problem of evil," hence, it arises out of this generalization; it is secondary, not primary; and the primary problem requires solution before the secondary one can be understood. And what else, under the circumstances, can the primary one be than this: "Why do men contradict their own experience?"

II

So put, the problem suggests its own solution. It indicates, first of all, that nature and human nature are not completely compatible, that consequently, conclusions are being forced by nature on human nature which human nature resents and rejects, and that traits are being assigned to nature by human nature which nature does not possess, but which, if possessed, would make her congenial to human needs. All this is so platitudinous that I feel ashamed to write it; but then, how can one avoid platitudes without avoiding truth? And truth here is the obvious fact that since human nature is the point of existence to which good and evil refer, what is called value has its seat necessarily in human nature, and what is called existence has its seat necessarily in the nature of which human nature is a part and apart. Value, in so far forth, is a content of nature, having its roots in her conditions and its life in her force, while the converse is not true. All nature and all existence is not spontaneously and intrinsically a content of value. Only that portion of it which is human is such. Humanly speaking, non-human existences become valuable by their efficacious bearing on humanity, by their propitious or their disastrous relations to human consciousness. It is these relations which delimit the substance of our goods and evils, and these, at bottom, are indistinguishable from consciousness. They do not, need not, and cannot connect all existence with human life. They are inevitably implicated only with those which make human life possible at all. Of the environment, they pertain only to that portion which is fit by the implicated conditions of life itself. It may therefore be said that natural existence produces and sustains some values,—at least the minimal value which is identical with the bare existence of mankind—on its own account, but no more. The residual environment remains—irrelevant and menacing, wider than consciousness and independent of it. Value, hence, is a specific kind of natural existence among other existences. To say that it is non-existent in nature, is to say that value is not coincident and coexistent with other existences, just as when it is said that a thing is not red, the meaning is that red is not copresent with other qualities. Conversely, to say that value exists in nature is to say that nature and human nature, things and thoughts, are in some respect harmonious or identical. Hence, what human nature tries to force upon nature must be, by implication, non-existent in nature but actual in mind, so that the nature of value must be held inseparable from the nature of mind.87

It follows that value is, in origin and character, completely irrational. At the foundations of our existence it is relation of their conditions and objects to our major instincts, our appetites, our feelings, our desires, our ambitions—most clearly, to the self-regarding instinct and the instincts of nutrition, reproduction, and gregariousness. Concerning those, as William James writes, "Science may come and consider their ways and find that most of them are useful. But it is not for the sake of their utility that they are followed, but because at the moment of following them we feel that it is the only appropriate and natural thing to do. Not a man in a billion when taking his dinner, ever thinks of utility. He eats because the food tastes good and makes him want more. If you ask him why he should want to eat more of what tastes like that, instead of revering you as a philosopher, he will probably laugh at you for a fool. The connection between the savory sensation and the act it awakens is for him absolute and *selbstverständlich*, an *a priori* synthesis of the most perfect sort, needing no proof but its own evidence.... To the metaphysician alone can such questions occur as 'Why do we smile when pleased, and not scowl? Why are we unable to talk to a crowd as we talk to a single friend? Why does a particular maiden turn our wits upside down?' The common man can only say '*of course* we smile, *of course* our heart palpitates at the sight of a crowd, *of course* we love the maiden, that beautiful soul clad in that perfect form, so palpably and flagrantly made from all eternity to be loved.' And so, probably, does each animal feel about the particular things it tends to do in the presence of particular objects.... To the broody hen the notion would probably seem monstrous that there should be a creature in the world to whom a nestful of eggs was not the utterly fascinating and precious and never-to-be-too-much-set-upon object it is to her." In sum, fundamental values are relations, responses, attitudes, immediate, simple, subjectively obvious, and irrational. But everything else becomes valuable or rational only by reference to them.

Study them or others empirically,88 and they appear as types of specific behavior, simple or complicated, consisting of a given motor "set" of the organism, strong emotional tone, and aggregates of connected ideas, more or less systematized. In the slang of the new medical psychology which has done so much to uncover their method and mechanism, they are called "complexes"; ethics has called them interests, and that designation will do well enough. They are the primary and morally ultimate efficacious units of which human nature is compounded, and it is in terms of the world's bearing upon their destiny that we evaluate nature and judge her significance and worth.

Now in interest, the important delimiting quality is emotional tone. Whatever else is sharable, that is not. It is the very stuff of our attitudes, of our acceptances and rejections of the world and its contents, the very essence of the relations we bear to these. That these relations shall be identical for any two human beings requires that the two shall be identical: two persons cannot hold the same relation to the same or different objects any more than two objects can occupy absolutely the same space at the same time. Hence, all our differences and disagreements. However socially-minded we may be, mere numerical diversity compels us to act as separate centers, to value things with reference to separate interests, to orient our worlds severally, and with ourselves as centers. This orienting is the relating of the environment to our interests, the establishment of our worlds of appreciation, the creation of our orders of value. However much these cross and interpenetrate, coincide they never can.

Our interests, furthermore, are possibly as numerous as our reflex arcs. Each may, and most do, constitute distinct and independent valuations of their objects, to which they respond, and each, with these objects, remains an irreducible system. But reflex arcs and interests do not act alone. They act like armies; they compound and are integrated, and when so integrated their valuations fuse and constitute the more complex and massive feelings, pleasures and pains, the emotions of anger, of fear, of love; the sentiments of respect, of admiration, of sympathy. They remain, through all degrees of complexity, appraisements of the environment, reactions upon it, behavior toward it, as subject to empirical examination by the psychologist as the environment itself by the physicist.

With a difference, however, a fundamental difference. When you have an emotion you cannot yourself examine it. Effectively as the mind may work in sections, it cannot with sanity be divided against itself nor long remain so. A feeling cannot be had and examined in the same time. And though the investigator who studies the nature of red does not become red, the investigator who studies the actual emotion of anger does tend to become angry. Emotion is infectious; anger begets anger; fear, fear; love, love; hate, hate; actions, relations, attitudes, when actual, integrate and fuse; as feelings, they constitute the sense of behavior, varying according to a changing and unstable equilibrium of factors *within* the organism; they are actually underneath the skin, and consequently, to know them alive is to have them. On the other hand, to know *things* is simply to have a relation to them. The same thing may be both loved and hated, desired or spurned, by different minds at the same time or by the same mind at different times. One, for example, values whiskey positively, approaches, absorbs it, aims to increase its quantity and sale; another apprehends it negatively, turns from it, strives to oust it from the world. Then, according to these direct and immediate valuations of whiskey, its place in the common world of the two minds will be determined. To save or destroy it, they may seek to destroy each other. Even similar positive valuations of the object might imply this mutual repugnance and destruction. Thus, rivals in love: they enhance and glorify the same woman, but as she is not otherwise sharable, they strive to eliminate each other. Throughout the world of values the numerical distinctness of the seats or centers of value, whatever their identity otherwise, keeps them ultimately inimical. They may terminate in the common object, but they originate in different souls and they are related to the object like two magnets of like polarity to the same piece of iron that lies between them. Most of what is orderly in society and in science is the outcome of the adjustment of just such oppositions: our civilization is an unstable equilibrium of objects, through the coöperation, antipathy, and fusion of value-relations.

Individuals are no better off; personality is constructed in the same way. If, indeed, the world had been made for us, we might have been spared this warfare to man upon earth. Life might have been the obvious irrational flow of bliss so vividly described by William James; nature and human nature would have been one; bridging the gulf between them would never have been the task of the tender-minded among philosophers. Unfortunately our mere numerical difference, the mere numerical difference of the interests which compose our egos, makes the trouble, so that we are compelled to devote most of our lives to converting the different into the same. The major part of our instincts serve this function recognizably, e.g., nutrition, and the "higher powers" do so no less, if not so obviously. Generalization is nothing more, thinking nothing else. It is the assimilation of many instances into one form, law, or purpose; the preservation of established contents of value, just as nutrition is the preservation of life by means of the conversion of foreign matter into the form and substance of the body. By bowels and by brain, what is necessary, what will feed the irrationally given interest, is preserved and consumed: the rest is cast off as waste, as irrelevance, as contradiction.

The relation may, of course, also reverse itself. Face to face with the immovable and inexorable, the mind may accept it with due resignation, or it may challenge its tyranny and exclude it from its world. It may seek or create or discover a substitute that it is content to accept, though this will in turn alter the course and character of the interest which in such an instance defines the mind's action. Thus, a way out for one of the lovers of the same girl might be to become a depressed and yearning bachelor, realizing his potential sexuality in the vicarious reproduction of reverie and sentiment; another might be to divert the stream of his affections to another girl, reorganizing his life about a different center and acquiring a new system of practical values determined by this center; a third might be a complete redirection of his sexual energies upon objects the interest in which we would call, abnormal and anti-social in one case, and in another lofty and spiritual. In the latter case sexuality would have been depersonalized; it would have changed into poetic and humanitarian passion; it would have become love as Plato means us to take the word. But each of these processes would have been a conversion, through the need defined by an identical instinct, of the *same into the different*; the human nature which existed at the beginning of the change would be deeply other than the human nature in which the change culminated. In each case a condition thrust upon the spirit by its environment would have occasioned the creation and maintenance of an environment demanded by the spirit. Yet in so far as it was not truly *the same* as that envisaged in the primitive demand, it would still imply the tragedy of the world not made for us and the "problem of evil," in which the life of the spirit is persistently a salvage of one of two always incompatible goods, a saving by surrender.

And this is all that a mind is—an affair of saving and rejecting, of valuing with a system of objects of which a living body and its desires and operations, its interests, are focal and the objects marginal, for its standard. Mind, thus, is neither simple, nor immutable, nor stable; it is a thing to be "changed," "confused," "cleared," "made-up," "trained." One body, I have written elsewhere,[89] "in the course of its lifetime, has many minds, only partially united. Men are all too often "of two minds." The unity of a mind depends on its consistent pursuit of *one* interest, although we then call it narrow; or on the coöperation and harmony of its many interests. Frequently, two or more minds may struggle for the possession of the same body; that is, the body may be divided by two elaborately systematized tendencies to act. The beginning of such division occurs wherever there is a difficulty in deciding between alternative modes of behavior; the end is to be observed in those cases of dual or multiple personality in which the body has ordered a great collection of objects and systematized so large a collection of interests in such typically distinct ways as to have set up for itself different and opposed "minds." On the other hand, two or fifty or a million bodies may be "of the same mind."

Unhappily, difference of mind, diversity and conflict of interests is quite as fundamental, if not more so, as sameness of mind, coöperation and unity of interests. This the philosophical tradition sufficiently attests. To Plato man is at once a protean beast, a lion, and an intellect; the last having for its proper task to rule the first and to regulate the second, which is always rebellious and irruptive.[90] According to the Christian tradition man is at once flesh and spirit, eternally in conflict with one another, and the former is to be mortified that the latter may have eternal life. Common sense divides us into head and heart, never quite at peace with one another. There is no need of piling up citations. Add to the inward disharmonies of mind its incompatibilities with the environment, and you perceive at once how completely it is, from moment to moment, a theater and its life a drama of which the interests that compose it are at once protagonists and directors. The catastrophe of this unceasing drama is always that one or more of the players is driven from the stage of conscious existence. It may be that the environment—social conditions, commercial necessity, intellectual urgency, allies of other interests—will drive it off; it may be that its own intrinsic unpleasantness will banish it, will put it out of mind; whatever the cause, it is put out. Putting it out does not, however, end the drama; putting it out serves to complicate the drama. For the "new psychology"[91] shows that whenever an interest or a desire or impulsion is put out of the mind, it is really, if not extirpated, put into the mind; it is driven from the conscious level of existence to the unconscious. It retains its force and direction, only its work now lies underground. Its life henceforward consists partly in a direct oppugnance to the inhibitions that keep it down, partly in burrowing beneath and around them and seeking out unwonted channels of escape. Since life is long, repressions accumulate, the mass of existence of feeling and desire tends to become composed entirely of these repressions, layer upon layer, with every interest in the aggregate striving to attain place in the daylight of consciousness.

Now, empirically and metaphysically, no one interest is more excellent than any other. Repressed or patent, each is, whether in a completely favorable environment or in a completely indifferent universe, or before the bar of an absolute justice, or under the domination of an absolute and universal good, entitled to its free fulfilment and perfect maintenance. Each is a form of the good; the essential content of each is good. That any are not fulfilled, but repressed, is a fact to be recorded, not an appearance to be explained away. And it may turn out that the existence of the fact may explain the effort to explain it away. For where interests are in conflict with each other or with reality, and where the loser is not extirpated, its revenge may be just this self-fulfilment in unreality, in idea, which philosophies of absolute values offer it. Dreams, some of the arts, religion, and philosophy may indeed be considered as such fulfilments, worlds of luxuriant self-realization of all that part of our nature which the harsh conjunctions with the environment overthrow and suppress. Sometimes abortive self-expressions of frustrated desires, sometimes ideal compensations for the shortcomings of existence, they are always equally ideal reconstructions of the surrounding evil of the world into forms of the good. And because they are compensations in idea, they are substituted for existence, appraised as "true," and "good," and "beautiful," and "real," while the experiences which have suppressed the desires they realize are condemned as illusory and unreal. In them humanity has its freest play and amplest expression.

III

This has been, and still to a very great extent remains, most specifically true of philosophy. The environment with which philosophy concerns itself is nothing less than the whole universe; its content is, within the history of its dominant tradition, absolutely general and abstract; it is, of all great human enterprises, even religion, least constrained by the direction and march of events or the mandate of circumstance. Like music, it expresses most truly the immediate and intrinsic interests of the mind, its native bias and its inward goal. It has been constituted, for this reason, of the so-called "normative" sciences, envisaging the non-existent as real, forcing upon nature pure values, forms of the spirit incident to the total life of this world, unmixed with baser matter. To formulate ultimate standards, to be completely and utterly lyrical has been the prerogative of philosophy alone. Since these standards reappear in all other reconstructions of the environment and most clearly in art and in religion, it is pertinent to enumerate them, and to indicate briefly their bearing on existence.

The foremost outstanding is perhaps "the unity of the world." Confronted by the perplexing menace of the variation of experience, the dichotomies and oppositions of thoughts and things, the fusion and diversifications of many things into one and one into many, mankind has, from the moment it became reflective, felt in the relation of the One and the Many the presence of a riddle that engendered and sustained uneasiness, a mystery that concealed a threat. The mind's own preference, given the physiological processes that condition its existence, constitution, and operation, could hardly come to rest in a more fundamental normation than Unity. A world which is *one* is easier to live in and with; initial adjustment therein is final adjustment; in its substance there exists nothing sudden and in its character nothing uncontrollable. It guarantees whatever vital equilibrium the organism has achieved in it, ill or good. It secures life in attainment and possession, insuring it repose, simplicity, and spaciousness. A world which is many complicates existence: it demands watchful consideration of irreducible discrete individualities: it necessitates the integration and humanization in a common system of adjustment of entities which in the last analysis refuse all ordering and reject all subordination, consequently keeping the mind on an everlasting jump, compelling it to pay with eternal vigilance the price of being. The preference for unity, then, is almost inevitable, and the history of philosophy, from the Vedas to the Brahma Somaj and from Thales to Bergson, is significantly unanimous in its attempts to prove that the world is, somehow, through and through one. That the oneness requires *proof* is *prima facie* evidence that it is a value, a desiderate, not an existence. And how valuable it is may be seen merely in the fact that it derealizes the inner conflict of interests, the incompatibilities between nature and man, the uncertainties of knowledge, and the certainties of evil, and substitutes therefore the ultimate happy unison which "the identity of the different" compels.

Unity is the common desiderate of philosophic systems of all metaphysical types—neutral, materialistic, idealistic. But the dominant tradition has tended to think this unity in terms of *interest*, of *spirit*, of *mentality*. It has tended, in a word, to assimilate nature to human nature, to identify things with the *values* of things, to envisage the world in the image of man. To it, the world is all spirit, ego, or idea; and if not such through and through, then entirely subservient, in its unhumanized parts, to the purposes and interests of ego, idea, or spirit. Why, is obvious. A world of which the One substance is such constitutes a totality of interest and purpose which faces no conflict and has no enemy. It is fulfilment even before it is need, and need, indeed, is only illusion. Even when its number is many, the world is a better world if the stuff of these many is the *same* stuff as the spirit of man. For mind is more at home with mind than with things; the pathetic fallacy is the most inevitable and most general. Although the totality of spirit is conceived as good, that is, as actualizing all our desiderates and ideals, it would still be felt that, even if the totality were evil, and not God, but the Devil ruled the roost, the world so constituted must be better than one utterly non-spiritual. We can understand and be at home with malevolence: it offers at least the benefits of similarity, of companionship, of intimateness, of consubstantiality with *will*; its behavior may be foreseen and its intentions influenced; but no horror can be greater than that of utter aliency. How much of religion turns with a persistent tropism to the consideration of the devil and his works, and how much it has fought his elimination from the cosmic scheme! Yet never because it loved the devil. The deep-lying reason is the fact that the humanization of Evil into Devil mitigates Evil and improves the world. Philosophy has been least free from this corrective and spiritizing bias. Though it has cared less for the devil, it has predominantly repudiated aliency, has sought to prove spirit the cause and substance of the world, and in that degree, to transmute the aliency of nature into sameness with human nature.

With unity and spirituality, *eternity* makes a third. This norm is a fundamental attribute of the One God himself, and interchangeable with his ineffable name: the Lord is Eternal, and the Eternal, even more than the One, receives the eulogium of exclusive realness. To the philosophical tradition it is the most real. Once more the reason should be obvious. The underlying urge which pushes the mind to think the world as a unity pushes it even more inexorably to think the world as timeless. For unity is asserted only against the perplexities of a manyness which may be static and unchanging, and hence comparatively simple. But eternity is asserted and set against mutability: it is the negation of change, of time, of novelty, of the suddenness and slaughter of the flux of life itself, which consumes what it generates, undermines what it builds and sweeps to destruction what it founds to endure. Change is the arch-enemy of a life which struggles for self-*preservation*, of an intellect which operates spontaneously by the logic of identity, of a will which seeks to convert others into sames. It substitutes a different self for the old, it falsifies systems of thought and deteriorates systems of life. It makes unity impossible and manyness inevitable. It upsets every actual equilibrium that life attains. It opens the doors and windows of every closed and comfortable cosmos to all transcosmic winds that blow, with whatever they carry of possible danger and possible ill. It is the very soul of chaos in which the pleasant, ordered world is such a little helpless thing. Of this change eternity is by primary intention the negation, as its philological form shows. It is *not-time*, without positive intrinsic content, and in its secondary significances, i.e., in those significances which appear in metaphysical dialectic, without meaning; since it is there a pure negation, intrinsically affirming nothing, of the same character as "not-man" or "not-donkey," standing for a nature altogether unspecific and indeterminable in the residual universe. By a sort of obverse implication it does, however, possess, in the philosophic tradition, a positive content which accrues to it by virtue of what it denies. This content makes it a designation for the persistence and perdurability of desiderated quality—from metaphysical unity and spirituality to the happy hunting-grounds or a woman's affection. At bottom it means the assurance that the contents of value cannot and will not be altered or destroyed, that their natures and their relations to man do not undergo change. There is no recorded attempt to prove that evil is eternal: eternity is *eternity of the good alone.*

Unity, spirituality, and eternity, then, are the forms which contents of value receive under the shaping hands of the philosophic tradition, to which they owe their metaphysical designation and of which the business has so largely and uniquely been to *prove* them the foundations and ontological roots of universal nature. But "the problem of evil" does not come to complete solution with these. Even in a single, metaphysically spiritual and unchanging world, man himself may still be less than a metaphysical absolute and his proper individuality doomed to absorption, his wishes to obstruction and frustration. Of man, therefore, the tradition posits *immortality* and *freedom*, and even the materialistic systems have sought to keep somehow room for some form of these goods.

To turn first to immortality. Its source and matrix is less the love of life than the fear of death—that fear which Lucretius, dour poet of disillusion, so nobly deplored. That he had ever himself been possessed of it is not clear, but it is perfectly clear that his altogether sound arguments against it have not abolished its operation, nor its effect upon human character, society, and imagination. Fear which made the gods, made also the immortality of man, the denial of death. What the fear's unmistakable traits may be has never been articulately said, perhaps never can be said. Most of us never may undergo the fear of death; we undergo comfort and discomfort, joy and sorrow, intoxication and reaction, love and disgust; we aim to preserve the one and to abolish the other, but we do not knowingly undergo the fear of death. Indeed, it is logically impossible that we should, since to do so would be to acquire an experience of death such that we should be conscious of being unconscious, sensible of being insensible, aware of being unaware. We should be required to be and not to be at the same instant, in view of which Lucretius both logically and wisely advises us to remember that when death is, we are not; and when we are, death is not.

Experience and feeling are, however, neither logical nor wise, and to these death is far from the mere non-being which the poet would have us think it. To these it has a positive reality which makes the fear of it a genuine cause of conduct in individuals and in groups, with a basis in knowledge such as is realized in the diminishing of consciousness under anæsthetic, in dreams of certain types, and most generally in the nascent imitation of the *rigor mortis* which makes looking upon the dead such a horror to most of us. Even then, however, something is lacking toward the complete realization of death, and children and primitive peoples never realize it at all. Its full meaning comes out as *an unsatisfied hunger in the living* rather than as a condition of the dead, who, alive, would have satisfied this hunger. And the realization of this meaning requires sophistication, requires a lengthy corporate memory and the disillusions which civilization engenders. Primitive peoples ask for no proof of immortality because they have no notion of mortality; civilized thinking has largely concerned itself about the proof of immortality because its assurance of life has been shaken by the realization of death through the gnawing of desire which only the dead could still. The *proof* which in the history of thought is offered again and again, be it noted, is not of the reality of life, but of the unreality and inefficacy of death. Immortality is like eternity, a negative term; it is *im*mortality. The experienced fact is mortality; and the fear of it is only an inversion of the desire which it frustrates, just as frustrated love becomes hatred. The doctrine of immortality, hence, springs from the fear of death, not from the love of life, and immortality is a value-form, not an existence. Now, although fear of death and love of life are in constant play in character and conduct, neither constitutes the original, innocent urge of life within us. "Will to live," "will to power," "struggle for existence," and other Germanic hypostases of experienced events which the great civil war in Europe is just now giving such an airing, hardly deserve, as natural data, the high metaphysical status that Schopenhauer, Nietzsche, and company have given them. They follow in fact upon a more primary type of living, acting form, a type to which the "pathetic fallacy" or any other manner of psychologizing may not apply. The most that can be said about this type is that its earlier stages are related to its later ones as potential is to kinetic energy. If, since we are discussing a metaphysical issue, we must mythologize, we might call it the "will to self-expression." Had this "will" chanced to happen in a world which was made for it, or had it itself been the substance of the world, "struggle for existence," "will to live," and "will to power," never could have supervened. All three of these expressions designate data which require an opposite, a counter-will, to give them meaning. There can be a struggle for existence only when there are obstacles thereto, a will to live only when there are obstructions to life, a will to power only when there is a resistance against which power may be exercised. Expression alone is self-implying and self-sufficient, and in an altogether favorable environment we might have realized our instincts, impulses, interests, appetites and desires, expressed and actualized our potentialities, and when our day is done, have ceased, as unconcerned about going on as about starting.

Metchnikoff speaks somewhere of an instinct toward death and the euphoria which accompanies its realization. He cites, I think, no more than two or three cases. To most of us the mere notion of the existence and operation of such an instinct seems fanciful and uncanny. Yet from the standpoint of biology nothing should be more natural. Each living thing has its span, which consists of a cycle from birth through maturation and senescence to dissolution, and the latter half of the process is as "fateful" and "inevitable" as the former! Dying is itself the inexpugnable conclusion of that setting free of organic potentialities which we call life, and if dying seems horrid and unnatural, it seems so because for most of us death is violent, because its occasion is a shock from without, not the realization of a tendency from within. In a completely favorable environment we should not struggle to exist, we should simply exist; we should not will to live, we should simply live, i.e., we should actualize our potentialities and die.

But, once more alas, our environment is not completely favorable, and there's the rub. That disorderly constellation of instincts and appetites and interests which constitutes the personality of the best of us does not work itself out evenly. At the most favorable, our self-realizations are lopsided and distorted. For every capacity of ours in full play, there are a score at least mutilated, sometimes extirpated, always repressed. They never attain the free fullness of expression which is consciousness, or when they do, they find themselves confronted with an opponent which neutralizes their maturation at every point.

Hence, as I have already indicated, they remain in, or revert to, the subterranean regions of our lives, and govern the making of our biographies from their seats below. What they fail to attain in fact they succeed in generating in imagination to compensate for the failure; they realize themselves vicariously. The doctrine of immortality is the generic form of such vicarious self-realization, as frequently by means of dead friends and relatives to whose absolute non-being the mind will not assent, as by means of the everlasting heaven in which the mind may forever disport itself amid those delights it had to forego on earth. Much of the underlying motive of the doctrine is a *sehnsucht* and nostalgia after the absent dead; little a concern for the continuity of the visible living. And often this passion is so intense that system after system in the philosophic tradition is constructed to satisfy it, and even the most disillusioned of systems—for example, Spinoza's—will preserve its form if not its substance.

That the "freedom of the will" shall be a particularized compensatory desiderate like the immortality of the soul, the unity, the spirituality, and the eternity of the world is a perversion worked upon this ideal by the historic accident we call Christianity. The assumptions of that theory concerning the nature of the universe and the destiny of man, being through and through compensatory, changed freedom from the possible fact and actual hope of Hellenic systems into the "problem" of the Christian ones. The consequent controversy over "free-will," the casuistic entanglement of this ideal with the notion of responsibility, its theological development in the problem of the relation of an omnipotent God to a recalcitrant creature, have completely obscured its primal significance. For the ancients, the free man and the "wise man" were identical, and the wise man was one who all in all had so mastered the secrets of the universe that there was no desire of his that was not actually realized, no wish the satisfaction of which was obstructed. His way in the world was a way without let or hindrance. Now freedom and wisdom in this sense is never a fact and ever a value. Its attainment ensues upon created distinctions between appearance and reality, upon the postulation of the metaphysical existence of the value-forms of the unity, spirituality, and the eternity of the world, in the realization of which the wise man founded his wisdom and gained his freedom. Freedom, then, is an ideal that could have arisen only in the face of *obstruction to action directed toward the fulfilling and satisfying of interests*. It is the assurance of the smooth and uninterrupted flow of behavior; the flow of desire into fulfilment, of thought into deed, of act into fact. It is perhaps the most pervasive and fundamental of all desiderates, and in a definite way the others may be said to derive from it and to realize it. For the soul's immortality, the world's unity and spirituality and eternity, are but conditions which facilitate and assure the flow of life without obstruction. They define a world in which danger, evil, and frustration are non-existent; they so reconstitute our actual environment that the obstructions it offers to the course of life are abolished. They make the world "rational," and in the great philosophic tradition the freedom of man is held to be a function of the rationality of the world. Thus, even deterministic solutions of the "problem of freedom" are at bottom no more than the rationalization of natural existence by the dialectical removal of obstructions to human existence. Once more, Spinoza's solution is typical, and its form is that of all idealisms as well. It ensues by way of identification of the obstruction's interest with those of the obstructee: the world becomes ego or the ego the world, with nothing outside to hinder or to interfere. In the absolute, existence is declared to be value *de facto*; in fact, *de jure*. And by virtue of this compensating reciprocity the course of life runs free.

Is any proof necessary that these value-forms are not the contents of the daily life? If there be, why this unvarying succession of attempts to *prove* that they are the contents of daily life that goes by the name of history of philosophy? In fact, experience as it comes from moment to moment is not one, harmonious and orderly, but multifold, discordant, and chaotic. Its stuff is not spirit, but stones and railway wrecks and volcanoes and Mexico and submarines, and trenches, and frightfulness, and

Germany, and disease, and waters, and trees, and stars, and mud. It is not eternal, but changes from instant to instant and from season to season. Actually, men do not live forever; death is a fact, and immortality is literally as well as in philosophic discourse not so much an aspiration for the continuity of life as an aspiration for the elimination of death, purely *im*mortality. Actually the will is not free, each interest encounters obstruction, no interest is completely satisfied, all are ultimately cut off by death.

Such are the general features of all human experience, by age unwithered, and with infinite variety forever unstaled. The traditional philosophic treatment of them is to deny their reality, and to call them appearance, and to satisfy the generic human interest which they oppose and repress by means of the historical reconstruction in imaginative dialectic of a world constituted by these most generalized value-forms and then to eulogize the reconstruction with the epithet "reality." When, in the course of human events, such reconstruction becomes limited to the biography of particular individuals, is an expression of their concrete and unique interest, is lived and acted on, it is called paranoia. The difference is not one of kind, but of concreteness, application, and individuality. Such a philosophy applied universally in the daily life is a madness, like Christian Science: kept in its proper sphere, it is a fine art, the finest and most human of the arts, a reconstruction in discourse of the whole universe, in the image of the free human spirit. Philosophy has been reasonable because it is so unpersonal, abstract, and general, like music; because, in spite of its labels, its reconstructions remain pure desiderates and value-forms, never to be confused with and substituted for existence. But philosophers even to this day often have the delusion that the substitutions are actually made.92

IV

It is the purity of the value-forms imagined in philosophy that makes philosophy "normative." The arts, which it judges, have an identical origin and an indistinguishable intent, but they are properly its subordinates because they have not its purity. They, too, aim at remodeling discordant nature into harmony with human nature. They, too, are dominated by value-forms which shall satisfy as nearly as possible all interests, shall liberate and fulfil all repressions, and shall supply to our lives that unity, eternity, spirituality, and freedom which are the exfoliations of our central desire—the desire to live. But where philosophy has merely negated the concrete stuff of experience and defined its reality in terms of desire alone, the arts acknowledge the reality of immediate experience, accept it as it comes, eliminating, adding, molding, until the values desiderated become existent in the concrete immediacies of experience as such. Art does not substitute values for existence by changing their rôles and calling one appearance and the other reality: art converts values into existences, it realizes values, injecting them into nature as far as may be. It creates truth and beauty and goodness. But it does not claim for its results greater reality than nature's. It claims for its results greater immediate harmony with human interests than nature. The propitious reality of the philosopher is the unseen: the harmonious reality of the artist must be sensible. Philosophy says that apparent actual evil is merely apparent: art compels potential apparent good actually to appear. Philosophy realizes fundamental values transcendentally beyond experience: art realizes them within experience. Thus, men cherish no illusions concerning the contents of a novel, a picture, a play, a musical composition. They are taken for what they are, and are enjoyed for what they are. The shopgirl, organizing her life on the basis of eight dollars a week, wears flimsy for broadcloth and the tail feather of a rooster for an ostrich plume. She is as capable of wearing and enjoying broadcloth and ostrich plume as My Lady, whose income is eight dollars a minute. But she has not them, and in all likelihood, without a social revolution she never will have them. In the novels of Mr. Robert Chambers, however, or of Miss Jean Libbey, which she religiously reads in the street-car on her way to the shop; in the motion picture theater which she visits for ten cents after her supper of corned beef, cabbage, and cream puffs, she comes into possession of them forthwith, vicariously, and of all My Lady's proper perquisites—the Prince Charming, the motor-car, the Chinese pug, the flowers, and the costly bonbons. For the time being her life is liberated, new avenues of experience are actually opened to her, all sorts of unsatisfied desires are satisfied, all sorts of potentialities realized. All that she might have been and is not, she becomes through art, here and now, and *continuously with* the drab workaday life which is her lot, and she becomes this without any compensatory derealization of that life, without any transcendentalism, without any loss of grip on the necessities of her experience: strengthened, on the contrary, and emboldened, to meet them as they are.

I might multiply examples: for every object of fine art has the same intention, and if adequate, accomplishes the same end— from the sculptures of Phidias and the dramas of Euripides, to the sky-scrapers of Sullivan and the dances of Pavlowa. But there is need only to consider the multitude of abstract descriptions of the æsthetic encounter. The artist's business is to create the other object in the encounter, and this object, in Miss Puffer's words, which are completely representative and typical, is such that "the organism is in a condition of repose and of the highest possible tone, functional efficiency, enhanced life. The personality is brought into a state of unity and self-completeness." The object, when apprehended, awakens the active functioning of the whole organism directly and harmoniously with itself, cuts it off from the surrounding world, shuts that world out for the time being, and forms a complete, harmonious, and self-sufficient system, peculiar and unique in the fact that there is no passing from this deed into further adaptation with the object. Struggle and aliency are at end, and whatever activity now goes on feels self-conserving, spontaneous, free. The need of readjustment has disappeared, and with it the feeling of strain, obstruction, and resistance, which is its sign. There is nothing but the object, and that is possessed completely, satisfying, and as if forever. Art, in a word, supplies an environment from which strife, foreignness, obstruction, and death are eliminated. It actualizes unity, spirituality, and eternity in the environment; it frees and enhances the life of the self. To the environment which art successfully creates, the mind finds itself completely and harmoniously adapted by the initial act of perception.

In the world of art, value and existence are one.

V

If art may be said to create values, religion has been said to conserve them. But the values conserved are not those created: they are the values postulated by philosophy as metaphysical reality. Whereas, however, philosophy substitutes these values for the world of experience, religion makes them continuous with the world of experience. For religion value and existence are on the same level, but value is more potent and environs existence, directing it for its own ends. The unique content of religion, hence, is a specific imaginative extension of the environment with value-forms: the visible world is extended at either end by heaven and hell; the world of minds, by God, Satan, angels, demons, saints, and so on. But where philosophy imaginatively abolishes existence in behalf of value, where art realizes value in existence, religion tends to control and to escape the environment which exists by means of the environment which is postulated. The aim of religion is salvation from sin. Salvation is the escape from experience to heaven and the bosom of God; while hell is the compensatory readjustment of inner quality to outer condition for the alien and the enemy, without the knowledge of whose existence life in heaven could not be complete.

In religion, hence, the conversion of the repressed array of interests into ideal value-forms is less radical and abstract than in philosophy, and less checked by fusion with existence than in art. Religion is, therefore, at one and the same time more carnal and less reasonable than philosophy and art. Its history and protagonists exhibit a closer kinship to what is called insanity93—that being, in essence, the substitution in actual life of the creatures of the imagination which satisfy repressed needs for those of reality which repress them. It is a somnambulism which intensifies rather than abolishes the contrast between what is desired and what must be accepted. It offers itself ultimately rather as a refuge from reality than a control of it, and its development as an institution has turned on the creation and use of devices to make this escape feasible. For religion, therefore, the perception that the actual world, whatever its history, is now *not* adapted to human nature, is the true point of departure. Thus religion takes more account of experience than compensatory philosophy; it does not de-realize existent evil. The outer conflict between human nature and nature, primitively articulated in consciousness and conduct by the distress engendered through the fact that the food supply depends upon the march of the seasons,[94] becomes later assimilated to the inner conflict between opposing interests, wishes, and desires. Finally, the whole so constituted gets expressed in the idea of sin. That idea makes outward prosperity dependent upon inward purity, although it often transfers the locus of the prosperity to another world. Through its operation fortune becomes a function of conscience and the one desire of religious thinking and religious practice becomes to bring the two to a happy outcome, to abolish the conflicts. This desiderated abolition is salvation. It is expressed in the ideas of a fall, or a separation from heaven and reunion therewith. The machinery of this reunion of the divided, the reconversion of the differentiated into the same, consists of the furniture of religious symbols and ceremonials—myths, baptisms, sacraments, prayers, and sacrifices: and all these are at the same time instruments and expressions of desires. God is literally "the conservation of values."[95] "God's life in eternity," writes Aristotle, who here dominates the earlier tradition, "is that which we enjoy in our best moments, but are unable to possess permanently: its very being is delight. And as actual being is delight, so the various functions of waking, perceiving, thinking, are to us the pleasantest parts of our life. Perfect and absolute thought is just this absolute vision of perfection."[96]

Even the least somnambulistic of the transcendental philosophies has repeated, not improved upon Aristotle. "The highest conceptions that I get from experience of what goodness and beauty are," Royce declares, "the noblest life that I can imagine, the completest blessedness that I can think, all these are but faint suggestions of a truth that is infinitely realized in the Divine, that knows all truth. Whatever perfection there is suggested in these things, that he must fully know and experience."

But this æsthetic excellence, this maximum of ideality is in and by itself inadequate. God, to be God, must *work*. He is first of all the invisible socius, the ever-living witness, in whose eyes the disharmonies and injustices of this life are enregistered, and who in the life everlasting redresses the balances and adjusts the account. Even his grace is not unconditional; it requires a return, in deed or faith; a payment by which the fact of his salvation is made visible. But this payment is made identical by the great religions of disillusion with nothing other than the concrete condition from which the faithful are to be saved. If the self is not impoverished, unkempt, and hungry, in fact, it is made so. Cleanliness may be next to godliness, but self-defilement is godliness; sainthood, if we are to trust the lives of saints, whether in Asia or in Europe, is coincident with insanitation; saintly virtues are depressed virtues,—humility, hope, meekness, pity; and such conditions of life which define the holy ones are unwholesome—poverty, asceticism, squalor, filth. Hence, by an ironic inversion, religions of disillusion, being other-worldly, identify escape from an actual unpropitious environment with submergence in it; that being the visible and indispensable sign of an operative grace. So the beatitudes: the blessed are the poor, the mourners, the meek. Beginning as a correction of the evils of existence, religion ends by offering an infallible avenue of escape from them through postulating a desiderated type of existence which operates to gather the spirit to itself. For this reason the value-forms of the spirituality or spiritual control of the universe and of the immortality of the soul have been very largely the practical concern of religion alone, since these are the instruments indispensable to the attainment of salvation. In so far forth religion has been an art and its institutional association with the arts has been made one of its conspicuous justifications. So far, however, as it has declared values to be operative without making them actually existent it has been only a black art, a magic. It has ignored the actual causes in the nature and history of things, and has substituted for them non-existent desirable causes, ultimately reducible to a single, eternal, beneficent spirit, omnipotent and free. To convert these into existence, an operation which is the obvious intent of much contemporary thinking in religion,97 it must, however, give up the assumption that they already exist *qua* spirit. But when religion gives up this assumption, religion gives up the ghost.

What it demands of the ghost, and of all hypostatized or anthropomorphized ultimate value-forms, is that they shall work, and its life as an institution depends upon making them work. Christian Science becomes a refuge from the failure of science, magic from mechanism, and by means of them and their kind, blissful immortality, complete self-fulfilment is to be attained— after death. There is a "beautiful land of somewhere," a happy life beyond, but it is beyond life. In fact, although religion confuses value and existence, it localizes the great value-forms outside of existence. Its history has been an epic of the retreat and decimation of the gods from the world, a movement from animism and pluralism to transcendentalism and monism; and concomitantly, of an elaboration and extension of institutional devices by which the saving value-forms are to be made and kept operative in the world.

VI

Let us consider this history a little.

Consciousness of feeling, psychologists are agreed, is prior to consciousness of the objects of feeling. The will's inward strain, intense throbs of sensation, pangs and pulses of pleasure and pain make up the bulk of the undifferentiated primal sum of sentience. The soul is aware of herself before she is aware of her world. A childish or primeval mind, face to face with an environment actual, dreamt, or remembered, does not distinguish from its privacy the objective or the common. All is shot through with the pathos and triumph which come unaccountably as desired good or evaded evil; all has the same tensions and effects ends in the same manner as the laboring, straining, volitional life within. These feelings, residuary qualities, the last floating, unattached sediment of a world organized by association and classified by activity, these subtlest of all its beings, finally termed mind and self, at first suffuse and dominate the whole. Even when objects are distinguished and their places determined these are not absent; and the so-called pre-animistic faiths are not the less suffused with spirit because the spiritual has not yet received a local habitation and name. They differ from animism in this only, not in that their objects are characterized by lack of animation and vital tonality. And this is necessary. For religion must be anthropopathic before it becomes anthropomorphic; since feeling, eloquent of good and evil, is the first and deepest essence of consciousness, and only by its wandering from home are forms distinguished and man's nature separated from that of things and beasts.

When practice has coördinated activity, and reflection distinguished places, animism proper arises. First the environment is felt as the soul's kindred; then its operations are fancied in terms dramatic and personal. The world becomes almost instinctively defined as a hegemony of spirits similar to man, with powers and passions like his, and directed for his destruction or conservation, but chiefly for their own glory and self-maintenance. The vast "pathetic fallacy" makes religion of the whole of life. It is at this point indistinguishable from science or ethics. It is, in fact, the pregnant matrix of all subsequent discourse about the universe. Its character is such that it becomes the determining factor of human adaptations to the conditions imposed by the environment, by envisaging the enduring and efficacious elements among these conditions as persons. The satisfaction of felt needs is rendered thereby inevitably social; and in a like manner fear of their frustration cannot be unsocial. Life is conceived and acted out as a miraculous traffic with the universe; and the universe as a band of spirits who monopolize the good and make free gifts of evil, who can be feared, threatened, worshiped, scolded, wheedled, coaxed, bribed, deceived, enslaved, held in awe, and above all, used for the prosecution of desiderated ends and the fulfilment of instinctive desires. The first recorded cognized order is a moral order in which fragmentary feelings, instinctive impulsions, and spontaneous imaginings are hypostatized, ideas are identified with their causes, all the contents of the immature, sudden, primitive, blundering consciousness receive a vital figure and a proper name. So man makes himself more at home in the world without,—that world which enslaves the spirit so fearfully and with such strangeness, and which just as miraculously yields such ecstasy, such power, such unaccountable good! In this immediate sense the soul controls the world by becoming symbolic of it; it is the world's first language. It is, however, an inarticulate, blundering, incoherent thing and the cues which it furnishes to the nature of the environment are as often as not dangerous and misleading. When bows and arrows, crystals and caves, clouds and waters, dung and dew, mountains and trees, beasts and visions, are treated as chiefs and men must be treated, then the moral regimen initiated, taking little account of the barest real qualities manifested by these things, and attributing the maximum importance to the characters postulated and foreign, is successful neither in allaying evil nor in extending good. Its benefits are adventitious and its malfeasance constant. Food buried with the dead was food lost; blood smeared upon the bow to make it shoot better served only to make the hands unskilful by impeding their activity. Initiation, ceremony, sacrificial ritual, fasting, and isolation involved privations for which no adequate return was recovered, even by the medicine-man whose absolute and ephemeral power needed only the betrayal of circumstances for its own destruction, taking him along with it, oftener than not, to disgrace or death.

As the cumulus of experience on experience grew greater, chance violations of tradition, or custom, or ritual, or formula achieving for the violator a mastery or stability which performance and obedience failed to achieve, the new heresy became the later orthodoxy, for in religion, as in all other matters human, nothing succeeds like success. An impotent god has no divinity; a disused potency means a dying life among the immortals as on the earth. And as the gods themselves seemed often to give their worshipers the lie, the futility of the personal and dramatic definitions of the immediate environment became slowly recognized, the recognition varying in extent, and clearer in practice than in discourse.

Accordingly the most primitive of the animisms underwent a necessary modification. The plasticity of objects under destructive treatment, the impotence of *taboo* before elementary needs, the adequate satisfactions which violations of the divine law brought,—these killed many gods and drove others from their homes in the hearts of things. The objects so purged became matters of accurate knowledge. Where animation is denied the *whole* environment, wisdom begins to distinguish between spirit-haunted matter and the purely material; knowledge of person and knowledge of things differentiate, and science, the impersonal and more potent knowledge of the environment, properly begins. Familiarity leads to control, control to contempt, and for the unreflective mind, personality is not, as for the sophisticated, an attribute of the contemptible. The incalculable appearance of thunder, the magic greed of fire, the malice, the spontaneity, the thresh and pulse as of life which seems to characterize whatever is capricious or impenetrable or uncontrollable are too much like the felt throbs of consciousness to become dehumanized. To the variable alone, therefore, is transcendent animation attributed. Not the seasonal variation of the sun's heat, but the joy and the sorrow of which his heat is the occasion made him divine. When the gods appear, to take the place of the immanent spirits immediately present in things, they appear, therefore, as already transcendent, with habitations just beyond the well-known: on high mountains, in the skies, in dark forests, in caves, in all regions feared or unexplored. But chiefly the gods inhabit those spaces whence issue the power of darkness and destruction, particularly the heaven, a word whose meaning is now, as it was primitively, identical with divinity. The savage becomes a pagan by giving concrete personality to the dreadful unknown. Thence it is that the ancient poet assigns the gods a lineage of fear; and fear may truly be said to have made the gods, in so far as the gods personify the fear which made them.

The moral level of these figments alters with the level of their habitation; their power varies with their remoteness; Zeus lives in the highest heaven and is arbiter of the destiny of both gods and man. To him and to his like there cannot be the relation of equality which is sustained between men and spirits of the lower order. His very love is blasting; interchange of commodities, good for good and evil for evil is not possible where he is concerned. Gods of the higher order he exemplifies, even all the gods of Olympus, of the Himalayas, of Valhalla, are literally beings invoked and implored, as well as dwellers in heaven. To them man pays a toll on all excellence he gains or finds; libations and burnt-offerings, the fat and the first fruits: he exists by their sufferance and serves their caprice. He is their toy, born for their pleasure, and living by their need.

But just because men conceive themselves to be play-things of the gods, they define in the gods the ideals of mankind. For the divine power is power to live forever, and the sum of human desire is just the desire to maintain its humanity in freedom and happiness endlessly. And exactly those capacities and instruments of self-maintenance,—all that is beauty, or truth, or goodness, the very essence of value in any of its forms,—the gods are conceived to possess and to control: these they may grant, withhold, destroy. They are as eternal as their habitations, the mountains; as ruthless as their element, the sea; as omnipresent as the heavens, their home. To become like the gods, therefore, the masters and fathers of men, is to remain eternally and absolutely human: so that who is most like them on earth takes his place beside them in heaven.

Hercules and Elias and Krishna, Çaka-Muni and Ishvara, Jesus and Baha Ullah. Nay, they are the very gods themselves, manifest as men! The history of the gods thus presents a double aspect: it is first a characterization of the important objects and processes of nature and their survival-values,—the sun, thunder, rain, and earthquakes; dissolution, rebirth, and love; and again it is the narration of activities native and delightful to mankind. Zeus is a promiscuous lover as well as a wielder of thunderbolts; Apollo not only drives the chariot of the sun; he plays and dances, discourses melody and herds sheep.

But while the portrait of the heart's desire in fictitious adventures of divinity endears the gods to the spirit, the exploration of the elements in the environment whose natures they dramatically express, destroys their force, reduces their number, and drives them still further into the unknown. Olympus is surrendered for the planets and the fixed stars. With remoteness of location comes transmutation of character. The forces of the environment which were the divinity are now conceived as instrumental to its uses. Its power is more subtly described; its nature becomes a more purely ideal expression of human aspiration. Physical remoteness and metaphysical ultimacy are akin. God among the stars is better than God on Olympus. If, as with the Parsees, the unfavorable character of the environment is expressed in another and equal being,—the devil, then the god of good must, in the symbolic struggle, become the ultimate victor and remain the more potent director of man's destiny. In religion, therefore, when the mind grows at all by experience, monism develops spontaneously. For the character of the god becomes increasingly more relevant to hope than to the conditions of hope's satisfaction. And what man first of all and beyond all aspires to, is that single, undivided good,—the free flow of his unitary life, stable, complete, eternal. There is hence always to be found a chief and father among the gods who, as mankind gain in wisdom and in material power, consumes his mates and his children like Kronos or Jahweh, inherits their attributes and performs their functions. The chief divinity becomes the only divinity; a god becomes God. But divinity, in becoming one and unique, becomes also transcendent. Monotheism pushes God altogether beyond the sensible environment. Personality, instead of being the nature of the world, has become its ground and cause, and all that mankind loves is conserved, in order that man, whom God loves, may have his desire and live forever. Life is eternal and happiness necessary, beyond nature,—in heaven. Finally, in transcendental idealism, the poles meet; what has been put eternally apart is eternally united; the immaterial, impalpable, transcendent heaven is made one and continuous with the gross and unhappy natural world. One *is* the other; the other the one. God *is* the world and transcends it; *is* the evil and the good which conquers and consumes that evil. The environment becomes thus described as a single, eternal, conscious unity, in which all the actual but transitory values of the actual but transitory life are conserved and eternalized. In a description of God such as Royce's or Aristotle's the environment is the eternity of all its constituents that are dearest to man. Religion, which began as a definition of the environment as it moved and controlled mankind, ends by describing it as mankind desires it to be. The environment is now the aforementioned ideal socius or self which satisfies perfectly all human requirements. Pluralistic and quarrelsome animism has become monistic and harmonious spiritism. Forces have turned to excellences and needs to satisfactions. Necessity has been transmuted to Providence, sin has been identified with salvation, value with existence, and existence with impotence and illusion before Providence, salvation, and value.

VII

With this is completed the reply to the question: Why do men contradict their own experience? Experience is, as Spinoza says, passion and action, both inextricably mingled and coincident, with the good and evil of them as interwoven as they. That piecemeal conquest of the evil which we call civilization has not even the promise of finality. It is a Penelope's web, always needing to be woven anew. Now, in experience desire anticipates and outleaps action and fact rebuffs desire. Desire realizes itself, consequently, in ideas objectified by the power of speech into independent and autonomous subjects of discourse, whereby experience is One, Eternal, a Spirit or Spiritually Controlled, wherein man has Freedom and Immortality. These, the constantly desiderated traits of a perfect universe, are in fact the limits of what adequacy environmental satisfactions can attain, ideas hypostatized, normative of existence, but not constituting it. With them, in philosophy and religion, the mind confronts the experiences of death and obstruction, of manifoldness, change and materiality, and denies them, as Peter denied Jesus. The visible world, being not as we want it, we imagine an unseen one that satisfies our want, declaring the visible one an illusion by its side. So we work a radical substitution of desiderates for actualities, of ideals for facts, of values for existences. Art alone acknowledges the actual relations between these contrasting pairs. Art alone so operates as in fact to convert their oppugnance into identity. Intrinsically, its whole purpose and technique consists of transmutation of values into existences, in the incarnation the realization of values. The philosophy and religion of tradition, on the contrary, consists intrinsically in the flat denial of reality, or at least, co-reality, to existence, and the transfer of that eulogium to value-forms as such.

Metaphysics, theology, ethics, logic, æsthetics, dialectic developments as they are of "norms" or "realities" which themselves can have no meaning without the "apparent," changing world they measure and belie, assume consequently a detachment and self-sufficiency they do not actually possess. Their historians have treated them as if they had no context, as if the elaboration of the ideal tendencies of the successive systems explained their origin, character, and significance. But in fact they are unendowed with this pure intrinsicality, and their development is not to be accounted for as exteriorization of innate motive or an unfoldment of inward implications. They have a context; they are crossed and interpenetrated by outer interests and extraneous considerations. Their meaning, in so far as it is not merely æsthetic, is *nil* apart from these interests and considerations of which they are sometimes expressions, sometimes reconstructions, and from which they are persistently refuges.

Philosophy and religion are, in a word, no less than art, social facts. They are responses to group situations without which they cannot be understood. Although analysis has shown them to be rooted in certain persistent motives and conditions of human nature by whose virtue they issue in definite contours and significances, they acquire individuality and specific importance only through interaction with the constantly varying social situations in which they arise, on which they operate, and by which they are in turn operated on. Philosophy has perhaps suffered most of all from nescience of those and from devoting itself, at a minimum, to the satisfaction of that passion for oneness, for "logical consistency" without which philosophic "systems" would never arise, nor the metaphysical distinction between "appearance" and "reality"; and with which the same systems have made up a historic aggregate of strikingly repugnant and quarrelsome units. It is this pursuit of consistency as against correctness which has resulted in the irrelevance of philosophy that the philosopher, unconscious of his motives and roots, or naïvely identifying, through the instrumentality of an elaborate dialectic, his instinctive and responsive valuations of existence with its categoric essences, confuses with inward autonomy and the vision of the "real." Consequently, the systems of tradition begin as attempts to transvalue social situations whose existence is troublesome and end as utterances of which the specific bearing, save to the system of an opponent, is undiscoverable. The attempt to correct the environment in fact concludes as an abolition of it in words. The philosophic system becomes a solipsism, a pure lyric expression of the appetites of human nature.

For this perversity of the philosophic tradition Plato is perhaps, more than any one else, answerable. He is the first explicitly to have reduplicated the world, to have set existences over against values, to have made them dependent upon values, to have assigned absolute reality to the compensatory ideals, and to have identified philosophy with preoccupation with these ideals. Behind his theory of life lay far from agreeable personal experience of the attitude of political power toward philosophic ideas. Its ripening was coincident with the most distressing period of the history of his country. The Peloponnesian War was the confrontation of two social systems, radically opposed in form, method, and outlook. Democracy, in Athens, had become synonymous with demagoguery, corruption, inefficiency, injustice and unscrupulousness in every aspect of public affairs. The government had no consistent policy and no centralized responsibility; divided counsel led to continual disaster without, and party politics rotted the strength within. Beside Athens, Sparta, a communistic oligarchy, was a tower of strength and effectiveness. The Spartans made mistakes; they were slow, inept, rude, and tyrannical, but they were a unit on the war, their policy was consistent, responsibilities were adequately centered, good order and loyalty designated the aims and habits of life.98 The Republic is the response to the confrontation of Spartan and Athenian; the attempt to find an adequate solution of the great social problem this confrontation expressed. The successful state becomes in it the model for the metaphysical one, and the difference between fact and ideal is amended by dialectically forcing the implications of existence in the direction of desire. Neither Athens nor Sparta presented a completely satisfactory social organization. There must therefore exist a type of social organization which is so satisfying. It must have existed from eternity, and must be in essence identical with eternal good, identical with that oneness and spirituality, lacking which, nothing is important. This archetypal social organization whose essence is excellence, it is the congenital vocation of the philosopher to contemplate and to realize. Philosophers are hence the paragons among animals, lovers of truth, haters of falsehood and of multiplicity, spectators of all time and all existence. In them the power to govern should be vested. Their nature is of the same stuff as the Highest Good with which it concerns itself, but being such, it appears, merely "appears" alas! irrelevant to the actual situations of the daily life. The philosopher is hence opposed and expelled by that arch-sophist, Public Opinion: the man on the street, failing to understand him, dubs him prater, star-gazer, good-for-nothing.99 He becomes an ineffectual stranger, an outlaw, in a world in which he should be master.

Plato's description of the philosopher and philosophy is, it will be seen, at once an apology and a program. But it is a program which has been petrified into a compensatory ideal. The confession of impotence, the abandonment of the programmatic intent is due to identification of the ideal with metaphysical fact, to the hypostasis of the ideal. With Christianity, that being a philosophy operating as a religion, world-weariness made the apology unnecessary and converted the hypostasis into the basis of that program of complete surrender of the attempt to master the problems of existence upon which ensued the arrest of science and civilization for a thousand years. The Greeks were not world-weary, and consequently, their joy in life and existence contributed a minimum of relevance to their other-worldly dreams. Need it be reasserted that the whole Platonic system, at its richest and best in the Republic, is both an expression of and a compensation for a concrete social situation? Once it was formulated it became a part of that situation, altered it, served as another among the actual causes which determined the subsequent history of philosophy. Its historic and efficacious significance is defined by that situation, but philosophers ignore the situation and accept the system as painters accept a landscape—as the thing in itself.

Now, the æsthetic aspect of the philosophic system, its autonomy, and consequent irrelevancy, are undeniable. Once it comes to be, its intrinsic excellence may constitute its infallible justification for existence, with no more to be said; and if its defenders or proponents claimed nothing more for it than this immediate satisfactoriness, there would be no quarrel with them. There is, however, present in their minds a sense of the other bearings of their systems. They claim them, in any event, to be *true*, that is, to be relevant to a situation regarded as more important because more lastingly determinative of conduct, more "real" than the situation of which they are born. Their systems are offered, hence, as maps of life, as guides to the everlasting. That they intend to define some method for the conservation of life eternally, is clear enough from their initial motivation and formal issue: all the Socratics, with their minds fixed on happiness or salvation according to the prevalence of disillusionment among them; the Christian systems, still Socratic, but as resolutely other-worldly as disillusioned Buddhists; the systems of Spinoza, of Kant, the whole subsequent horde of idealisms, up to the contemporary Germanoid and German idealistic soliloquies,— they all declare that the vanity and multiplicity of life as it is leads them to seek for the permanent and the meaningful, and they each find it according to the idiosyncrasies of the particular impulses and terms they start with. That their Snark turns out in every case to be a Boojum is another story.

Yet this story is what gives philosophy, like religion, its social significance. If its roots, as its actual biography shows, did not reach deep in the soil of events, if its issues had no fruitage in events made over by its being, it would never have been so closely identified with intelligence and its systematic hypostasis would never have ensued. The fact is that philosophy, like all forms of creative intelligence, is a tool before it is a perfection. Its autonomy supervenes on its efficaciousness; it does not precede its efficaciousness. Men philosophize in order to live before they live in order to philosophize. Aristotle's description of the self-sufficiency of theory is possible only for a life wherein theory had already earned this self-sufficiency as practice, in a life, that is, which is itself an art, organized by the application of value-forms to its existent psycho-physical processes in such a way that its existence incarnates the values it desiderates and the values perfect the existence that embodies them.

The biography of philosophy, hence, reveals it to have the same possibilities and the same fate that all other ideas have.

Today ideas are the patent of our humanity, the stuff and form of intelligence, the differentiæ between us and the beasts. In so far forth, they express the surplusage of vitality over need, the creative freedom of life at play. This is the thing we see in the imaginings and fantasies of childhood, whose environment is by social intent formed to favor and sustain its being. The capacity for spontaneity of idea appears to decrease with maturity, and the few favored healthy mortals with whom it remains are called men of genius. William James was such a man, and there are a few still among the philosophers. But in the mass and in the long run, ideas are not a primary confirmation of our humanity; in the mass and long they are warnings of menace to it, a sign of its disintegration. Even so radical an intellectualist as Mr. Santayana cherishes this observation to the degree of almost suggesting it as the dogma that all ideas have their origin in inner or outer maladjustment.100 However this may be, that the dominant philosophic ideas arise out of radical disharmonies between nature and human nature need not be here reiterated, while the provocative character of minor maladjustments is to be inferred from the fertility of ideas in unstable minds, of whatever type, from the neurasthenic to the mad. Ideas represent in these cases the limits of vital elasticity, the attempt of the organism to maintain its organic balance; it is as if a balloon, compressed on one side, bulged on the other.

Ideas, then, bear three types of relations to organic life, relations socially incarnated in traditional art, religion, and philosophy. First of all they may be an expression of innate capacities, the very essence of the freedom of life. In certain arts, such as music, they are just this. In the opposite case they may be the effect of the compression of innate capacities, an outcome of obstruction to the free low of life. They are then compensatory. Where expressive ideas are confluent with existence, compensatory ideas diverge from existence; they become pure value-forms whose paramount realization is traditional philosophy. Their rise and motivation in both these forms is unconscious. They are ideas, but not yet intelligence. The third instance falls between these original two. The idea is neither merely a free expression of innate capacities, nor a compensation for their obstruction or compression. Arising as the effect of a disharmony, it develops as an enchannelment of organic powers directed to the conversion of the disharmony into an adjustment. It does not *use up* vital energies like the expressive idea, it is not an abortion of them, like the compensatory idea. It uses them, and is aware that it uses them—that is, it is a program of action upon the environment, of conversion of values into existences. Such an idea has the differentia of intelligence. It is creative; it actually converts nature into forms appropriate to human nature. It abolishes the Otherworld of the compensatory tradition in philosophy by incarnating it in this world; it abolishes the Otherworld of the religionist, rendered important by belittling the actual one, by restoring the working relationships between thoughts and things. This restoration develops as reconstruction of the world in fact. It consists specifically of the art and science which compose the efficacious enterprises of history and of which the actual web of our civilization is spun.

Manifest in its purity in art, it attends unconsciously both religion and philosophy, for the strands of life keep interweaving, and whatever is, in our collective being, changes and is changed by whatever else may be, that is in reach. The life of reason is initially unconscious because it can learn only by living to seek a reason for life. Once it discovers that it can become self-maintaining alone through relevance to its ground and conditions, the control which this relevance yields makes it so infectious that it tends to permeate every human institution, even religion and philosophy. Philosophy, it is true, has lagged behind even religion in relevancy, but the lagging has been due not to the intention of the philosopher but to the inherent character of the task he assumed. Both art and religion, we have seen, possess an immediacy and concreteness which philosophy lacks. Art reconstructs correlative portions of the environment for the eye, the ear, the hopes and fears of the daily life. Religion extends this reconstruction beyond the actual environment, but applies its saving technique at the critical points in the career of the group or the individual; to control the food-supply, to protect in birth, pubescence, marriage, and death. All its motives are grounded in specific instincts and needs, all its reconstructions and compensations culminate with reference to these. Philosophy, on the other hand, deals with the *whole* nature of man and his *whole* environment. It seeks primaries and ultimates. Its traditional task is so to define the universe as to articulate thereby a theory of life and eternal salvation. It establishes contact with reality at no individual, specific point: its reals are "real in general." It aims, in a word, to be relevant to all nature, and to express the whole soul of man. The consequence is inevitable: it forfeits relevance to everything natural; touching nothing actual, it reconstructs nothing actual. Its concretest incarnation is a dialectic design woven of words. The systems of tradition, hence, are works of art, to be contemplated, enjoyed, and believed in, but not to be acted on. For, since action is always concrete and specific, always determined to time, place, and occasion, we cannot in fact adapt ourselves to the aggregate infinitude of the environment, or that to ourselves. Something always stands out, recalcitrant, invincible, defiant. But it is just such an adaptation that philosophy intends, and the futility of the intention is evinced by the fact that the systems of tradition continue side by side with the realities they deny, and live unmixed in one and the same mind, as a picture of the ocean on the wall of a dining room in an inland town. Our operative relations to them tend always to be essentially æsthetic. We may and do believe in them in spite of life and experience, because belief in them, involving no action, involves no practical risk. Where action is a consequence of a philosophic system, the system seems to dichotomize into art and religion. It becomes particularized into a technique of living or the dogma of a sect, and so particularized it becomes radically self-conscious and an aspect of creative intelligence.

So particularized, it is, however, no longer philosophy, and philosophy has (I hope I may say this without professional bias) an inalienable place in the life of reason. This place is rationally defined for it by the discovery of its ground and function in the making of civilization; and by the perfection of its possibilities through the definition of its natural relationships. Thus, it is, in its essential historic character at least, as fine an art as music, the most inward and human of all arts. It may be, and human nature being what it is, undoubtedly will continue to be, an added item to the creations wherewith man makes his world a better place to live in, precious in that it envisages and projects the excellences and perfections his heart desires and his imagination therefore defines. So taken, it is not a substitution for the world, but an addition to it, a refraction of it through the medium of human nature, as a landscape painting by Whistler or Turner is not a substitution for the actual landscape, but an interpretation and imaginative perfection of it, more suitable to the eye of man. A system like Bergson's is such a work, and its æsthetic adequacy, its beauty, may be measured by the acknowledgment it receives and the influence it exercises. Choosing one of the items of experience as its medium, and this item the most precious in the mind's eye which the history of philosophy reveals, it proceeds to fabricate a dialectical image of experience in which all the compensatory desiderates are expressed and realized. It entices minds of all orders, and they are happy to dwell in it, for the nonce realizing in the perception of the system the values it utters. By abandoning all pretense to be true, philosophic systems of the traditional sort may attain the simple but supreme excellence of beauty, and rest content therewith.

The philosophic ideal, however, is traditionally not beauty but truth: the function of a philosophic system is not presentative, but *re*presentative and causal, and that the systems of tradition have had and still have consequences as well as character, is obvious enough. It is, however, to be noted that these consequences have issued out of the fact that the systems have been specific items of existence among other equally and even more specific items, thought by particular men, at particular times and in particular places. As such they have been programs for meeting events and incarnating values; operative ideals aiming to recreate the world according to determined standards. They have looked forward rather than backward, have tacitly acknowledged the reality of change, the irreducible pluralism of nature, and the genuineness of the activities, oppugnant or harmonizing, between the items of the Cosmic. Many they ostensibly negate. The truth, in a word, has been experimental and prospective; the desiderates they uttered operated actually as such and not as already existing. Historians of philosophy, treating it as if it had no context, have denied or ignored this rôle of philosophy in human events, but historians of the events themselves could not avoid observing and enregistering it.

Only within very recent years, as an effect of the concept of evolution in the field of the sciences, have philosophers as such envisaged this non-æsthetic aspect of philosophy's ground and function in the making of civilization and have made it the basis for a sober vision which may or may not have beauty, but which cannot have finality. Such a vision is again nothing more than traditional philosophy become conscious of its character and limitations and shorn of its pretense. It is a program to execute rather than a metaphysic to rest in. Its procedure is the procedure of all the arts and sciences. It frankly acknowledges the realities of immediate experience, the turbulence and complexity of the flux, the interpenetrative confusion of orders, the inward self-diversification of even the simplest thing, which "change" means, and the continual emergence of novel entities, unforeseen and unprevisible, from the reciprocal action of the older aggregate. This perceptual reality it aims to remould according to the heart's desire. Accordingly it drops the pretense of envisaging the universe and devotes itself to its more modest task of applying its standards to a particular item that needs to be remade. It is believed in, but no longer without risk, for, without becoming a dogma, it still subjects itself to the tests of action. So it acknowledges that it must and will itself undergo constant modification through the process of action, in which it uses events, in their meanings rather than in their natures, to map out the future and to make it amenable to human nature. Philosophy so used is, as John Dewey somewhere says, a mode and organ of experience among many others. In a world the very core of which is change, it is directed upon that which is not yet, to previse and to form its character and to map out the way of life within it. Its aim is the liberation and enlargement of human capacities, the enfranchisement of man by the actual realization of values. In its integrate character therefore, it envisages the life of reason and realizes it as the art of life. Where it is successful, beauty and use are confluent and identical in it. It converts sight into insight. It infuses existence with value, making them one. It is the concrete incarnation of Creative Intelligence.

FOOTNOTES:

1 The word relation suffers from ambiguity. I am speaking here of *connexion*, dynamic and functional interaction. "Relation" is a term used also to express logical reference. I suspect that much of the controversy about internal and external relations is due to this ambiguity. One passes at will from existential connexions of things to logical relationship of terms. Such an identification of existences with *terms* is congenial to idealism, but is paradoxical in a professed realism.

2 There is some gain in substituting a doctrine of flux and interpenetration of psychical states, *à la* Bergson, for that of rigid discontinuity. But the substitution leaves untouched the fundamental misstatement of experience, the conception of experience as directly and primarily "inner" and psychical.

3 Mathematical science in its formal aspects, or as a branch of formal logic, has been the empirical stronghold of rationalism. But an empirical empiricism, in contrast with orthodox deductive empiricism, has no difficulty in establishing its jurisdiction as to deductive functions.

4 It is a shame to devote the word idealism, with its latent moral, practical connotations, to a doctrine whose tenets are the denial of the existence of a physical world, and the psychical character of all objects—at least as far as they are knowable. But I am following usage, not attempting to make it.

5 See Dr. Kallen's essay, below.

6 The "they" means the "some" of the prior sentence—those whose realism is epistemological, instead of being a plea for taking the facts of experience as we find them without refraction through epistemological apparatus.

7 It is interesting to note that some of the realists who have assimilated the cognitive relation to other existential relations in the world (instead of treating it as an unique or epistemological relation) have been forced in support of their conception of knowledge as a "presentative" or spectatorial affair to extend the defining features of the latter to all relations among things, and hence to make all the "real" things in the world pure "simples," wholly independent of one another. So conceived the doctrine of external relations appears to be rather the doctrine of complete externality of *things*. Aside from this point, the doctrine is interesting for its dialectical ingenuity and for the elegant development of assumed premises, rather than convincing on account of empirical evidence supporting it.

8 In other words, there is a general "problem of error" only because there is a general problem of evil, concerning which see Dr. Kallen's essay, below.

9 Compare the paper by Professor Bode.

10 As the attempt to retain the epistemological problem and yet to reject idealistic and relativistic solutions has forced some Neo-realists into the doctrine of isolated and independent simples, so it has also led to a doctrine of Eleatic pluralism. In order to maintain the doctrine the subject makes no difference to anything else, it is held that *no* ultimate real makes any difference to anything else—all this rather than surrender once for all the genuineness of the problem and to follow the lead of empirical subject-matter.

11 There is almost no end to the various dialectic developments of the epistemological situation. When it is held that all the relations of the type in question are cognitive, and yet it is recognized (as it must be) that many such "transformations" go unremarked, the theory is supplemented by introducing "unconscious" psychical modifications.

12 Conception-presentation has, of course, been made by many in the history of speculation an exception to this statement; "pure" memory is also made an exception by Bergson. To take cognizance of this matter would, of course, accentuate, not relieve, the difficulty remarked upon in the text.

13 Cf. *Studies in Logical Theory*, Chs. I and II, by Dewey; also "Epistemology and Mental States," Tufts, *Phil. Rev.*, Vol. VI, which deserves to rank as one of the early documents of the "experimental" movement.

14 Cf. "The Definition of the Psychical," G. H. Mead, *Decennial Publications of the University of Chicago.*

15 Cf. *The Logic of Hegel-Wallace*, p. 117.

16 *Bosanquet's Logic*, 2nd Ed., p. 171. The identification of induction and procedure by hypothesis occurs on p. 156.

17 *Ibid.*, p. 14 (italics mine).

18 Perhaps the most complete exhibition of the breakdown of formal logic considered as an account of the operation of thought apart from its subject-matter is to be found in Schiller's *Formal Logic.*

19 Cf. Stuart on "Valuation as a Logical Process" in *Studies in Logical Theory.*

20 *The New Realism*, pp. 40-41.

21 Cf. Montague, pp. 256-57; also Russell, *The Problems of Philosophy*, pp. 27-65-66, *et passim*; and Holt's *Concept of Consciousness*, pp. 14ff., discussed below.

22 Cf. Angell, "Relations of Psychology to Philosophy," *Decennial Publications of University of Chicago*, Vol. III; also Castro, "The Respective Standpoints of Psychology and Logic," *Philosophic Studies, University of Chicago*, No. 4.

23 I am here following, in the main, Professor Holt because he alone appears to have had the courage to develop the full consequences of the premises of analytic logic.

24 *The Concept of Consciousness*, pp. 14-15.

25 It is interesting to compare this onlooking act with the account of consciousness further on. As "psychological" this act of onlooking must be an act of consciousness. But consciousness is a cross-section or a projection of things made by their interaction with a nervous system. Here consciousness is a function of all the interacting factors. It is in the play. It *is* the play. It is not in a spectator's box. How can consciousness be a function of all the things put into the cross-section and yet be a mere beholder of the process? Moreover, what is it that makes any particular, spectacle, or cross-section "logical"? If it be said all are "logical" what significance has the term?

26 Cf. Russell's *Scientific Methods in Philosophy*, p. 59.

27 Holt, *op. cit.*, pp. 128-30.

28 In fact, Newton, in all probability, had the Cartesian pure notions in mind.

29 Holt, *op. cit.*, p. 118 (italics mine). Cf. also Perry's *Present Philosophical Tendencies*, pp. 108 and 311.

30 The character of elements and the nature of simplicity have been discussed in the preceding section.

31 *Ibid.*, p. 275.

32 *Ibid.*, p. 275.

33 This lack of continuity between the cognitive function of the nervous system and its other functions accounts for the strange paradox in the logic of neo-realism of an act of knowing which is "subjective" and yet is the act of so palpably an objective affair as a nervous system. The explanation is that the essence of all deprecated subjectivity is, as before pointed out, functional isolation. That this sort of subjectivity should be identified with the "psychical" is not strange, since a living organism is very difficult to isolate, while the term "psychical," in its metaphysical sense, seems to stand for little else than just this complete isolation. Having once appealed to the nervous system it seems incredible that the physiological continuity of its functions with each other and with its environment should not have suggested the logical corollary. Only the force of the prepossession of mathematical atomism in analytic logic can account for its failure to do so.

34 But it would be better to use the term "logically-practical" instead of "subjective" with the psychical implications of that term.

35 An analysis which has been many times carried out has made it clear that scientific data never do more than approximate the laws and entities upon which our science rests. It is equally evident that the forms of these laws and entities themselves shift in the reconstructions of incessant research, or where they seem most secure could consistently be changed, or at least could be fundamentally different were our psychological structure or even our conventions of thought different. I need only refer to the *Science et Hypothèse* of Poincaré and the *Problems of Science* of Enriques. The positivist who undertakes to carry the structure of the world back to the data of observation, and the uniformities

appearing in the accepted hypotheses of growing sciences cannot maintain that we ever succeed in isolating data which must remain the same in the kaleidoscope of our research science; nor are we better served if we retreat to the ultimate elements of points and instants which our pure mathematics assumes and implicitly defines, and in connection with which it has worked out the modern theory of the number and continuous series, its statements of continuity and infinity.

36 In other words, science assumes that every error is *ex post facto* explicable as a function of the real conditions under which it really arose. Hence, "consciousness," set over against Reality, was not its condition.

37 C. Judson Herrick, "Some Reflections on the Origin and Significance of the Cerebral Cortex," *Journal of Animal Behavior,* Vol. III, pp. 228-233.

38 *Psychology,* Vol. I, p. 256.

39 H. C. Warren, *Psychological Review,* Vol. XXI, Page 93.

40 *Principles of Psychology,* I, p. 241, note.

41 *Ibid.,* p. 258.

42 *Psychology. Briefer Course.* P. 468.

43 Angell, *Psychology,* p. 65.

44 *Psychology,* Vol. I, p. 251.

45 Thorstein Veblen: *The Instinct of Workmanship,* p. 316.

46 It may still be argued that we must depend upon analogy in our acceptance or rejection of a new commodity. For any element

of novelty must surely suggest something to us, must *mean* something to us, if it is to attract or repel. Thus, the motor-car will whirl us rapidly over the country, the motor-boat will dart over the water without effort on our part. And in such measure as we have had them hitherto, we have always enjoyed experiences of rapid motion. These new instruments simply promise a perfectly well-known *sort* of experience in fuller measure. So the argument may run. And our mental process in such a case may accordingly be held to be nothing more mysterious than a passing by analogy from the *old* ways in which we got rapid motion in the past to the *new* way which now promises more of the same. And more of the same is what we want.

"More of the same" means here intensive magnitude and in this connection at all events it begs the question. Bergson's polemic seems perfectly valid against such a use of the notion. But kept in logical terms the case seems clearer. It is said that we reason in such a case by "analogy." We do, indeed; but what is analogy? The term explains nothing until the real process behind the term is clearly and realistically conceived. What I shall here suggest holds true, I think, as an account of analogical inference generally and not simply for the economic type of case we have here to do with. Reasoning is too often thought of as proceeding from given independent premises—as here (1) the fact that hitherto the driving we have most enjoyed and the sailing we have most enjoyed have been *fast* and (2) the fact that the motor-car is *fast*. But do we accept the conclusion because the premises suggest it in a way we cannot resist? On the contrary, stated thus, the premises clearly do *not* warrant the conclusion that the motor-car will be enjoyable. Such a statement of the premises is wholly formal and *ex post facto*. What, then, is our actual mental process in the case? The truth is, I think, that we simply—yes, "psychologically"— wish to try *that promised unheard-of rate of speed!* That comes first and foremost. But we mean to be reasonably prudent on the whole, although we are avowedly adventurous just now in this particular direction! We, therefore, ransack our memory for *other fast things* we have known, to see whether they have encouragement to give us. We try to supply ourselves with a major premise because the new proposal in its own right interests us—instead of having the major premise already there to coerce us by a purely "logical" compulsion as soon as we invade its sphere of influence. And confessedly, in point of "logic," there is no such compulsion in the second figure: there is only a timid and vexatious neutrality, a mere "not proven."

Why, then, do we in fact take the much admired "inductive leap," in seeming defiance of strict logic? Why do we close our eyes to logic, turn our back upon logic, behave as if logic were not and had never been? In point of fact, we do nothing of the sort. The "inductive leap" is no leap away from logic, but the impulsion of logic's mainspring seen only in its legitimate event. Because we have not taken care to see the impulse coming, it surprises us and we are frightened. And we look about for an illusive assurance in some "law of thought," or some question-begging "universal premise" of Nature's "uniformity." We do not see that we were already conditionally committed to the "leap" by our initial interest. Getting our premises together is no hurried forging of a chain to save us from our own madness in the nick of time. We are only hoping to rid ourselves of an excess of conservative ballast. To reason by analogy is not to repress or to dispense with the interest in the radically novel, but to give methodical and intelligent expression to that interest.

47 Aristotle's *Nicomachaean Ethics* (Welldon's transl.), Book VIII.

48 Cf. Aristotle's *Politics* (Jowett's trans.) III. 9. §6 ff. and elsewhere; *Nicom. Ethics*, I, Chap. III (end).

49 Cf. Veblen: *op. cit.*

<u>50</u> W. McDougall in his *Social Psychology* (Ed. 1912, pp. 358 ff.) recognizes "incomplete anticipation of the end of action" as a genuine type of preliminary situation in human behavior, but appears to regard this as in so far a levelling-down of man to the blindness of the "brutes." But "incompleteness" is a highly ambiguous term and seems here to beg the question. "Incompleteness" may be given an emphasis in which it imports conjecture and hypothesis—almost anything, in fact, but blindness. Rather do the brutes get levelled up to man by such facts as those McDougall cites.

<u>51</u> I take *routine* to be the essence and meaning of hedonism. There are two fundamental types of conduct—routine and constructiveness. Reference may be made here to Böhm-Bawerk's pronouncement on hedonism in *Kapital und Kapitalzins*, 1912 (II-2, pp. 310 ff.): "What people love and hate, strive towards or fight off—whether only pleasure and pain or other 'lovable' and 'hatable' things as well,—is a matter of entire indifference to the economist. The only thing important is that they do love and hate certain things.... The deductions of marginal utility theory lose no whit of their cogency even if certain ends (dependent for their realization upon a supply of goods inadequate to the fulfillment of all ends without limit) are held to have the character not of pleasure but of something else. The marginal utility may be a least pleasure or a competing least utility of some other sort...." (p. 317). This is a not uncommon view. As W. C. Mitchell has suggested, it is too obvious to be wholly convincing. (*Journ. Pol. Ec.*, Vol. XVIII. "The Rationality of Economic Activity.") Veblen has made it perfectly clear that particular matters of theory are affected by the presupposition of hedonism. (*Journ. Pol. Ec.*, Vol. XVII, *Quart. Journ. Econ.*, Vol. XXII, p. 147 ff.) The matter is too complex for a footnote, but I think it of little consequence whether "pleasure" be in any case regarded as substantively the end of desire or not. This is largely a matter of words. What is important is the practical question whether a thing is *so habitual with me that when the issue arises I cannot or*

will not give it up and take an interest in something new the "utility" of which I cannot as yet be cognizant of because it partly rests with me to create it. If this is the fact it will surely look as if pleasure or the avoidance of pain were my end in the case. Hedonism and egoism are in the end convertible terms. There is conduct wearing the outward aspect of altruism that is egotistic in fact—not because it was from the first insincere or self-delusive, but because it has become habitual and may in a crisis be held to for the sake of the satisfaction it affords. Genuine altruism, on the other hand, is a form of constructiveness.

52 Until after this essay was finished I had not seen John A. Hobson's book entitled *Work and Wealth, A Human Valuation* (London, 1914). My attention was first definitely called to this work by a friend among the economists who read my finished MS. late in 1915, and referred me in particular to the concluding chapter on "Social Science and Social Art." On now tardily reading this chapter I find that, as any reader will readily perceive, it distinctly anticipates, almost *verbatim* in parts, what I have tried, with far less success, to say in the foregoing two paragraphs above. Hobson argues, with characteristic clearness and effect, for the qualitative uniqueness and the integral character of personal budgets, holding that the logic of marginality is "an entirely illusory account of the psychical process by which a man lays out his money, or his time, or his energy" (p. 331). "So far as it is true that the last sovereign of my expenditure in bread equals in utility the last sovereign of my expenditure in books, that fact proceeds not from a comparison, conscious, or unconscious, of these separate items at this margin, but from the parts assigned respectively to bread and books in the organic plan of my life. Quantitative analysis, inherently incapable of comprehending qualitative unity or qualitative differences, can only pretend to reduce the latter to quantitative differences. What it actually does is to ignore alike the unity of the whole and the qualitativeness of the parts" (p. 334). Hobson not only uses the analogy of the artist and the picture (p. 330) precisely as I have done, but offers

still other illustrations of the principle that seem to me even more apt and telling. Though not indebted to him for what I have put into the above paragraphs, I am glad to be able to cite the authority of so distinguished an economist and sociologist for conclusions to which I found my own way. Other parts as well *of Work and Wealth* (e.g., Chapter IV, on "The Creative Factor in Production") seem to have a close relation to the main theme of the present discussion.

<u>53</u> It may be worth while to glance here for the sake of illustration at an ethical view of preference parallel with the economic logic above contested. "The act which is right in that it promotes one interest, is, by the same principle," writes R. B. Perry, "wrong in that it injures another interest. There is no contradiction in this fact ... simply because it is possible for the same thing to possess several relations, the question of their compatibility or incompatibility being in each case a question of empirical fact. Now ... an act ... may be doubly right in that it conduces to the fulfillment of two interests. Hence arises the conception of comparative goodness. If the fulfillment of one interest is good, the fulfillment of two is better; and the fulfillment of all interests is best.... Morality, then, is *such performance as under the circumstances, and in view of all the interests affected, conduces to most goodness.* In other words, that act is morally right which is most right." (*Present Philosophical Tendencies*, p. 334. Cf. also *The Moral Economy*). It is evident that constructive change in the underlying system (or aggregate?) of the agent's interests gets no recognition here as a matter of moral concern or as a fact of the agent's moral experience. Thus Perry understands the meaning of freedom to lie in the fact that "*interests operate*," i.e., that interests exist as a certain class of operative factors in the universe along with factors of *other* sorts. "I can and do, within limits, *act as I will*. Action, in other words, is governed by desires and intentions." (pp. 342 ff.). The cosmical heroics of Bertrand Russell are thus not quite the last word in Ethics (p. 346). Nevertheless, the "free man," in

Perry's view, apparently must get on with the interests that once for all initially defined him as a "moral constant" (p. 343).

<u>54</u> In a recent interesting discussion of "Self-interest" (T. N. Carver, *Essays in Social Justice*, 1915, Chap. III) occurs the following: "We may conclude ... that even after we eliminate from our consideration all other beings than self, there is yet a possible distinction between one's present and one's future self. It is always, of course, the present self which esteems or appreciates all interests whether they be present or future. And the present self estimates or appreciates present interests somewhat more highly than it does future interests. In this respect the present self appreciates the interests of the future self according to a law quite analogous to, if indeed it be not the same law as that according to which it appreciates the interests of others" (p. 71). This bit of "subjective analysis" (p. 60), a procedure rather scornfully condemned as "subjective quibbling" on the following page, must be counted a fortunate lapse. It could be bettered, I think, in only one point. Must the future self "of course" and "always" get license to live by meeting the standards of the present self? Has the present self no modesty, no curiosity, no "sense of humor"? If it is so stupidly hard and fast, how can a self new and qualitatively different ever get upon its feet in a man? In some men no such thing can happen—but must it be in all men impossible and impossible "of course"? And what of the other self? Carver has not applied the "methods of subjective analysis" to *change* from self *to* self or from interest in self *to* interest in others. The present tense of formal logic governs fundamentally throughout the whole account.

If this essay were a volume I should try to consider, from the point of view of constructive intelligence, the explanation of interest as due to the undervaluation of future goods.

<u>55</u> Fite, *Introductory Study of Ethics*, pp. 3-8.

<u>56</u> Dewey and Tufts, *Ethics*, pp. 205-11.

<u>57</u> The term "egocentric predicament" (cf. R. B. Perry: *Present Philosophical Tendencies*, p. 129 ff.) has had, for a philosophic term, a remarkable literary success. But at best it conveys a partial view of the situation it purports to describe. The "egocentricity" of our experience, viewed in its relation to action, seems, rightly considered, less a "predicament" than an opportunity, a responsibility and an immunity. For in relation to *action*, it means (1) that an objective complex situation has become, in various of its aspects, a matter of my cognizance in terms significant to me. That so many of its aspects have come into relations of conflict or reënforcement significant *for me* is *my* opportunity for reconstructive effort if I choose to avail myself of it. Because, again, I am thus "on hand myself" (*op. cit.*, p. 129) and am thus able to "report" upon the situation, I am (2) responsible, in the measure of my advantages, for the adequacy of my performance. And finally (3) I cannot be held to account for failure to reckon with such aspects of the situation as I cannot get hold of in the guise of "ideas, objects of knowledge or experiences" (*Ibid.*). Our egocentricity is, then, a predicament only so long as one stubbornly insists, to no obvious positive purpose, on thinking of knowledge as a self-sufficing entitative complex, like a vision suddenly appearing full-blown out of the blue, and as inviting judgment in that isolated character on the representative adequacy which it is supposed to claim (cf. A. W. Moore, "Isolated Knowledge," *Journ. of Philos., etc.*, Vol. XI). The way out of the predicament for Perry and his colleagues is to attack the traditional subjective and representative aspects of knowledge. But, this carried out, what remains of knowledge is a "cross-section of neutral entities" which *still* retains all the original unaccountability, genetically speaking, and the original intrinsic and isolated self-sufficiency traditionally supposed to belong to knowledge. The ostensible gain achieved for knowledge is an alleged proof of its ultimate self-validation or the meaninglessness of any suspicion of its validity (because there is no uncontrolled

and distorting intermediation of "consciousness" in the case). But to wage strenuous war on subjectivism and representationism and still to have on hand a problem calling for the invention *ad hoc* of an entire new theory of mind and knowledge seems a waste of good ammunition on rather unimportant outworks. They might have been circumvented.

But what concerns us here is the ethical parallel. The egocentric predicament in this aspect purports to compel the admission by the "altruist" that since whatever he chooses to do must be his act and is obviously done because he wishes, for good and sufficient reasons of his own, to do it, therefore he is an egoist after all—perhaps in spite of himself and then again perhaps not. The ethical realism of G. E. Moore (*Principia Ethica*, 1903) breaks out of the predicament by declaring Good independent of all desire, wish or human interest and *indefinable*, and by supplying a partial list of things thus independently good. What I do, I do because it seems likely to put me in possession of objective *Good*, not because it accords with some habit or whim of mine (although my own pleasure is undoubtedly *one* of the good things). It is noteworthy that Perry declines to follow Moore in this (*op. cit.*, p. 331 ff.). Now such an ethical objectivism can give no account of the motivation, or the process, of the individual's efforts to attain, for guidance in any case, a "more adequate" apprehension of what things are good than he may already possess, just as the objectivist theory of consciousness (=knowledge) can supply no clue as to how or whether a *more* or a *less* comprehensive or a qualitatively *different* "cross-section of entities" can or should be got into one's "mind" as warrant or guidance ("stimulus") for a contemplated response that is to meet a present emergency (cf. John Dewey, "The Reflex Arc Concept in Psychology," *Psychol. Rev.*, Vol. IV). Thus neither sort of deliverance out of the alleged predicament of egocentricity abates in the least the only serious inconvenience or danger threatened by subjectivism.

58 Cf. W. Jethro Brown, *The Underlying Principles of Modern Legislation* (3d ed., London, 1914), pp. 165-68.

59 Bosanquet: *Principle of Individuality and Value*, pp. 13, 15, 20, 24, 27, 30.

60 The case against the Austrian explanation of market-price in terms of marginal utility has been well summed up and re-enforced by B. M. Anderson in his monograph, *Social Value* (Boston, 1911). Anderson finds the fatal flaw in the Austrian account to consist in the psychological particularism of the marginal utility theory. The only way, he holds, to provide an adequate foundation for a non-circular theory of price is to understand the marginal estimates people put upon goods as resultants of the entire moral, legal, institutional, scientific, æsthetical, and religious state of society at the time. This total and therefore absolute state of affairs, if I understand the argument, is to be regarded as focussed to a unique point in the estimate each man puts upon a commodity. Thus, presumably, the values which come together, summed up in the total demand and supply schedules for a commodity in the market, are "social values" and the resultant market-price is a "social price." This cross-sectional social totality of conditions is strongly suggestive of an idealistic Absolute. The individual is a mere focussing of impersonal strains and stresses in the Absolute. But the real society is a radically temporal process. The real centers of initiation in it are creatively intelligent individuals whose economic character as such expresses itself not in "absolute" marginal registrations but in price estimates.

On the priority of price to value I venture to claim the support of A. A. Young, "Some Limitations of the Value Concept," *Quart. Journ. Econ.*, Vol. XXV, p. 409 (esp. pp. 417-19). Incidentally, I suspect the attempt to reconstruct ethical theory as a branch of what is called *Werttheorie* to be a mistake and likely to result only in useless and misleading terminology.

<u>61</u> *Positive Theory of Capital* (Eng. trans.). Bk. IV, Ch. II. The passage is unchanged in the author's latest edition (1912).

<u>62</u> It is pointed out (e.g., by Davenport in his *Economics of Enterprise*, pp. 53-54) that, mathematically, in a market where large numbers of buyers and sellers confront each other with their respective maximum and minimum valuations on the commodity this interval within which price must fall becomes indefinitely small to the point of vanishing. This is doubtless in accord with the law of probability, but it would be an obvious fallacy to see in this any manner of proof or presumption that therefore the assumptions as to the nature of the individual valuations upon which such analysis proceeds *are true*. In a large market where this interval is supposed to be a vanishing quantity is there more or less higgling and bargaining than in a small market where the interval is admittedly perceptible? And if there *is* higgling and bargaining (*op. cit.*, pp. 96-97), what is it doing that is of price-fixing importance unless there be supposed to be a critical interval for it to work in? Such a use of probability-theory is a good example of the way in which mathematics may be used to cover the false assumptions which have to be made in order to make a mathematical treatment of certain sorts of subject-matter initially plausible as description of concrete fact.

<u>63</u> As I have elsewhere argued ("Subjective and Exchange Value," *Journ. Pol. Econ.*, Vol. IV, pp. 227-30). By the same token, I confess skepticism of the classical English doctrine that cost can affect price only through its effect upon quantity produced. "If all the commodities used by man," wrote Senior (quoted by Davenport, *op. cit.*, p. 58), "were supplied by nature without any interference whatever of human labor, but were supplied in precisely the same amounts that they now are, there is no reason to suppose either that they would cease to be valuable or would exchange at any other than the present proportions." But is this inductive evidence or illustrative rhetoric? One wonders, indeed, whether private property would ever have developed or how long

modern society would tolerate it if all wealth were the gift of nature instead of only some of it (that part, of course, which requires no use of produced capital goods for its appropriation).

64 Certain points in this discussion have been raised in two papers, entitled, "The Present Task of Ethical Theory," *Int. Jour. of Ethics*, XX, and "Ethical Value," *Jour. of Phil., Psy., and Scientific Methods*, V, p. 517.

65 Cf. also John Dewey, *Influence of Darwin upon Philosophy*, and Dewey and Tufts, *Ethics*, Ch. XVI.

66 *International Journal of Ethics*, XXV, 1914, pp. 1-24.

67 *Dreams of a Spirit Seer.*

68 Cf. A. W. Moore, *Pragmatism and Its Critics*, 257-78.

69 Croce, *Philosophy of the Practical*, pp. 312 f.

70 G. E. Moore, *Principia Ethica*, p. 147.

71 *Ethics*, ch. V.

72 G. E. Moore, *Principia Ethica*, p. 149.

73 Rashdall, *Is Conscience an Emotion?* pp. 199 f.

74 *Ibid.*, 177.

75 G.E. Moore, *Ethics*, Ch. III.

76 Dewey and Tufts, *Ethics*, pp. 334 f.

77 *Methods of Ethics*, p. 380.

78 *Individualism*, 55, 61, 62.

79 Lectures III and IV, especially 175, 176, 235-39.

80 Pp. 111 ff., 172-75, 329 ff.

81 Pp. 73, 186, 236, 261 f., 267, 269.

82 124, 182, 301.

83 263 ff., 123.

84 Pp. 180, 241.

85 P. 180.

86 Art and religion have doubtless their important parts in embodying values, or in adding the consciousness of membership in a larger union of spirits, or of relation to a cosmic order conceived as ethical, but the limits of our discussion do not permit treatment of these factors.

87 Cf. my paper, "Goodness, Cognition, and Beauty," *Journal of Philosophy, Psychology, and Scientific Methods*, Vol. IX, p. 253.

88 Cf. Thorndike, *The Original Nature of Man*; S. Freud, *Die Traumdeutung, Psychopathologie des Alltagsleben*, etc.; McDougall, *Social Psychology*.

89 *The Journal of Philosophy, Psychology, and Scientific Methods*, Vol. IX, p. 256.

90 Cf. Plato, *Republic*, IX, 571, 572, for an explicit anticipation of Freud.

91 This "new psychology" is not so very new.

92 Cf. Hocking, *The Meaning of God in Human Experience*, for the most recent of these somnambulisms. But any idealistic system will do, from Plato to Bradley.

93 Cf. James, *The Varieties of Religious Experience*.

94 Cf. Jane Harrison, *Ancient Art and Ritual*.

95 Cf. my paper, "Is Belief Essential in Religion?", *International Journal of Ethics*, October, 1910.

96 "Metaphysics," *Book Lambda*.

97 This is accomplished usually by ignoring the differentia of the term of religion, and using it simply as an adjective of eulogy, as in the common practice the term "Christian" is made coextensive with the denotation of "good," or "social." For example, a "Christian gentleman" can differ in no discernible way from a gentleman not so qualified save by believing in certain theological propositions. But in usage, the adjective is simply tautologous. Compare R. B. Perry, *The Moral Economy*; E. S. Ames, *The Psychology of Religious Experience*; J. H. Leuba, *A Psychological Study of Religion*; H. M. Kallen, *Is Belief Essential in Religion?*

98 The condition of England and Germany in the present civil war in Europe echoes this situation.

99 Cf. *Republic*, Books V and VI.

100 Cf. *Winds of Doctrine* and *Reason in Common Sense*.

Made in the USA
Lexington, KY
01 June 2011